Illinois Central College
Learning Resource Center

AMAZING MONUMENT

BARDOLATER—SHAW AT STRATFORD

AMAZING MONUMENT

A SHORT HISTORY OF THE
SHAKESPEARE INDUSTRY

BY

JOHN CARNEGIE

IVOR BROWN & GEORGE FEARON

'1891—

KENNIKAT PRESS
Port Washington, N. Y./London

AMAZING MONUMENT

First published in 1939
Reissued in 1970 by Kennikat Press
Library of Congress Catalog Card No: 73-113362
ISBN 0-8046-1009-6

Manufactured by Taylor Publishing Company   Dallas, Texas

To
TWO IRENES

CONTENTS

ILLUSTRATIONS

ACKNOWLEDGMENT

Our debt to those possessing special information and experience has been very great. In every case we have been met with the most generous assistance. Especially would we mention the time, trouble, and knowledge bestowed on us by Mr. F. C. Wellstood, the Secretary of the Shakespeare Birthplace Trustees, who has been particularly helpful, not only concerning the history of the Birthplace, but with regard to the Shakespeare Clubs. Our list of benefactors includes Sir Archibald Flower (High Steward of the Borough of Stratford-upon-Avon), whose kindly given information concerning the American Shakespeare Foundation Fund and the building of the present Memorial Theatre has been invaluable, Sir Frank Benson, Mr. B. Iden Payne (Director of The Stratford Festival Company), Mr. Henry Tossell (Manager and Secretary of The Shakespeare Memorial Theatre), Mr. Geoffrey Whitworth (Secretary of the National Theatre Committee), Mr. T. C. Kemp (of the *Birmingham Post*), Mr. A. Acton-Bond (Vice-President of the British Empire Shakespeare Society), the Staff of the Stratford-upon-Avon Public Library for their unflagging patience in putting us in contact with several long-forgotten books and pamphlets, Councillor and Mrs. T. N.

Waldron (Mayor and Mayoress of Stratford-upon-Avon), Mr. H. E. Seward and Mr. Waller Jeffs (both of Stratford-upon-Avon), Mr. Rupert Boyden (of the *Stratford-upon-Avon Herald)*, Mr. John H. Bird (of the *Evesham Journal* at Stratford), Mr. J. C. Higgins of The Shakespeare Hotel, Mr. R. Urwin of The Falcon Hotel and Mr. R. R. Owens of The Washington Irving Hotel, all of Stratford-upon-Avon, Miss Fanny Bradshaw (of New York City), Mr. Bertram G. Theobald, the President, and Mr. Percy Walters, the Librarian of the Bacon Society, and Mr. Robert Jorgensen for help with the Danish section.

In a book of this kind, dealing with a wide variety of facts, many buried in a misty past and others the subject of continual dispute, it is inevitable that some of the statements should be challenged. If inaccuracies or errors of judgment there be, the friends mentioned above are in no way responsible. The merit for what is correct is theirs; the mistakes, if any, are our own.

I.B.

G.F.

CHAPTER I

"Then longen folk to go on pilgrimages."—CHAUCER, *Canterbury Tales*. Prologue.

THOSE who enter Stratford-upon-Avon by road, coming in by way of Leamington and Warwick, will pass, as they near their goal, a petrol and service station for cars whose proprietor has made a gesture and an intimation. In front of his premises he displays a statue of the head of William Shakespeare. At night he reverently removes the same and gives it shelter. Once in Stratford you will see that head on every coign of vantage, outside banks, as though it were a symbol of the Gold Standard, while, inevitably, in all sizes and materials, it dominates the shop-windows. Should you wish the local beer, the same face confronts you on the bottle. The garage-man gets in the first blow. Now it is not customary in Britain thus to mingle sculpture with salesman-ship, art with oil. But the displayer of the famous beard and brow is showing his awareness of the facts. The traveller knows, of course, that he is entering, in the Guide Book's romantic lingo, "The Heart of the Shakespeare Country." The petrol-pump proclaims a

1

further fact, which only realists will appreciate, that we are entering the Headquarters of the Shakespeare Industry.

For not in Stratford only but all over the world Shakespeare has passed far beyond his old status of poet and playwright. He is now, on the grand scale, a commercial magnet, a trade-sign for garages, a pillar of finance, a Warwickshire and a British staple. As raw material, available without cost and without cease, he everywhere sustains actors and their critics, musicians and stage-decorators, costumiers and scene-shifters, electricians and box-office staffs, teachers and lecturers, librarians, publishers and editors of texts, controversialists who say that he was not Stratford William at all, but Bacon or Oxford or any of Queen Bess's brighter boys, booksellers, examiners, creators of educational curricula, compilers of quotation dictionaries, preachers in search of a "tag," writers in search of a title or a phrase, and even Prime Ministers departing on desperate quest to pluck this flower safely from the nettle danger. He has more recently supplied Hollywood with the matter for some "super-films" and he has constantly supplied scholars, as well as actors, with reputations. Furthermore, the business of Remembering the Mighty Name has provided jobs for Appeal Secretaries and vastly enriched the Post Office, the Printing, and the Stationery trades. It has also inflicted on listeners of all kinds more Public Speeches than one dares to contemplate.

2

In Warwickshire, he is still and increasingly the prop of his own town. He draws to its theatre some fifteen hundred pounds every week of the summer and he attracts thousands of pounds more to the local museums, show-places, hotels, lodgings, garages, cafés, shops, bathing-pools, camping-grounds, boating jetties, public-houses, and ice-cream barrows. That this thing could happen the poet himself can never have foreseen. His generation and his descendants would have been equally astonished at such curious antics of Fame. There was no burial in Westminster Abbey for Stratford's William, as there was for Chaucer, Spenser, Beaumont, and Jonson. A grave and a bust in the local church were his meed. He was liked and esteemed, he became a Gentleman. He made money. He seems to have liked the money and handled it prudently. The great poet was no less successful as a small investor. And there they left him, a country gentleman decently buried, with complimentary verses, among his kin and kindred. It was not until a century and a half after Shakespeare's death that the simple monument grew into a shrine, the honoured name became a tradesman's talisman, the "harlotry player" a national hero, almost a national saint, the bard an immortal, and the cult of that Immortal Bard an industry which has ramifications all over the world.

That state of affairs is the more astonishing because the British people, judged by their general conduct and methods of personal expenditure, are by no means addicted to the two articles with which this William Shakespeare of Stratford so efficiently supplied them—namely, poetry and drama. The English have been rich in poets and, intermittently, in the taste for poetry. The Elizabethan public relished it to such an extent that a little-known poet who happened to win their ear, as Shakespeare did in 1593 with the sumptuously mannered narrative of "Venus and Adonis," might collect a good reward as well as good renown. Again, in the times of Byron and of Scott, ballads, satires, and even demi-epics were greedily purchased. Tennyson was another who could make poetry pay. But nowadays new poetry seems only to appeal to a very small minority of readers. Volumes of poems by men with some standing in their craft may fail to attract more than a few hundred purchasers. It is fairly safe to say that of the hundreds of thousands who flock into Stratford every year scarcely any regard poetry as a pleasure to be purchased with eagerness and to be enjoyed with affection. They were confronted with the stuff at school. It was called "Eng. Lit." Under duress they learned it by heart and wrote notes on the unusual words. They informed the examiners that the Rialto was not a cinema, or perhaps, with malice, that it was. They were heartily glad when it was all over.

The same is true of drama, to which the English have to be coaxed by the tricks of publicity, by kindly, even flattering, reviews, and by everlasting appeals to support this or that play-house of good intentions. In the case of popular entertainment such as musical comedy, they are willing to look and listen without suasion or bullying. But, with a few happy exceptions, the serious drama has to be put to them, very often and usually with disastrous results, as a duty. There is certainly not one visit made to the theatre for every twenty made to the film, and nineteen out of twenty of those who will flock to Stratford and pack its theatre, which offers Shakespeare only, through the summer from April to September, would never think of attending a Shakespeare play in their own town, should it by some chance happen to arrive there, just as they would never think of buying a book of modern poetry. But now the name of Shakespeare seems to act like a strange intoxicant upon the very people whom one thought to be totally immune from any such Dionysiac infection.

So the astonishing thing has occurred. The Shakespeare Industry goes on and on and up and up. The sales of his texts are prodigious. Of the first Temple Shakespeare, for example, now replaced by Mr. Ridley's recension of the text and new introductory comments, the house of Dent sold more than a million volumes. Yet the same publishing house was also responsible for the three-volume Shakespeare in the Everyman Library, which also had colossal sales. Still it is worth while for another firm to offer Shakespeare with Dr. G. B. Harrison's scholarship thrown in for sixpence a play, a venture pre-supposing myriads of buyers if there is to be any profit at all. Year in, year out, Shakespeare must be easily the next best-seller of the English-reading world; that is presuming the Bible still to be first on the list.

The Industry's headquarters become continually more busy and more prosperous. Nothing will keep people out of the Memorial Theatre at Stratford-upon-Avon whose Shakespeare Festivals now run from April till September; except for a week or so in May, just after the Easter holidays, the house is constantly packed, although the level of some of the performances has been severely criticised, and the standard, as some maintain, is not so high as to give the company the international reputation to which Stratford might aspire. That there should be keen debate on the merits of each year's company is all to the good.

Of course, there are occasional slumps. The Shakespeare Industry is part of the national economy and rises and falls with the general prosperity. The statistics of the Stratford shrines reveal the interdependence of the Shakespeare Industry with general commerce. When trade is best, the worship is most brisk. The Bard and the markets soar together. The record attendance at the Birthplace, for example, occurred in 1928–9, before the great international collapse of markets and the consequent restrictions upon currency and travel. In that year over 118,000 pilgrims passed through the house in Henley Street, where Shakespeare is said to have been born. This establishment holds preference in public favour over the museum (with Shakespearean garden) at New Place and Anne Hathaway's cottage at Shottery. The confident assumption, incidentally, that Shakespeare is the local industry is proved by the Stratford Town Council's habit of writing up in large letters about the town: "To the Birthplace." No name of any infant is specified. One might even gather from this notice that nobody except Shakespeare has ever been born in the district. On the other hand, an innocent stranger might reasonably assume that Stratford owns and wishes to advertise some famous and exemplary hospital for the treatment of maternity cases.

It is the object of this book to chronicle and, if possible, to analyse and to explain this growth of a local loyalty into a local cult and of the local cult into a cosmic industry, which, despite occasional ups and downs in the numbers of Stratford's sight-seers consequent upon the vicissitudes of international finance, seems to be developing new phases and widening its appeal every year. After all, Stratford, where they put up the bust of a poet as an encouragement to the purchase of petrol and will sell you any Shakespearean gew-gaw from a Hamlet cigarette-case to a Shylock nut-cracker, is the home town only. London has been for many years its rival in the cult and the commerce. It is true that it no longer ridicules Stratford's claim to the status of a shrine, as it once did with some bitterness, dismissing the Stratfordians as rustic oafs with ideas beyond their station. But it has built and worshipped in its own temples at the "Old Vic" and "Sadler's Wells." The latter recently defaulted to opera and ballet, but it is now further proposed to erect the true Cathedral of the cult on the South Kensington site recently purchased by the Shakespeare Memorial National Theatre Committee. Again there is a movement to associate the honouring of Shakespeare's name with the section of London where so much of his work was done: the south bank of the Thames. The Globe-Mermaid Association hopes to establish modern versions of the old Shakespearean theatre and tavern, if not upon the original spots (the Mermaid was north of the river) at least upon the southern bank, where the players had their liberty and made their living.

Let us now suppose that we have passed the bust of Shakespeare on the road from Leamington. As we come near to Stratford-upon-Avon we shall see on the left a municipal bathing-place where any, even the profane, may dip in waters deemed so holy that American Shakespeareans will actually send for bottles of this magic fluid believing it to be an elixir, fructifying the arts wherever it be spilt. There are Christian believers who set special store on the veritable waters of Jordan. There are the faithful in Texas who place a similar value on the stream into which the young William may have gone splashing as a child. This is the more strange because, while the poet's plays contain many English place-names, especially of the Midlands, they never once mention the River Avon. Ben Jonson's allusion to the Swan of Avon in his complimentary verses in the First Folio has so impinged itself upon the public mind that many seem to think of Shakespeare as constantly sitting with his feet in the river and his hand composing verses in its praise. Commentators may think of Avon when they read of pale streams gilded with heavenly alchemy, of willows, sedges, and young women drowned. But the odd fact remains that in none of the plays or poems attributed to William Shakespeare is Stratford or the Avon mentioned.

However that may be, there are many who find "big magic" in Stratford's earth and Avon's water. If Stratford were really eager to sell Shakespeare in a shameless way—a commerce which, with a very few exceptions, it now creditably declines—it could retail bottled Avon at most satisfactory prices. Consider what occurred not long ago.

In the spring of 1936 the Director of the Stratford Festival Company received the following cable: "Please send earth Shakespeare's Garden water River Avon for dedication Shakespeare Theatre, Dallas, Texas, July 1st." The playhouse, for which this pious supplication was made, was a model of the old Globe Theatre on the Bankside, which was erected as

9

part of the Great Texas Fair. Stratford rose—or rather dug and dipped—to the occasion. Proper ceremony was observed in making the retort courteous. Within a few days a number of townsmen and actors gathered in the garden of Shakespeare's Birthplace to meet America's nearest official representative, the Vice-Consul in Birmingham. Then some earth was dug up by Alderman Winter of Stratford, placed in a small box of charred wood (a relic of the burned Memorial Theatre) and handed, with suitable observations, to the Vice-Consul.

The party then moved on from gas to water. They went to the premises of the Stratford Rowing Club on the banks of the Avon. Here Mr. Fordham Flower accompanied the Vice-Consul on to a small raft and dipped into the sacred stream an aluminium bottle on which was painted Shakespeare's coat of arms. As aluminium is an important element in Stratford's light metal industry, the marriage of two trades was thus symbolised. After more suitable observations the Vice-Consul received the precious fluid, which, with the no less precious earth, he handed to the representative of the Cunard-Star Shipping Company. The latter removed the treasure to Liverpool, where he passed it—still, let us hope, with observations strictly suitable—to the Captain of one of the Company's liners.

It was conveyed (free of charge) to New York, received by a member of the British Consulate, and despatched to Dallas. The reception at Dallas was held in the best ceremonial manner. The whole affair was broadcast, the new stage on an old model was sprinkled with the earth and water, and what was not used of those precious elements was not wasted. The undistributed divots of Shakespeare's Birth-soil and the remaining drops of Stratford's Avon were exposed in Dallas for general veneration.

The addiction of mankind to relics and the belief that some especial grace may be communicated by contact therewith is common in all religions, Bardolatry not least. We have ourselves noticed in Stratford's parish church, after the announcement by some unscrupulous guide that Shakespeare was here a choir-boy and sat in a certain stall, the thrill of excitement which animated the bosoms, even the entire frames, of a conducted party of young American womanhood. Dallas may worship afar the transported elements of Stratford's soil and river: these, blessed above women, were on the actual spot, and there had the opportunity to "contact"—as they themselves would have said—Shakespeare's reputed seat. "Contact" it they most eagerly did, each placing her rump for one glorious moment on the sacred oak and evidently deriving—such was the air of rapture on each face—a sense of inspiration, of instant and glowing community with genius, *a posteriori*.

Of course there is not the shadow of evidence that Shakespeare ever did sing in the choir or that he sat in a particular stall. (He was obviously musical and may have been a chorister.) Nor do we suggest that Stratford habitually retails such pleasant yarns for the comfort of its visitors. But comforted they visibly were: indeed, exalted is not too strong a word. It is a nice point for casuistry to settle whether guides at shrines like this are entitled to take a chance with such a tale as that of Shakespeare's choir-stall, seeing what deep innocuous bliss, what veritable ecstasy even, may be conveyed to the meekest of pilgrim spinsters by the belief that she has shared the seats of the mighty.

Continuing our journey beside the sacred stream we shall see, in high summer, what appears to be an army encamped. On both sides of the water are tents and caravans of all kinds. That the inhabitants are all worshippers is unlikely to be true: they engage themselves, for sport, in bathing, fishing, and turning on the gramophone. But Stratford has drawn them. It is a place to know, a sight to have seen, and so they come. Many, indeed, are Shakespearean campers who have arrived for some course of instruction and play-going. A little way upstream is the recently founded Stratford College of Drama: downstream is the new Memorial Theatre, with its Conference Hall on the site of the old theatre. Here are held a constant succession of Summer Schools, whose members meet to practise elocution or the rustic dance, to distribute and absorb Shakespearean news and views, and generally to make Stratford a shrine of the lecturer's dais and the cultural water-bottle as well as of Sir Toby Belch and of canakin's clink.

The first thing you will notice on entering Stratford on a summer day, especially at the week-end, is the enormous number of people who are driving in, driving round, driving out, or just standing and staring. The town itself has a population of less than 12,000. Like many English places of its size and sense, it brews its own liquor and its beer has become justly famous and esteemed in London as well as all over the middle and west of England. It has a light metal industry and has recently taken up the tinning of fruit and vegetables which grow abundantly in the Avon valley, one of England's finest orchard-grounds. On the analogy of the ordinary English market-town one would expect Stratford to have two fair-sized inns with twelve or fifteen bedrooms each and a number of beer-houses supplying a Farmer's Ordinary along with plentiful ale on market-days. Instead it has seven or eight major hotels, one of which announces over a hundred rooms. There are numerous private hotels or boarding-houses, residential hostels for students, and lodging-houses of all kinds. There are theatre-minded pilgrims from the New World enjoying a Shakespeare Fortnight of play-going, sight-seeing, lectures, and, let us hope, a little beer and skittles too, in suitably Old-World surroundings. If we assume that at least half of the hotel bedrooms are double rooms, Stratford can accommodate (and actually does on a great many summer nights, when the town is "playing to capacity," as theatre-people would say) as many as a thousand visitors. This is far more than the accommodation readily available in some of the great industrial cities which have permanent populations fifty times as large as Stratford. This reckoning makes no count of the swarms of campers and caravanners. Stratford has none of the ordinary stock-in-trade of a "resort," save a quite ordinary Midland river. It has neither mountains nor sea. For popularity it depends on a poet whose name can draw pilgrims from the five continents and the seven seas.

Yet it is but a tithe of the visitors to Stratford and its theatre who stay there for the night. The motor-car has opened up what used to be a lonely and quiet town to the myriads of the Midlands and Stratford has also become a favourite calling-place for the north-country tourist on his way south. It is served by two railways, on both of which excursions are run. Why, you may ask, these crowds? Why this trek of hundreds of thousands of people every year, most of them completely antipathetic to poetry and drama, in order to see the Birthplace of a dramatic poet? The truth is that the Shakespeare Industry has benefited enormously by an accident: the discovery and cheap distribution of mechanical road-transport. The historian who starts to consider the effect on society of

14

the invention of the petrol-engine must devote some
chapters to the new liberty of travel, the destruction
of distance which that involves, and the general desire
to keep on the move which the ability to go fast and
far and cheaply at once evokes in all owners of such
means of transport. The Midlands are the main
centres of England's motor-car industry. Coventry, in
particular, has been triumphantly associated with the
car-trade. Its population rose from 180,000 in 1933
to 220,000 in 1938 and it is a prosperous population.
The Midlands teem with private cars as well as offer-
ing excellent long-distance services in public bus and
motor-coach.

It is inevitable that the owners of all this horse-
power should want to set those horses going. Ours is
an age in which everybody wants to use his or her
car. Hence young people who could perfectly well
go to swim, drink and dance in their own towns are
continually found scurrying across country in order to
swim, drink and dance some thirty or forty miles away.
Their elders, with a car in the garage, look for more
modest entertainment and their eyes light on
announcements of Beauty Spots, Places of Historic
Interest, and the like. The cult of the Beauty Spot is
now enormous, not because motorists and motor-
cyclists have discovered a sudden passion for Beauty,
but because they have an engine throbbing in front
of or beneath them and do not know what to do with
the thing. Off they must pelt. Now the Midlanders

are some way from hills (of any size) and from the sea. So any pretty place or site of historic interest is gladly taken for a target by the organisers of excursions. Broadway, in the Cotswolds, has, to the great unhappiness of all its more sensitive residents, been made an acknowledged Beauty Spot. It is a Cotswold Gem. Therefore, on a summer afternoon, motor-coaches and private cars pour in and disgorge a horde of people who care nothing whatever for jewels of architecture, the niceties of the Cotswold style, or the loveliness of Cotswold stone. They have been taken for a ride. Here is a Beauty Spot, which means a place where you get out. They dismount to ease their cramp; they stand and stare and smoke and spit. Some look for beer, others for tea. Then they are rounded up and off they go.

The same sort of thing has befallen Stratford. It has become a place to visit, both shrine and tripper-dump. Stratford-upon-Avon has become Stratford-on-petrol. On the other hand, Shakespeare does mean more than Cotswold architecture to the average man in the motor-coach. He heard of the fellow at school. The English public is not æsthetically-minded. But it has, deep in its bosom, a queer kind of moral urge about artistic matters, an instinctive feeling that certain things are good and proper and ought to be done. The Puritan who is still in us has no particular taste, but he has a conscience. The man who hates music or pictures can sometimes be "got at" if you tell him

that it is his duty to support the thing which bores
him. Because Shakespeare has been dinned into the
general ear as one of the best and noblest of Englishmen, the general curiosity is attracted by Shakespeare's town.

So calculation is made. One ought to go there. If
the car is ready or the motor-coach invites, why not?
There's a nice river with punts and boats and canoes,
and you can get tea on the terrace beside it and that's
not too bad. One might even stop and go to the play.
That's more serious. But it might be faced. Anyhow,
play or no play, the party can go home aglow with
satisfaction and the sense of duty done. Merely to buy
trinkets in the town, to stand beside the Avon, and to
throw cigarette-ends into the holy water bestows a
slight and agreeable feeling of having done something
which is morally worth while. That, of course, is the
lowest form of Shakespearean "tripping." Above it
are all grades and variations of travellers' motive,
from intelligent curiosity to the most odious and
pretentious forms of intellectual snobbery.

These remarks should not deflect the intending
visitor to the Headquarters of the Shakespeare
Industry. (It would be as well to avoid Bank Holiday,
unless you are a practitioner of Mass-Observation.)
Stratford in its normal state remains a pleasant
specimen of Midland market-town. The agricultural
foundations abide. When pigs come to market on a
Tuesday, bacon, not Shakespeare, is the staple of the

place. There are some atrocious architectural experiments in Bogus Tudor, but the amount of genuine old building is considerable and its quality first-rate. The curve of the river from Clopton Bridge to the church draws a bow of serene, agreeable English beauty, with its quiet glow of old brick-work and coolness of its natural green. The Trustees of the Birthplace and kindred shrines look after them well and do not permit romancing caretakers to seek tips by telling tall stories. The people who repeat that Stratford is nothing but a riot of Ye Olde Jacobethan Hocusse-Pocusse are completely wrong. Most of Stratford is still a typical town of the Cotswold fringe. There is no better time to see it than October: the players will have gone and the pilgrims are few. The timbered houses are lit by the comfortable warmth of the westering sun. The creepers blaze scarlet on the walls of the Old Town. The pleasures of the Great Mop Fair, an old hiring festival, but now a jollification only, are rampant in the streets. Later comes Runaway Mop, a survival of the second hiring-day when disgusted masters and fugitive servants tried to suit themselves better. Do not suppose that the Shakespeare Industry has driven cattle and horses and cricket and football from the Stratford mind. Enter a tavern and listen to the talk. There are Warwickshire lads still.

The Shakespeare Industry, too, has its own agreeable aspects. The season starts in April and on April

23rd, which is accepted as the Bardic Birthday, there is all manner of ceremonial. The Governors of the Memorial Theatre meet and, unlike most Governors of an artistic enterprise, they nowadays consider a balance-sheet which is always satisfactory. The Town is packed and not the shrillest of the east winds, which so often sear and torture England at the latter end of April, will empty the streets. There is a public procession of people carrying flowers to the poet's tomb in the church and this, prudently, is not too closely organised. Anybody can join in behind the dignitaries and officials: you can look for Dogberry and Verges, Bottom and Quince and Dull among the wearers of municipal insignia, the bandsmen bearing powerful brass, the marching rank and file. A generation has passed since C. E. Montague wrote so finely of this annual and spontaneous parade:

"Each year on April 23rd, when Shakspere died, and may have been born, there is a little rite in the Church. A parson gives an address, and then anyone who chooses may bring flowers to Shakspere's grave in the chancel. One trembles at the thought of an unsymbolistic race essaying this joint act of emotional symbolism, unhelped by the Gallic passion for such efforts. Yet all goes well and is simple and not hugger-mugger. The time I saw it a couple of thousand persons were there, mostly women; most of them carried little bunches of daffodils, wallflowers, primroses — anything. The divine who had to say a few words about Shakspere extricated himself with credit, and then every one filed past the poet's grave, all looking, in a surprising degree, as if it mattered to them that he had lived. . . ."

Those words do still apply.

Then there is the unveiling of the Flags of All the Nations (or Nearly All—Germany and Russia were kept on the Black List for a while). If possible the banners are unfurled at the masts in Bridge Street by official representatives. The Embassies and Ministries are sent free first-class tickets from London for their deputies and invitations to visit the theatre at night. A few top-hatted gentry of this order may be seen, cowering from the sleety blast and nervously fingering a cord below their national emblem. Many nations, however, must find understudies, and the local worthies, even visiting journalists, have been accepted as volunteers and honoured with the charge of a South American banner or an emblem of the gorgeous East. These things accomplished and the flags in colourful mid-air, the Shakespeare Birthday Committee generously entertains eminent strangers to luncheon. The responses of the eminent to the various toasts are delivered into microphones and transmitted to all listeners by the B.B.C. The public praise of Shakespeare is one of the most popular of

WORSHIPFUL PERSONS.   THE BIRTHDAY AT STRATFORD

Photo: J. H. Bird

English pastimes. Some of the speakers so relish their opportunity that no amount of sighs, groans, nods and winks will persuade them to abandon their platitudes and resume their seats. The Birthday Luncheon in Stratford has often prolonged itself, as a feast of oratory, almost until tea-time. But the devout are no weaklings. They not only sit it through: they pay their ten shillings and sixpence again next year and come up eagerly for more. None shall ever say of British Bardolatry, that it "is yellow and cannot take it."

At night there is the Birthday Play, which is just like any other play in the Shakespearean repertory except that it is given its first showing of the season on April 23rd. The house, of course, is packed, there is much hasty swallowing of hotel dinners in order to be seated by eight o'clock, and those who do not wear evening-dress in the stalls are made to feel that they have under-estimated the solemnity of the occasion. Some of the diplomatic foreigners are there in full fig and look and listen patiently until the hour of eleven brings release. In the morning they discover that their invitations did not cover their hotel accommodation. Confronted with unexpected hotel bills, they have been known to swear in many languages, terrifying the innocent young ladies at cash-desks, and vowing to go no more on Stratford's pilgrimage of grace which is not, as they hoped, entirely gratuitous.

We need not, in any case, pay too much attention

to Stratford and London. Shakespearean zeal runs infinitely far afield. The Industry knows no bounds. There are clubs and producing societies and study circles and reading-groups all over the globe. The British Empire Shakespeare Society alone has many branches and nearly ten thousand members.

That leads to considerations of finance. It is a sign of the almost universal contempt in which art and literature are held by ruling persons (the representatives of democracy are quite as much to blame as autocrats and tyrants) that no property is allowed to exist in these things shortly after an author's or composer's death. (Our British law of copyright only protects property in writing during the author's lifetime and for fifty years subsequent to publication.) Property in land and shares is heavily taxed by death and succession duties, but the right to own does continue. If you are in the true line of heirs to a piece of land, nothing, except a sale forced by inability to pay the taxes, can keep you out of it. But if you are legal heir to a piece of drama, poetry, or music, you very soon are pushed out of your inheritance and get nothing whatever. The propertied classes may rage against the villainies of Communism, but, with regard to art and literature, they permit total expropriation of the legitimate owner, presumably because they regard the property—mere words, noises, and thoughts —as so much inconsiderable trash.

Let us suppose for a moment that Shakespeare's

literary and dramatic rights had been defined and regarded in his own time and then vested in a Shakespeare Trust on behalf of his descendants. Nobody knows who the present recipient would be, since direct descent failed with the death of the poet's grandchild, Lady Barnard. But whoever the rightful heir may be, he or she ought to be one of the richest persons in the world. If Shakespeare had, anticipating modern practice, created a Shakespeare Trust to be financed by his royalties on books and plays, the Trust's income to-day would certainly be no less than £100,000 a year and might be far more. If the Trustees had put a quarter of the annual income to reserve in the past and invested it at compound interest the income would probably have risen to the half-million. If Shakespeare's royalties had been paid over to a Shakespeare Memorial Fund we could have peppered the land with National Theatres, at no expense to ourselves, instead of feebly failing to build one in so wealthy a capital as London.

Of course, estimates of Shakespearean royalties are extremely hard to make. If the Trust sold one play a year to Hollywood for "super-film" purposes the text should be worth at least £30,000. Royalties on stage-performances depend on the percentage which the author can claim as well as on box-office receipts. Averaging Shakespeare's percentages at ten (Mr. Bernard Shaw often gets as much as fifteen), the year's income on the Stratford-upon-Avon and Old Vic seasons alone would run to £5,000 or £6,000. (Stratford is playing to upwards of £1,500 a week in the height of the season.) If the Open Air Theatre in London took £12,000 by its Shakespearean productions in the middle and late summer, that would mean another £1,200 in royalties. If a popular actor like Mr. Gielgud puts on a West-End Shakespearean production, that should mean another £150 a week to the Trust. If he does the same in New York the royalty might be double that. Then there are touring rights, repertory productions, amateur performances, ubiquitous and perennial. Of course, one has to remember that, if a royalty were charged, some of these performances might not be given. But on the whole, the necessary subtraction on that account is not large. So far we have not left Great Britain and New York. Yet the entire universe reads and acts Shakespeare. There is scarcely a town of any size in any civilised nation which does not see Shakespeare performed from time to time. Moreover, the Trust would have its dues from operatic versions of Shakespeare's plays and from the adaptations popular in many countries.

Then there come broadcasting, a trifle of gramophone rights on words of Shakespearean songs and speeches delivered by actors, and last, an enormous item, the book-rights. The magnitude of these is incalculable. Shakespeare has been translated (and is continually being re-translated) into every written language. The number and price and sale of these translations cannot be accurately traced. The number, price and sale of school texts is another vast and not easily assessable feature. Simply ·on the orthodox book-sales in Great Britain alone, including all editions from the sixpenny with its tiny dues to the luxury editions with their large ones, many thousands a year would accrue to the Trust. But Britain supplies only a small fraction of the Shakespearean reading-public, be they happy volunteers or conscripts for whom the plays are hard labour. Statisticians, with some knowledge of the book and theatre worlds, could amuse themselves for a long time with these calculations about a single facet of the Shakespeare Industry.

We have gleaned so far but a few scattered aspects of the mighty commerce arising from an article which is often deemed to be hopelessly uncommercial. We have offered a few surmises about Shakespearean finance: we have cursorily examined the Industry in its local manifestations, with its votive offerings, its ceremonial homage, and its revels at the natal shrine. Here is an amazing monument of veneration, raised to a poet in a world where poetry is more commonly left to starve in neglect than promoted to the fame and flesh-pots of society's High Table. How that monument first was slowly built and how it is being incessantly enlarged we hope, in the following chapters, to describe and to explain.

CHAPTER II

"Yon fane
Enshrines his ashes, and the lowliest hind
Holds in his breath with awe, as though 'twould stain
The slabs where sleeps the Monarch of the Mind.
And would they waft o'er Transatlantic foam
This cot—as sacred as Palladium old?
No! where his heart had glow'd, shall rest his home,
Though every brick might gain its weig'.t in gold!
England, whose lamp was kindled from His fire
Will never let the sacred flame expire."

Verses, signed "L," composed on the Sale of
Shakespeare's Birthplace in 1847.

WILLIAM SHAKESPEARE died at Stratford on April 23rd, 1616, and was buried in the parish church. The cause of death was unknown. His will, drawn up first in January of that year, declared him to be in "perfect health and memory." His son-in-law, Dr. John Hall, who married Susanna, later on left notes on many of his cases; nothing, unfortunately, was said of Shakespeare. We can believe, if we like, that

"Shakespeare, Drayton, and Ben Jonson had a merry meeting and, it seems, drank too hard, for Shakespeare died of a fever then contracted."

The authority for this anecdote lies in a note written by John Ward, Vicar of Stratford, some half-century later (1662–1681). Ward is not reliable. He naïvely confessed that he knew little or nothing of Shakespeare's works and must "remember to peruse them." That the Vicar of Stratford could admit such ignorance of the town's immortal son and Avon's matchless Swan shows how little progress had been made locally by the Shakespeare Industry within the fifty years after the poet's death.

As Judith Shakespeare, the second daughter, was married to Thomas Quyney in February, 1616, there was doubtless a celebration of some kind. This Drayton may have attended, since he stayed often at Clifford Chambers near-by. He was a patient of the poet's son-in-law, Dr. Hall, and was cured by him of a tertian fever with an infusion of violets. It was a pity that the doctor could not do as much for his wife's father, who was only fifty-two when he died.

Shakespeare's grave was in the chancel, which was a place of honour. "The earth can yield me but a common grave," he himself had written in early life. But in the end, though he never reached Westminster, he fared as well as might be for a Stratford man. The honorific site of his tomb, however, had no direct connection with his poetry and plays. His town was rapidly becoming Puritanical, and many of the citizens, who may privately have been proud of Shakespeare's renown and may have liked him as a

27

neighbour and a man, would have denounced his profession and the source of his wealth. As early as 1602
the Corporation of Stratford had voted against
receiving plays or interludes in the town. As Fripp,
in *Shakespeare, Man and Artist,* two most valuable
volumes especially rich in local research, has pointed
out, the poet had a right to lie in the Chancel, not
because of his immortal verse, but as a lessee of tithes.
As ever in England, property was more than poetry.
The well-known sonnet of one William Basse,
beginning:

"Renowned Spencer, lye a thought more nye
 To learned Chaucer, and rare Beaumont lye
 A little neerer Spenser, to make roome
 For Shakespeare in your threefold, fowerfold
     Tombe,"

had been taken as proof that the London-Stratford
battle, of which we shall have more to say later on,
had already begun and that there was a plan to take
Shakespeare's coffin to Westminster, despite the
doggerel on the tomb which implored a curse on all
disturbing the poet's bones. There is no chance of
certainty here. It is probable that London was not
greatly concerned about Shakespeare. He had retired
from its life and his status, though high among his
colleagues, was not one of strong pre-eminence.
Webster in his introductory epistle to *The White*

Devil (1612) mentioned, after Jonson, Beaumont, and Fletcher, "the right happy and copious industry of M. Shake-speare, M. Decker, and M. Heywood." Webster paid compliments all round. To him Shakespeare was just one of the top class. The pyramid of praise was yet to come.

Others of the period who mentioned Shakespeare as one of a talented group, but not predominant in genius, were Richard Carew (1614)—he regarded Sidney as "the miracle of the age"—Edmund Howes (1615), Edmund Bolton (1616) and John Taylor (1620). There was general fondness for the man and admiration of his work, but there was little or no idea that posterity would regard him as a colossal giant among normal creatures. Jonson then seemed most likely to be the Immortal Bard of that busy, brilliant world. Now a production of a Jonson play is quite a scarce event. The mighty Laureate and monarch of the Jacobean and Caroline tavern-wits is to-day little read and less acted. Too rare Ben Jonson! A bitter irony is here. Ben had, with justice, a good conceit of himself. How he would have roared at the suggestion of a Shakespeare Cult so intense in its fervour and so widely spread as to constitute an international Shakespeare Industry!

So Westminster went without Shakespeare. But London, in the person of his old colleagues, did come to Stratford six years later. The King's Men, his own company, toured the Midlands in the summer of

1622. Among their "dates" were Leicester, June 8th, and Coventry, August 9th. At Stratford they were paid six shillings for *not* performing in the Guild Hall.

Their visit to Stratford was surely made for personal reasons. The players must have known that Stratford was now becoming sternly anti-theatrical. The Council's resolution of 1602 had been strengthened in 1612. The penalty of 10s. imposed on convicted play-actors was increased to £10, following, it was stated, the example of other well-governed cities and boroughs. Yet, even so, the law was occasionally broken, as Fripp points out. Some players got 5s. in Stratford in 1618 and the owners of a puppet-show 3s. 4d. The King's Men did not play during their visit in 1622, but they were very decently treated with a grant of 6s. for doing nothing, a gift which must have considerably infuriated the Puritan party.

What were they doing in Stratford? Heminge and Condell, in process of editing the First Folio, were doubtless in quest of papers and may have found some at Shakespeare's house, New Place, into which Dr. and Mrs. Hall had moved. Fripp also connects this journey with the well-known monumental effigy in the church:

"This was the work of Gerard Johnson, the sculptor of John Combe's tomb. It occupied him in his workshop at Southwark near the Globe, where the Poet's old friends could drop in to criticise it, and eventually was brought down to Stratford and put up in the restored Chancel for the admiration of his relatives and neighbours— and, if our conjecture is right, of the King's Men on tour that summer in Warwickshire."

The bust executed by G. Janssen, or Johnson, a Flemish mason working on the Bankside in London, is generally disparaged. It is a heavy dull presentment of a heavy dull person and Shakespeare, whatever else he may have been, simply cannot have been heavy and dull. It may be summarised that it was based on the death-mask of a dying man: in that case it is not the Shakespeare we would choose to remember. Certainly it is a dreadful effigy on which to found a cult and an industry of veneration. Professor Dover Wilson in his brilliant essay on "The Essential Shakespeare" likes the frame of it. "The proportions of it are admirable, and the architectural design, with its pillars and canopy, its mantled shield, and its twin cherubs, is even beautiful," but the face, he believes, "might suit well enough with an affluent and retired butcher, but does gross wrong to the dead poet. 'Some men there are love not a gaping pig,' and for half the unlearned world this Shakespeare simply will not do." He further quotes Mr. H. Spielmann on "its wooden appearance and vapid expression" and "its coarsely-shaped, half-moon eyebrows, more like

George Robey's than anybody else's," and its "nose too small for the face."

Good or ill, this effigy, originally painted over in colours, has caused a deal of argument. It has had strange adventures. In 1746 it was said to have become "much impaired and decayed." A company of players led by the grandfather of Mrs. Siddons gave a performance in aid of a Repair Fund and a "Mr. John Hall, limner," was later set to work. Sir Edmund Chambers in his *William Shakespeare,* Vol. II, page 183, suggests that Hall touched up the colouring as part of his job. In 1793 Malone persuaded the Vicar of Stratford to have it brought back to its original state by painting it stone-colour. In 1861 a Mr. Simon Collins put on the present colours, the gown black, the cushion green and red, the doublet scarlet, and the hair and beard auburn. But the adventures of the poet's colour-scheme are a trifle compared with the Dugdale mystery. Dugdale was a traveller of some scholarship who published in his *Antiquities of Warwickshire* (1656) his own drawing of the monument. And it is radically different from the bust as we know it now. As Chambers puts it:

"The allegorical figures, one with an hour-glass, the other with a spade, are poised at the extreme ends of the cornice, where no Renaissance sculptor would have placed them. The bust itself is

elongated; the elbows project angularly; there are
no pen and paper; the face is narrow and
melancholy, more like that of a tailor than of a
humorist; the moustache droops, instead of following a straight line with an uptwist at each end."

This naturally supplied plentiful raw material to
what one may call the "argle-bargle" side of the
Shakespeare Industry, and has given vast employment
to authors, publishers, printers, and paper-makers.
Was Dugdale just an incompetent draughtsman?
Were the 1748 repairs an entire reconstruction and,
if so, why and what model did they follow? Or was
there some great "plant"? The Baconians naturally
smell conspiracy and a sinister hand at work here.
Chambers cites some of the literature on the problem,
which it is not our business to unravel. One thing
at any rate the effigy has achieved. It has helped to
build up the Shakespeare Mystery and what a blessing that has been to many phases of the Shakespeare
Industry! The poet not only bequeathed no papers
and no diaries that survived. He has actually left us
with a graven image which looked utterly different
three hundred years ago, that is if we can trust Dugdale. There, as they say, the matter rests, with debate
unrestfully and unceasingly rumbling round those
auburn locks and about the puffy, pudding-like face.

The three players remembered in Shakespeare's
will were Burbage, Heminge, and Condell. Burbage,

the chief player of the King's Men, "created," as
actors say, most of the "big leads,"

"Young Hamlet, old Hieronimo,
Kind Lear, the grievèd Moor and more beside,"

as a funeral elegy informs us.

He did not long survive his author and colleague.
He had a seizure on March 12th, 1619, and died
almost at once. Condell lived on till 1627, Heminge
till 1630. Both were buried in St. Mary's, Alderman-
bury; indeed, one might describe them as cremated
there, since the old church was destroyed in the Great
Fire and rebuilt by Wren in 1677. Both had lived
for many years in the parish. To its population they
had added generously, begetting no less than twenty-
three children between them. To its fame they also
added much, as editors of the First Folio of Shakespeare's collected plays. In the churchyard was set,
in 1895, a memorial pedestal which includes a representation of the Folio's title-page carved in stone. It
is well that they are remembered. For, by editing
Shakespeare, albeit in a slovenly way, they contributed more to drama and scholarship as well as to
the Shakespeare Industry than did any others of the
time. Our obligation to them is incalculable.

When the King's Men were at Stratford in 1622
Heminge and Condell must surely have inquired at
New Place for help with manuscripts and papers and
may have received some. If not, they were strangely

remiss. The Folio appeared in the following year. We can surmise that Shakespeare, in his partial retirement, was looking over his writings with a view to putting them in order and into a single volume. Ben Jonson had recently set the fashion for collection and recension of one's plays. That Shakespeare, in his leisure, might attempt the same is a fair conjecture. So far there had been published, in quarto form, the text of nineteen of Shakespeare's plays. Some of these texts were stolen, many were imperfect. The two editors of the Folio claimed to present the maimed versions "cured and perfect of their limbs." The perfection was more of a boast than a reality. The printing, by Isaac Jaggard and Edward Blount, was a careless piece of work and contained many thousands of misprints. Isaac Jaggard was just taking over from his father William, who was in failing health and losing his sight at the time, and died immediately after the appearance of the volume. The finance of the venture was supplied by two others, Smithweeke and Apsley, as well as by Jaggard and Blount. To them, as well as to Heminge and Condell, we owe the text of eighteen plays of Shakespeare which would otherwise have vanished, including "The Tempest" and two of the major tragedies, "Macbeth" and "Antony and Cleopatra." It is a mighty debt.

Ben Jonson contributed to the Folio verses of seemingly ungrudging admiration (some have read them as ironic) and these are so well known as to be not

worth quoting afresh. Jonson, too, had some responsibility for the Folio, because he had already set the
new example of treating playhouse texts as potential
literature worthy to be preserved, and of collecting
and editing them for posterity. It is not known how
many copies of the First Folio were printed; probably
as many as a thousand, of which less than two hundred, most of them damaged copies, survive. (First
Folio prices now vary according to the condition of
the book and the prosperity of the U.S.A. Ten
thousand dollars is a fair average.) Another edition
was demanded within nine years and so a Second
Folio, printed by Cotes, appeared in 1632. There
were no more Folios until after the Restoration. The
Third, which carried "Pericles" and the "apocryphal"
pieces, "The London Prodigal," "Thomas, Lord
Cromwell," "The Puritan," "Sir John Oldcastle,"
"The Yorkshire Tragedy," and "Locrine," appeared
in 1664 and many copies were destroyed in the Great
Fire. It is a noteworthy sign of some growth in the
Shakespeare Industry that it was now thought worth
while to include as Shakespearean six plays of dubious
authorship. These had been printed in his own time
with his name and initials, but the fact that his colleagues, who knew all his work intimately, did not
include them in the First Folio, strongly suggests that
these attributions were baseless. Piratical printers
were simply usurping a good name: it is possible,
however, that Shakespeare contributed something to

each or some of these pieces, and the ingenious can pore over them with pleasure for traces of the master's hand.

The First Folio contained a copperplate engraving of the poet by a young and incompetent artist called Droeshout. The bust in the church, which Dugdale reproduced in so radically different a form from its present one, has caused trouble enough. The wretched Droeshout portrait has caused almost as much discussion. Those who think that the name of "Shakespeare" was a mask for another personality, perhaps that of some highly-placed person who could not admit that he mixed with the "Harlotry players" and wrote stage-plays, can point to the Droeshout picture as aid for their cause. Whatever the reason may have been, the Droeshout face has the look of a dummy propped up on a pole and certainly does not suggest the head of a genius supported on a real neck. There is something queer, too, about the body and its clothing. The doublet suggests that both the arms are left arms. The portrait exists in a "proof" and an improved form, but the differences do not affect the generally unsatisfactory nature of the work. As Chambers puts it: "The head is too large for the body. The line of the jaw is too hard. There is bad drawing in the hair, eyes, nose, ear and mouth, which is too much to the right. The lines of the dress are distorted. The lighting comes from more than one direction." Worse still, for the ordinary lover of

Shakespeare, is the utter prosaic flatness of the thing. It is as bad as the effigy in the church and may have been taken from it. Professor Dover Wilson will not have Droeshout any more than Janssen and puts a kind of tentative faith in an unidentified Tudor portrait of a young man now hanging in the Rylands Library at Manchester:

"As the inscription at the top shows, he was Shakespeare's exact contemporary, and a comparison with the Droeshout engraving reveals the further coincidence that the relative distances from the chin to the lower lip, from the lower lip to the tip of the nose, from the tip of the nose to the lower eyelid, from the lower eyelid to the eyebrow, and from the eyebrow to the top of the forehead, are identical in both portraits, a fact which is not to be despised seeing that honest Droeshout and Janssen would take a pride in getting their faces right by the squier.' The similarity too of the great foreheads is particularly striking. Beyond these coincidences there is nothing whatever to connect the unknown youth of the wonderful eyes and the oval Shelley-like face with the poet who was also twenty-four years old in 1588."

Professor Dover Wilson can fairly claim that the Rylands picture reveals the kind of man who could have written "Hamlet." The Droeshout-Janssen head

is that of a "puddin'-headed" William who could
never have written anything except a note of hand to
buy malt on a rising market, which Master Shakespeare of New Place apparently did do as a side-line
in life but not, unless the Baconians or Oxfordians
are right after all, as his main occupation.

Opposite the Droeshout Portrait in the First Folio
"B.I.," i.e. Ben Jonson, set these somewhat equivocal
lines:

To the Reader.

> This Figure, that thou here seest put,
>   It was for gentle Shakespeare cut;
> Wherein the Grauer had a strife
>   With Nature, to out-doo the life:
> O, could he but haue drawne his wit
>   As well in brasse, as he hath hit
> His face; the Print would then surpasse
>   All, that was euer writ in brasse.
> But, since he cannot, Reader, looke
>   Not on his Picture, but his Booke.

Various interpretations have been set on that advice
to prefer the text to the illustration. It is advice that
all wise people will take. In "his Booke" lies Shakespeare's true image for those who have eyes to discern
it. However, as was said before, there is nothing like
a mystery to make men happy. The Shakespeare
Industry has dealt lavishly in oil and canvas. The discovery of "Genuine Shakespeare Portraits" has been

going on briskly ever since the eighteenth century. The most reputable of the rivals to Droeshout has been the Chandos Portrait, now in the National Portrait Gallery and alleged to have been painted by Burbage and passed to us through the hands of Sir William Davenant, the Poet Laureate of Charles II, who used to boast that he was Shakespeare's bastard. That is as may be. So are all the Shakespeare Portraits. These are not quite as common as fools, of whom there is said to be one a minute on the arrival list. But there is usually a new Shakespeare Portrait turning up every six months. The zeal of the eighteenth century, which even forged new Shakespeare plays, set a brisk pace in portraits of the Bard. We still continue their creativity, faint perhaps, but busily pursuing.

In London Shakespeare's plays continued to be acted; "Othello," "Henry VI," and "A Winter's Tale" were especially favoured. Charles I is said to have "Well liked 'Cymbeline.' " But Ben was the monarch, reigning with his vast bulk throned in the Apollo Room of Simon Wadloe's Old Devil Tavern. At the Mermaid he and Shakespeare had met and wrangled as equals: in later years Jonson was supreme, his admirers countless and sealed as "The Tribe of Ben." When he died, twenty-one years after Shakespeare, crowds followed his body to Westminster. There could be no Shakespeare Industry while Ben was alive.

In Stratford, too, there could be no organised remembrance. The Puritans were winning and the players were not wanted. Shakespeare's son-in-law was himself a leader of the Puritans and it is quite conceivable that members of his family were more glad to forget one who had lived and laboured in the motley than to remember his triumphs in that cloth. The new Vicar of Stratford, Wilson, was a strong and eloquent Puritan. There was much conflict in the town about a Maypole, whose ancient rituals and phallic suggestion would naturally be abhorrent to the stricter moralists. There was a Royal permit, issued by King James in the "King's Book of Sports" for the use of Maypoles. But many in Stratford put conscience before King and would rather join in an anti-Maypole riot for righteousness' sake than indulge in the old revels of the spring-time dance.

Dr. Hall, son-in-law of the poet, settled in New Place, favoured the Puritans, and prospered greatly in medicine. His counsel was sought far and wide. He wrote, in Latin, a record of his more interesting cases which was translated into English by a colleague called Cooke and published in 1657, long after Hall's death, which occurred in 1635. The volume had the charming title of *Select Observations on English Bodies.* Unfortunately the English body of William Shakespeare was not mentioned, though Hall describes the cure of Mrs. Hall, the poet's daughter Susanna, from colic, scurvy, and melan-

41

cholia, and of his other daughter, Elizabeth, whose mouth, after a convulsion, was somehow set crooked in her face, "struck so," as the nursemaids say. This was owing to a chill caught on April 22nd. Visitors to the Birthday Celebrations know those Stratford Aprils. Let them beware of East Winds, wrap up accordingly, and not return from pilgrimage with their mouths apparently nibbling their own ears.

The learned doctor's loyalty to the new religion did not prevent him from having aristocratic and Papist clients. When in pain they would turn to the clever Puritan of Stratford. Fripp quotes: "Such as hated him for his religion often made use of him!" Among the English bodies of Hall's "select observations" was "Lady Smith, Roman Catholic, cruelly afflicted with wind." It was a tight-laced time. "Cut my lace, Charmian," said Shakespeare's Cleopatra when faint at ill news. The bodices worn by ladies of quality in the seventeenth century must have borne very hardly on victims of flatulence, and one can easily imagine poor Lady Smith anxious rather to be relieved by a skilful Puritan than to have no ease at all from the agonies of her distension.

The direct line of the poet's succession died out with his granddaughter Elizabeth Hall, who married twice and had no issue. The connection with New Place was lost, but visitors to Stratford were beginning to regard the tomb in the Church as an essential "sight." A Lieutenant Hammond of the Military

Company of Norwich was the first to leave a record
of Shakespearean sight-seeing. This was in 1634.
Among things "worth observing" at Stratford he
found, and duly observed: "A Neat Monument of the
famous English poet, Mr. William Shakespeere, who
was borne heere." He also saw the verses, attributed
to Shakespeare, on the grave of the greedy old usurer
Combe, ten-per-cent Combe.

"Tenn in the hundred here lyeth engraved
A hundred to tenn his soule is now saved,
If anny one aske who lyeth in this Tombe
Oh ho quoth the Divell tis my John a Combe."

One Dobyns, another Stratford visitor nearly forty
years later, noted Shakespeare's and Combe's
sepulchres and added:
"Since my being at Stratford the heires of Mr.
Combe have caused these verses to be razed, so that
now they are not legible." No, there was no careful
Shakespeare Industry then. Fancy permitting to be
"razed" anything associated with the Bard! Visiting
the poet's grave became fairly common at the end
of the century. There are several travellers' allusions
to it in letters preserved.

The Commonwealth put the theatre out of action.
The Restoration restored William Shakespeare as
well as Charles Stuart. But he came back, like
Hamlet's father's ghost, in questionable shape. It was

the age of adaptation and titivation. Dryden, regarding Shakespeare as a talented barbarian, the voice of a Dark Age, rewrote "Antony and Cleopatra" and "The Tempest," to suit the new epoch of illumination.

Nahum Tate was another adapter. The liberties taken were enormous. New characters were freely introduced. Song and dance were added even to the tragedies. Pepys liked greatly "the variety of dancing and music" in "Macbeth" and saw a version of "Measure for Measure" in which Benedick and Beatrice arrived. The history of Shakespearean adaptation and revision, an appalling record of outrages and vulgarities, has been fully related by Professor Odell in his *Shakespeare from Betterton to Irving.*

Betterton was more faithful than the others. Born in 1635 and playing until he was 75, he was the first of the post-Shakespearean actors to make a Stratford pilgrimage; this he probably did in 1708. He inherited the traditions of the Shakespearean Globe. Theatre itself, for he was a pupil and colleague of Sir William Davenant, in turn a pupil and colleague of the King's Men whom Shakespeare knew. John Downes in 1708 said that Betterton's Hamlet was directed by Davenant who saw Mr. Taylor of the Blackfriars Company act it and Taylor had been "instructed by the Author, Mr. Shaksepeur." Betterton also drew on William Beeston for information as to the way in which the great parts were first performed. Beeston's father, Christopher, is mentioned as acting with Shakespeare in Jonson's *Every Man in his Humour* in 1598. He did not stay with Shakespeare's company, but much later in life was manager of the Cockpit, where many of Shakespeare's plays were given in the reign of King Charles I. In 1636, for example, "Julius Cæsar" and "The Merry Wives of Windsor" were given there.

If old Beeston talked to his son William and the latter remembered and did not add to what he heard, Aubrey, the author of *Brief Lives* (1681), was going to the right source when he mentioned Beeston as the man to give him information. Aubrey probably got from Beeston, whose authority as one "who knows most of him" (Shakespeare) he mentions in a note, the remark that Shakespeare was not a company-keeper and "would not be debauched: if invited to, writ: he was in paine." That Shakespeare should have pleaded one kind of headache in order to avoid another is likely enough. He was an actor and administrator in London, a landlord and dealer in property at home. And he had to get those plays written sometime. So the message "Sorry, engaged with a headache," or words to that effect, must have been serviceable many times. Debauchery in those days was hard work. The standard of consumption and absorption seems to have been high, judged by the menus of feasts. The food was heavily spiced:

the wine was rich. Let anyone who wishes to acquire
a specialised knowledge of liver attacks or to write a
learned History of Hangovers apply himself freely
to the sweet sticky stuff called "sack," so memorably
appraised by Shakespeare's Falstaff. Shakespeare's
claim to be "in pain," when called to a long, wet
evening, must often have been prudent.

The interest in Shakespeare as a man was at last
growing. Aubrey is the first of his biographers and
sums up the Shakespeare legend as it had so far taken
shape. He spoke of young William as a butcher's boy
who would rant over a dying calf and left Stratford
for London at eighteen. "He was a handsome well-
shapt man: very good company and of a very readie
and pleasant smooth Witt." According to Aubrey, he
returned to the country every year. Aubrey says of
Davenant, the leading figure of the Restoration
Theatre, that his father was a Vintner in Oxford:—

"a very grave and discreet Citizen: his mother
was a very beautifull woman, and of a very good
witt and of conversation extremely agreable. . . .
Mr. William Shakespeare was wont to goe into
Warwickshire once a yeare, and did commonly in
his journey lye at this house in Oxon: where he was
exceedingly respected. (I have heard parson
Robert D[avenant] say that Mr. W. Shakespeare
here gave him a hundred kisses.) Now Sr. Wm.
would sometimes when he was pleasant over a glasse

46

of wine with his most intimate friends e.g. Sam:
Butler (author of *Hudibras*) &c. say, that it seemed
to him that he writt with the very spirit of Shakespeare, and seemed contented enough to be
thought his Son: he would tell them the story as
above. (in which way his mother had a very light
report, whereby she was called a whore.)"

Some tactful person has scored out the now bracketed
observations about Davenant's mother's "light
report" and the poet's curious addiction to embracing
the Church in no metaphorical sense. It is no doubt
as well. Aubrey was a gossip before he was a historian
and the smile which he himself derived from this odd
century of holy kisses may have been his chief motive
for recording such tittle-tattle. The story of the poet
and the parson may still be gratifying news to those
who regard the author of the Sonnets as the lover of
a ship's cook called Willie Hughes, but otherwise it
is wanting in taste as it is in evidence or probability.

After Aubrey the lives and legends of Shakespeare
grow apace. Rowe's Life appeared in 1709, and after
that the ceaseless flow of rumour and anecdote begins.
There were yarns about the deer-stealing in Lucy's
park, about the local carousing at various villages,
notably "Drunken Bidford," about the flight to
London and the holding of horses' heads outside the
theatre, about the rhymes he made on Stratford
characters, about his adventures and amours in

47

London, his rivalries with Burbage in love-affairs and with Jonson in his work, about his relations with Queen Bess and King James. How much of it is true? Tradition exaggerates, but it often has a central core of truth. True or not, the provision of anecdotes began to pay. The Industry was growing. The hunger for gossip and relics was profitably fed. Local figures were beginning to profit by Stratford's Shakespearean fame. There was John Jordan, who was born at Tiddington, near Stratford, and trained as a wheelwright. Mr. John Mair, in his excellent study of that early pioneer on the shady side of the Industry, William Ireland, "The Fourth Forger," naturally pays some attention to this humbler adventurer in the art and craft of Shrine-Guidance. Jordan, he says:

"possessed a deep and muddled enthusiasm for history and the arts without the education or abilities to perfect himself in either. The Stratford Jubilee stirred his ambitions, and he presented Garrick with a poetical address of unparalleled dullness and mediocrity, following up this attempt eight years later with an historical poem based on the legends surrounding Welcombe Hills, near Stratford. But his poetry was not a success, and he soon found that Shakespeare offered him far the greater possibilities." . . .

"With his dark, heavy face, fuzzy black hair and ploughman's physique, Jordan gave a deceptive

48

impression of honest stupidity, and William con-
descendingly describes him as 'an honest fellow'
and a 'civil inoffensive creature.' Actually he was
a quick-witted romancer with an extraordinary gift
of judging exactly how much each enquirer would
swallow."

At any rate, Jordan did better by telling good stories
than by writing bad verses. In 1793 he was guide to
the two Irelands, father and son, at a profit. He led
them up Anne Hathaway's garden, where Samuel
Ireland, a passionate antiquarian, actually bought "a
bugle-purse given by Shakespeare during his courting
and the very oak chair in which the poet used to sit
holding Anne upon his knee." The authenticity of
these articles was, of course, wholly unproven. But
Samuel Ireland was a fish ready to rise at any
sufficiently antiquated bait. Stratford, under the
leadership of a quick salesman called Sharp, was turning up its sleeves and getting to work on its new
staple. It was now fully realised that the relics and
anecdotes of a mere poet could, by some miracle, sell
better than grain and beasts.

CHAPTER III

THE GOLDEN BOUGH

"And from his touchwood trunk the mulberry tree
Supplied such relics as devotion holds
Still sacred, and preserves with pious care . . .
So 'twas a hallowed time."
—COWPER.

DURING the early part of the eighteenth century there was no great enthusiasm for the veneration of antiques. Complacence with the present was blithely maintained. Dryden had deemed Shakespeare "scarce intelligible to a refinéd age" and rewritten him accordingly. The subsequent Age of Reason considered itself equally refined and preferred its Shakespeare to be brought up to date. The First Georgians did not found Societies for the Preservation of Tudor or of Stuart England or regard Elizabethan texts as sacrosanct. They knew better. It was a century, indeed, in which vandalism had a free hand. We may regard our own period as atrocious in the misuse of destructive power, but at least we manage to stop some crimes and make a worthy fuss about others. The greatest megalithic temple of Europe, which England was lucky to possess at Avebury on Salisbury Plain, was

50

destroyed by a few stone-hungry farmers with none
to raise a hand or voice in its defence. To be antique
was to be barbarous. Shrines were not yet in fashion;
not yet had ruins and relics become the raw materials
of a thriving industry.

But, as the century came into its middle reaches,
there was a noticeable change of attitude. Shakespeare's plays, in versions suitably amended by
Cibber and Garrick, following the first essays in this
kind by Tate and Dryden, were presented to the
refinéd age and commended. The tragedies had
happy endings. Juliet lived on to love, and Lear to
be a Methuselah. Yet there was a new phase of
opinion which, instead of despising a barbarous
antiquity, began to patronise it. An appetite for the
old-world was growing. Noblemen of wealth and
cultivation started to remember the glories of the
past and admitted that a Gothic revival might help
to embellish and enliven the serene civilities of the
classical style which ruled in architecture and in
decoration. It became necessary to have, secreted in
the parks which surrounded the Palladian mansions
of the eighteenth-century grandee, a set of ruins, some
ivy-mantled towers, and an outfit of the newfangled
"canals," an aquatic crazy pavement with which the
gentry sought to diversify and to romanticise their
grounds and pleasaunces. In Coleman's comedy,
"The Clandestine Marriage," there is much allusion
to the new vogue for Gothic in and around a noble-

man's seat. Straight lines were losing favour. The new mode was "crinkle-crankle," as Lord Ogleby remarked.

The backward-looking glance, which was now permissible or even obligatory in men of breeding and of culture, did not miss Stratford and its Shakespeare. Even before Garrick imposed upon that town his famous Jubilee and Jamboree of 1769, and so presented England with its first great essay in Mass-Bardolatry, the attention of many had been directed to the banks of the Avon where the architecture was sufficiently "crinkle-crankle" to evoke considerable raptures from the devotees of sentimental history. In 1709 the dramatist Rowe had provided the public not only with an edition of Shakespeare but also with a Life. This contained a good deal of anecdote which has since been discredited. The poaching, for example, of Sir Thomas Lucy's deer cannot have taken place because the Lucy family at the time had neither park nor herd. Richard Davies, Vicar of Sapperton in Gloucestershire from 1695 to 1708, had started the story: he was an ignorant man, thought Shakespeare's Justice Shallow was Justice Clodpate, and made every possible kind of misstatement in telling the story. But the eighteenth century began at last to like this kind of antiquarian gossip and to "take-up" Shakespeare and his legends very much as a modern hostess might take up a Bloomsbury poet, beard, bunkum, and all.

Accordingly sight-seeing and relic-hunting began to be a popular pastime. One reason of several why Shakespeare's home, New Place in Chapel Street, Stratford, and the mulberry-tree alleged to have been planted by his hand were destroyed was their excessive popularity with the pushers and peepers who are now so large and turbulent a section of society. The coach-and-horses were already anticipating the motor-coach in the seventeen-fifties. The tripper was on the move and the "rubber-neck" was arriving before Garrick brought the London blades and wits and beauties to observe his antics at the shrine. The first detachments of the great army of standers-and-starers who now occupy Stratford in force every summer week-end, one might almost say on every summer afternoon, had begun their operations. The owner of the property, so long left to peace and privacy but now at length deemed sacrosanct, was a testy, quarrel-some man who could not get on with Stratford people at the best of times. The visitors added to his rage. He was ready to cut down both house and tree in order to spite their infuriating faces.

The history of New Place had been complicated. The house had been built by the local laird, Sir Hugh Clopton, Knight, in the reign of Henry VII. The Cloptons, whose name still attaches to a local mansion and to Stratford's famous and lovely bridge across the Avon, were wealthy folk and did things well. Leland in 1542 saw New Place and praised its looks. Dugdale, in the following century, called it a "fair house of brick and timber." It was the chief house of the town, having ten rooms and a frontage of sixty feet, a breadth in one place of seventy, and a height of twenty-eight. (Its importance was proved by the fact that when, during the Civil War, Queen Henrietta arrived in the town, she was quartered there.) During Elizabeth's reign it passed from the hands of the seigneurial Cloptons to a lawyer named Bott and from him to another local lawyer, William Underhill of Idlicote. Shakespeare, newly enriched by his London successes in poetry and drama, and by the generous favours of Southampton, bought the property for £60 in 1597 and remained in possession till his death. How much, if any, of his work was done there nobody can say for certain. Tradition held that he went into Warwickshire once a year and certainly much of his later writing seems to have been coloured by garden-tints and mellowed by green thoughts in such green shades as Stratford might provide. Naturally then, if Stratford were to develop Shakespearean salesmanship and the new kind of visitor needed something at which to stare, New Place was a strong attraction and took its place in the centre of the Stratfordian shop-window.

By the poet's will New Place and the lands which went therewith passed to his elder married daughter, Susanna Hall, for life, and then to her daughter, Elizabeth. She became the wife of Thomas Nash, who

54

died in 1647. Mistress Nash did not remain lonely for long. Two years later she married John Barnard, Lord of the Manor of Abington near Northampton, a patron of letters and owner of a library. At the Restoration he was made a baronet and Shakespeare's granddaughter was consequently titled. Lady Barnard died in 1670, Sir John in 1674. Among his goods and chattels were "books" to the value of £29 11: od. and "old goods and lumber at Stratford-upon-Avon" worth £4. As Barnard was a literary man, inheriting direct from Shakespeare by his daughter and heir, Susanna Hall, and her child and heir Elizabeth, the books and lumber may very well have included volumes and papers which would now be worth enormous sums of money. It is difficult to imagine the saleable value to-day, with serial and all translation rights, of a Shakespeare Diary. But there was no Shakespeare Industry in those days and the treasure, if there was any, was dispersed. Lady Barnard seems to have been somewhat lacking both in family piety and in that financial acumen which would properly assess the value of her grandfather as a lock-up investment. She left New Place in 1653, and appointed trustees for its sale.

In 1675 the house, whose value had now risen to over £1,000, was in the hands of a Sir Edward Walker. His only daughter, Barbara, married one of the Cloptons. So the wheel had come full circle. The property was once more in the hands of its original builders and owners. They, too, had no conception of its potential value and there was a drastic reconstruction early in the eighteenth century. This action may have conferred on New Place the existing notions of "all modern comforts" and it certainly provided the famous old house with an entirely new front. It was no mere case of gentle face-lifting. The Tudor building became frankly Georgian. Those who curse the parson Gastrell for his vandalism in destroying the house altogether half a century later should remember that the Cloptons had already got rid of the building as Shakespeare knew it. The chief local family it was that so wastefully dissipated the greatest possible asset in what was soon to be the chief local industry.

The last Clopton owner, Sir Hugh, died in 1751. His trustee and son-in-law then disposed of New Place to the Rev. Francis Gastrell, Vicar of Frodsham in Cheshire, on whose head posterity has poured a stream of curses not wholly justified. He seems to have been a highly irritable divine and lacking in the Christian virtues of patience and peacefulness. He quarrelled with the Town Council on several points of law about property and his dislike for the people of his new home appears to have been amply returned. The tourist trade was then starting and Gastrell, as the occupant of New Place, was in some degree its victim. In his rage he smashed two of the borough's chief Shakespeare Relics. In 1756 he cut down the Shakespeare Mulberry Tree. In 1759 he razed the entire building of New Place to the ground and left the town, as the villain in melodrama should leave the stage, amidst a storm of hisses. And rightly. For Gastrell, with the Cloptons, had committed a commercial as well as a cultural rape.

The mulberry-tree at New Place had begun to acquire sacrosanctity because of the tradition that Shakespeare had planted it, which shows how the temper of Bardic veneration and of relic-worship had risen by the middle of the eighteenth century. The evidence for the belief is merely a report of a statement made by an interested party, Thomas Sharp, of whose lively ability to exploit a commercial opportunity we shall hear more presently. Sharp swore on oath that Sir Hugh Clopton had told him that Shakespeare planted the tree. There is no reason whatever why Shakespeare should not have done so. The mulberry is a pleasant and useful tree. It thrives abundantly in Stratford and a noble specimen has flourished through the centuries in the garden of Hall's Croft, the lovely house in Old Town, once occupied by Shakespeare's son-in-law, Dr. Hall, the husband of his elder child, Susanna.

It is interesting to note that the connection of mulberries with the Dramatic Muse has been sustained at another Midland town, which, if not already hallowed, is at least a potential shrine. Mr. Bernard Shaw once assailed Bardolatry in his journalistic youth, but he established Shaviolatry at Malvern in his play-writing maturity by his constant attendance at, and contributions to, the dramatic festivals held in that town. He took up the trowel, in the best manner of a local hero, and planted a Shaw Mulberry Tree in the Public Gardens of Malvern Spa. This he did by public invitation, and to the great public delight, in order to celebrate his eightieth birthday in July, 1936. The task was executed amid a battery of cine-cameras and a vast tangle of news-reel apparatus. The art and craft of planting cultural mementoes has notably advanced since the days when Shakespeare may quietly have added a mulberry-tree to his garden at New Place. Nobody at any rate will ever be able to dispute the authenticity of the Shavian timbers. There is this to be said for modern publicity: it will save posterity from a deal of tiresome argument. If Shakespeare had been continually pursued by recorders, interviewers, and photographers, as Mr. Shaw has been, our scholars would now be spared enormous amounts of research and the stress of ceaseless disputation.

But to return to Gastrell. The parson from Cheshire had thought to live quietly in the house. He had not realised the consequence of entering a nascent temple. There is no evidence that he cared anything for Shakespeare's work: he took the house as a house, not as a shrine. But the Shakespeare Industry had been founded and Gastrell, who might have profited vastly by it, was merely rendered peevish and destructive. Trying to live quietly at New Place, he was aggravated by what Wheler, who published a history of Stratford fifty years later, called "the frequent importunities of travellers." What these early clients of the Shakespeare Industry did we can only guess. Presumably they stole the fruit in due season, thus hoping to absorb some precious essence of the poet-planter's genius. Or they carved their names on its trunk, as even the most exalted, Schiller, Sir Walter Scott and the great Duke of Wellington were later on to scribble their names on the wall of the Birthplace. They may have taken their meals untidily in the vicinity and made a filthy mess in the accepted manner of those who first dote upon and then befoul beauty-spots and sites of historic interest.

Gastrell seems to have been as short-sighted as he was short of temper. He was, as other facts show, fond of money. But instead of exploiting his good fortune by charging visitors a fee and initiating the "Bob-a-nob" demand now levelled at visitors by the Birthplace Trustees and the Governors of the Memorial Theatre, instead of selling the mulberries at special prices and ingeniously stimulating a demand for silk made by silk-worms fed on the true Shakespearean mulberry-leaf, instead of turning a piece of ordinary timber into a golden bough, he furiously ordered the axe to be set at the foot of the tree and the whole thing to be disposed of as so much firewood. Thus, he thought, he would be rid of the trippers and also of the dampness which he believed to be invading his house because the tree deprived it of sun and air.

Three years later this reckless and improvident priest destroyed the very house itself. The motive in this case appears to have been meanness rather than hatred of the tourist, a fact which makes even more astonishing his failure to extract profit from the mulberry-tree which he carelessly sold to one of the earliest Stratford profiteers. Gastrell had become engaged in the ancient, popular, but exhausting practice of dodging the tax-gatherer. According to Wheler: "Being compelled to pay the monthly assessments for the maintenance of the poor (some of which he thought to escape because he resided part of the year in Lichfield, though his servants continued in the house during his absence), in the heat of his anger he declared that his house should never be assessed again." Gastrell was a man of quick action as well as of quick temper. The thought of the Stratford poor battening on his rates and taxes so incensed the choleric and thrifty parson that he actually had the famous house entirely destroyed. This deed of foolish violence can only have saved Gastrell in taxes a fraction of what he lost in capital. But he was ready to lose in pocket in order to gratify his spite. Certainly he managed to inflict tremendous loss upon the town which he had come to hate as well as upon all Shakespearean devotees.

True, it was not Shakespeare's own New Place. But it was the next best thing from the relic-lover's point of view: a continuously occupied house which was in the hands of the poet and his family for over half a century and had been reconstructed by a descendant of the original owners, a family which had been paramount in Stratford for centuries. Therefore, had New Place survived it would have become, with the rise of the Shakespeare Industry, the most venerated and most frequented building in the town. The Birthplace, although it has had many adventures and alterations since Shakespeare's time, is now the first attraction. New Place is now a museum mainly exemplifying the Shakespearean way of life, and there is an exquisite garden on the site of the old building, a garden which especially and cunningly displays the flowers mentioned by the poet. But the house, even the reconstructed Cloptonian house of the eighteenth century, would have been another great asset to the town. The angry Gastrell, who so bitterly resented contributing to the meagre social services of the time, as well as undergoing the importunities of the new regiment of cultured pilgrims, inflicted a Parthian shot of the first magnitude when he reduced New Place to dust the better to shake Stratfordian dust off his feet.

Meanwhile, the destruction of New Place had by

no means destroyed the new commerce. Shakespeare's Mulberry Tree had been cut down as firewood, but Stratford prudence was not going to make so wasteful a use of it. A certain Mr. Thomas Sharp bought the object of Gastrell's rage and began a trade in curios which, in one form or another, has been thriving ever since. He carved up the famous mulberry into toys, trinkets and mementoes of all kinds and "A Present from Stratford" of a suitable order was put on the market as soon as the tree had vanished from the garden. Sharp, according to Wheler, turned the tree to much advantage by "converting every fragment into small boxes, goblets, toothpick-cases, tobacco-stoppers and numerous other articles." The golden bough from New Place had the additional merit of being apparently inexhaustible, and the flow of trinkets from Sharp's workshop continued briskly during the following years. In 1769, for example, David Garrick received the freedom of Stratford in a box of this sacred wood, while Mr. George Keat, who "attended Mr. Garrick" with the honourable gift, received a "neat writing-standish" carved from the same tree. In 1769 Garrick received a further medal and wand, also of the Bard's own wood. The tree was certainly being coaxed into an auriferous immortality, sprouting in its death a fine spread of golden boughs. The number of Bardic devotees who in future might be inclined to ponder gratefully upon William and his wood-notes wild whenever they picked their teeth or rammed their tobacco home grew steadily as the years rolled on.

It was scarcely surprising that the Shakespearean Mulberry became, in the course of decades, something of a laughing-stock and even of a scandal. Time marched or galloped on and still the curios emerged from Sharp's memento-factory. It was naturally rumoured that other and less sacred raw material was being utilised. But Sharp stood by his assertions of its authenticity and refused to let the local gossip shiver his profitable timbers. That the controversy was burning brightly forty-three years after the cutting of the tree is a strong tribute to the productivity of its trunk and branches. Still Sharp, who only claimed to have purchased the larger part of the tree and not the whole of it, swore to the genuine nature of his wares. In 1799, near to dying, when his conscience might have been tenderest and his scruples rendered more acute by the shape of things to come, he made an affidavit upon the Four Evangelists, before the Mayor of Stratford and a Justice of the Peace.

Here is Wheler's account of the event and transcription of Sharp's statement:

> Mr. Sharp, being informed that hints were thrown out of his having expended all the *original* tree, in the fabrication of his curiosities, and had purchased other mulberry wood, to furnish him with a sufficiency of toys, called in the Mayor, and

one of the standing Justices of the Peace for the borough, and ordered a friend to draw up an affidavit; wishing to convince the world to the contrary of such insinuations, and enable them to set a proper value upon the relics of the celebrated tree. The affidavit, of which the following is an exact copy, was voluntarily made upon his death-bed, a few days before his dissolution:—

This is to certify, That I, Thos. Sharp, of the borough of Stratford-upon-Avon, in the county of Warwick, clock and watch-maker, was born in the Chapel Street, & baptiz'd Feby. 5th 1724, that I was personally acquainted with Sir Hugh Clopton, Knight, Barrister at Law, & one of the Heralds at Arms; who was son of Sir John Clopton, Knight, that purchased a certain messuage or house near the Chapel, in Stratford, called the New Place, of the executors of Lady Elizabeth Barnard and grand-daughter of Shakespear; and that I have often heard the said Sir Hugh Clopton solemnly declare, that the Mulberry-tree, which growed in his garden, was planted by Shakespear, and he took pride in show-ing it to, and entertaining persons of distinction, whose curiosity exited them to visit the spot, known to be the last residence of the immortal Bard; and, after the decease of the said Sir Hugh, in 1753 the premises were sold to the Reverend *Jno* (Francis) *Gastrel;* who in 1756 cut down the said Mulberry-tree, and cleft it as fire-wood; when the greatest part of it was purchased by me, the said Thos. Sharp; who, out of a sincere veneration for the memory of its celebrated planter, employed one John Luckman to convey it to my own premises;

where I have worked it into many curious toys and usefull articles from the same. And I do hereby declare, & take my solemn oath, upon the four Evangelists, in the presence of Almighty God, that I never had worked, sold, or substituted any other wood, than that what came from, & was part of the same tree, as or for Mulberry-wood. Signed, and a true affidavit made by me,

THOS. SHARP.

Taken and sworn at and in the borough
of Stratford-upon-Avon, this 14th day
of October 1799; before us,

RICHD. ALLEN, Mayor
THOS. NOTT.

It would be unkind to think of perjury in the case of Thomas Sharp, whose picture should have a place of honour were there a Board Room of the Shakespeare Industry decorated with the portraits of the pioneers. We can only conclude that it was a very big tree indeed.

After the mulberry, the crab. This fruitful apple-tree was given sacrosanctity by Jordan, the Stratford contemporary of Sharp who was mentioned in the last chapter as a picker-up and salesman of legends, relics, and the like. One of Jordan's lines was to portray Shakespeare as a hearty drinker and to associate his "pub-crawls" with the neighbouring villages, especially Bidford, an Avonside hamlet with a lovely bridge and some inns not unknown to thirsty tourists to-day. Here are Jordan's own words written about 1770:

"Our Poet was extremely fond of drinking hearty draughts of English Ale, and glory'd in being thought a person of superior eminence in that proffession if I may be alowed the phrase. In his time, but at what period it is not recorded, There were two companys or fraternitys of Village Yeomanry who used frequently to associate together at Bidford a town pleasantly situate on the banks of the Avon about 7 Miles below Stratford, and Who boasted themselves Superior in the Science of drinking to any set of equal number in the Kingdom and hearing the fame of our Bard it was determined to Challenge him and his Companions to a tryal of their skill which the Stratfordians accepted and accordingly repaired to Bidford which place agreeable to both parties was to be the Scene of Contention. But when Shakespeare and his Companions arrived at the destined spot, to their disagreeable disappointment they found the Topers were gone to Evesham fair and were told that if they had a mind to try their strength with the Sippers, they were ther ready for the Contest, Shakespeare and his compainions made a Scoff at their Opponents, but for want of better Company they agreed to the Contest and in a little time

66

42704

our Bard and his Companions got so intollerable intoxicated that they was not able to Contend any longer and accordingly set out on their return to Stratford. But had not got above half a mile on the road e'er the (y) found themselves unable to proceed any farther, and was obliged to lie down under a Crabtree which is still growing by the side of the road where they took up their repose till morning when some of the Company roused the poet and intreated him to return to Bidford and renew the Contest he declined it saying I have drunk with

'Piping Pebworth, Dancing Marston,
Haunted Hillborough, Hungry Grafton,
Dadgeing Exhall, Papist Wicksford,
Beggarly Broom, and Drunken Bidford.' "

The crab-tree cannot have enjoyed much longer life after that. The antiquarian's axe was profitably applied to it and these Bidford timbers began to yield another portentous flow of cups, walking-sticks, and knick-knacks of all kinds. There was a further legend of the Jordan era, and no doubt of Jordan's making, that Shakespeare spent much time and drank heavily at the Falcon Inn, opposite New Place, whose landlord was Julius Shaw, a witness to his will. There appears to be no sort of confirmation for this yarn.

Even, however, before Sharp was swearing before God and the Mayor of Stratford that his toothpick-holders were true mulberry from the one and only sacred stem, the new Industry had begun to lead young minds astray, and had started an evil wave of fibbing and fabrication. It was now worth while to fake up Shakespearean anecdotes and alleged signatures and writings, so keen had become the interest in the man of Stratford, so ready was the public to buy. Chambers, in his schedule of Shakespeare-Fabrications, cites no less than six people probably guilty on this count before the daring efforts of young William Ireland, a conveyancing clerk who had the run of some old deed-boxes and used them to produce an incredible series of Shakespeareana.* His father, an antiquary, seems to have had a charming faith in his son's story of an anonymous gentleman who saved Shakespeare from drowning and was given the manuscripts by the gratified and generous poet. Old Ireland asked no questions and was told a lot of lies. His son, to meet the public appetite for such tit-bits, actually produced such artificial pearls of pastiche as Shakespeare's verses to Miss Hathaway and a letter of Queen Elizabeth to the poet, bidding him to "Hamptowne," a spelling she would never have used and one seized upon by the learned Malone, who ultimately and with great forensic skill as well as scholarship exposed the whole ludicrous business. What seems strange now is that Ireland's "dis-

* Mr. John Mair goes two less and names his clever study of Ireland *The Fourth Forger*. This volume, published in 1938, gives the whole amazing story in detail and renders unnecessary a further investigation oi the young man's activities.

coveries," with their over-worked medievalism, in the manner of Chatterton, ever took in anybody.

However, before the neurotic youngster, feeding his own fantasies of grandeur, had been exposed and disgraced, he had had his fling. It is a common feature of the Shakespeare Industry to snatch the poet's soul in sectarian fervour from the clutching hands of the other sects. The Roman Catholics have frequently laid hands on Shakespeare and not long ago the ingenious and learned Mr. Fripp very nearly equipped the poet with a Noncomformist conscience. Young Ireland was a keen churchman as well as a powerful liar and he sought to save Shakespeare from the Papists by fabricating a "Profession of Faith," which proved him a good Anglican. The most astonishing of Ireland's efforts in Shakespearean exploitation were the supply of bogus MSS. of sections of "Hamlet" and "King Lear," and the actual provision of entire fakes, that is to say, two hitherto unknown Shakespeare plays: "Vortigern and Rowena" and "Henry II." With his effrontery unchecked young Ireland in 1796 persuaded the Drury Lane directors to produce "Vortigern" with Kemble in the lead. There was already suspicion abroad, but Sheridan, who was in charge at the Lane, was no Shakespearean scholar, and what must have been the strangest "first night" in the whole history of the English Stage at last arrived. A huge crowd came to see the novelty, found itself bored by the inadequacy of Ireland's mock-Shakespearean verse, and finally shouted the actors down. The piece was immediately withdrawn. Meanwhile, Malone had built up his case against Ireland and his exposure of the whole business was final. But the game, which seems sometimes to have been played as much for the fun of the thing or in vanity as for profit, was carried on by John Payne Collier (1789–1883), a scholar and librarian who entertained himself by forging old archives in order to produce new information about Shakespeare. Even as late as 1926 a man was sent to prison for similar attacks on public credulity. Portraiture is now the most frequent form of Shakespearean "discovery." A new "Shakespeare Portrait" was only recently on view in Stratford-upon-Avon.

That the trade in relics continued to flourish in the most ingenious forms is shown by the account of William Howitt, whose *Visits to Remarkable Places* was written in 1839 and published in the following year. Howitt had greatly enjoyed Stratford and had stimulated the Shakespeare Industry in various ways. For example, while strolling to Shottery, he met a schoolmaster with some boys and brightly rallied the usher (as he would have phrased it) on the presence of another Shakespeare in the class. The master was not missing a chance like this:

"'I have a Shakspeare here,' said the master with evident pride and pleasure. 'Here, boys, here!' He quickly marshalled his laddish troop in a row, and said to me: 'There now, sir, can you tell which is a Shakspeare?' I glanced my eye along the line, and instantly fixing it on one boy, said: 'That is the Shakspeare.' 'You are right,' said the master; 'that is the Shakspeare: the Shakspeare cast of countenance is there. That is William Shakspeare Smith, a lineal descendant of the poet's sister.' "

Howitt was so pleased with his own sagacity in dis-covering an inheritor of the Bardic Brow that he gave Master Smith sixpence.

"The Boy's eyes sparkled at the sight of the money, and the healthful joyous colour rushed into his cheeks; his fingers continued making acquaint-ance with so large a piece of money in his pocket, and the sensation created by so great an event in the school was evident. It sounded oddly enough, as I was passing along the street in the evening, to hear some of these same schoolboys say to one another, 'That is the gentleman who gave Bill Shakspeare sixpence.' "

It may be surmised that henceforward many a Strat-ford urchin spent his hours in the parish church, with his mind abstracted from the liturgy and greedily wondering how best he could twist his features into resemblance of the famous bust and so put himself among possible collectors of fortuitous small silver.

Howitt further described a house opposite to the Town Hall occupied by a gentleman named Mr. Reason. Reason advertised the ownership and display of articles originally at the poet's Birthplace. These had belonged to his mother-in-law, Mary Hornby, who had left the Birthplace because the owner, aware of the unearned increment brought in by the growth of the Shakespeare Industry, continually raised the rent against her. So Mary went off and set up her show of relics opposite the Town Hall, having first blotted out the famous and precious signatures on the Birthplace walls with a spiteful coat of white-wash. Howitt gives a list of the kind of relics which a visitor to Stratford might then (in the eighteen-thirties) expect to see for his money. As a catalogue of shameless impositions it is rich and strange (they are described in detail in our chapter on the Birthplace) and it is worth remarking that this effrontery was being practised on the English in their own country. The idea that the Americans are the only gullible tourists is complete nonsense. Despite the influence of Washington Irving the Americans can hardly have been visiting Stratford in large numbers in the days of the most primitive steamships and before the arrival of the railway beside the Avon.

In the middle of the nineteenth century the intervention of the Birthplace Trustees, applying proper standards of evidence to the alleged relics, put an end to the major part of these pretences. But the going was evidently good when Howitt was marking down and endowing (to the extent of sixpence) the boyish descendants of the Bard. It would be interesting to know, but it is impossible to discover, when the tree so detested by Gastrell and so wisely purchased by Sharp, yielded its last chip of the sacred timber. It is safe to think, however, that the Golden Bough was fruitful for something like a century, during which it provided incessant material for Warwickshire's new and strange addition to rural England's arts and crafts, namely that of making poetry pay.

CHAPTER IV

"Garrick, no more of jubilees and stuff,
Your acting gives your Shakespeare praise enough,
Let others urge his fame these vulgar ways,
Yours is the most sincere and lasting praise."
—From SHAKESPEARE'S *Garland*.

THE "Garrick Jubilee" of 1769 was the first great effort to organise Shakespearean celebration on the spot. The habit of going piously to Stratford, of which Betterton had been an early practitioner, was growing. Garrick went with the actor Macklin in 1742 and sat talking, it is believed, under the Mulberry Tree with Clopton at New Place. After that, ideas of doing something on the grand scale at and for Stratford began to be constantly in his mind. The chance came in the seventeen-sixties, when Stratford, robbed of New Place and with its precious mulberry-tree in Sharp's prolific workshop, began to realise the potentialities of the Shakespeare Industry and the need for fresh action.

Jubilee—"season of rejoicing; exultant joy." Thus the Oxford Dictionary. There is no reason why a jubilee should be connected with a period of years: the word is derived from a Hebrew term for a ram's

74

horn and suggests trumpet-blowing of a powerful order. The Stratford Jubilee in 1769 had no particular chronological significance. It came five years after the tercentenary of the Poet's birth. But the word was justified. Nobody could have blown his own trumpet louder than did David Garrick.

In 1768 Stratford celebrated the erection of its new Town Hall by granting the freedom of the borough to Mr. Garrick. This honourable document was ordered to be conveyed to him in a "small neat chest" constructed from the inevitable segment of Shakespeare's mulberry and engraved with the images of Shakespeare and Garrick. Garrick thanked the Corporation both for the compliment and for its container—"an elegant and inestimable box"—and out of these exchanged civilities grew the plans for the Jubilee.

The Corporation meanwhile asked for a statue or bust of Shakespeare out of Garrick's collection. Garrick commissioned Gainsborough at a fee of sixty guineas to paint Shakespeare. Gainsborough held the usual views about the Droeshout engraving and the Stratford bust; "I think a stupider face I never beheld," he said. Having damned Droeshout heartily, he said that he would paint the spirit of Shakespeare by study of his works, but evidently the mighty line and wood-notes wild worked feebly on the artist's imagination. Other contracts, with more urgent clients, had to be fulfilled. After four years the effort

75

thus to capture on canvas the genius of the Poet was still fruitless and the project was abandoned. So Garrick had to give Stratford Benjamin Wilson's portrait of Shakespeare, a now dark and unimpressive canvas hanging in the Town Hall, and the statue by Roubiliac which is set above the entrance and gazes down upon the tramping Bardolaters in High Street. Meanwhile, the Corporation, stirred by this generosity, purchased Gainsborough's portrait of Garrick propped against a bust of Shakespeare and set it also on the walls of the Town Hall.

Meanwhile, the Great Event was being prepared by the Avon. Shakespeare's Birthday was not yet a date of importance. The Horse Races were a far greater magnet, so Race Week, in September, was chosen. At Garrick's expense, a Rotunda to be known as Shakespeare's Hall and designed to please the prevailing taste, was built on the Bankcroft. The architect, a Mr. Latimore, came from London. The Rotunda was built to take a thousand spectators and an orchestra of one hundred. (It was called Shakespeare's Hall, but there was no idea of acting Shakespeare's plays in it). Wheler thus describes the glories of the place in which Garrick planned to recite his own poetry: "In the amphitheatre, which was supported by a circular colonnade of columns of the Corinthian order, was built a noble orchestra, large enough to contain upwards of one hundred performers. From the centre of the dome was suspended

GARRICK-UPON-SHAKESPEARE. THE GAINSBOROUGH
PORTRAIT AT STRATFORD-UPON-AVON

an amazingly large chandelier, consisting of eight hundred lights, which had a beautiful effect; in fine, the gilding of the capitals and bases of the columns, the paintings of the ceiling and cornice, the curious pilasters at the angles, and the side ornaments altogether appeared with such symmetry and elegance, 'that it would' (says a contemporary writer), 'make a lover of art sigh to think how soon it would be demolished.'* No person that could be conveyed into it without viewing the outside, could ever conceive it was a building of boards."

Meanwhile, a suitable mobilisation of artillery was made. On the river-bank were set thirty cannon, twelve cohorns, and some mortars which were to be discharged at intervals and made so colossal a din that some attributed the disastrous downpours of rain to their shattering effect upon the clouds. Further preparation was made for a dazzling display of fireworks. That ingenious Italian, Signor Domenico Angelo, arrived from London with two special wagon-loads of rockets, squibs and fairy lamps and busily toiled that Stratford might be "all lit up."

The attention attracted was enormous. "Incredible multitudes," is Wheler's description of the crowds who swarmed in. Lodgings were unobtainable. Prices soared. For the Stratford landladies there never have been such days in the whole history of the Industry.

---

* Immediately after the jubilee, this elegant amphitheatre was taken down, and the materials sold by auction.

Samuel Foote, Garrick's rival and enemy, came down to observe the goings-on and had good reason to be peevish if he was indeed charged "nine guineas for six hours sleep." Thoughtless grandees, who had neglected to book rooms in advance, had to spend the night in their carriages and their weight added to their troubles and to the laughter of the less charitable lookers-on. For, when the rain came down in torrents, the carriages stuck in the river-side mud, and were only extricated after enormous labours. Foote may have been charged heavily for his bed, but he was given plenty to laugh at and laugh he did.

Dr. Arne was the superintendent of the music. Mr. George Garrick, the actor's impecunious brother, helped to supervise the arrangements and managed to find scope for a favourite hobby, which was borrowing money. The idea of a decoration, comparable to an Old Shakespearean Tie, was executed. This was the Jubilee Ribbon which united all the colours of the rainbow, as the emblem of the universality of genius. Boswell regretted in his life of Johnson that the great doctor was an absentee. "Johnson's connection both with Shakespeare and Garrick founded a double claim to his presence and it would have been highly gratifying to Mr. Garrick." He added:

"When almost every man of eminence in the literary world was happy to partake in this festival of genius, the absence of Johnson could not but be

78

wondered at and regretted. The only trace of him there was in the whimsical advertisement of a haberdasher, who sold Shaksperian ribbands of various dyes: and, by way of illustrating their appropriation to the bard, introduced a line from the celebrated Prologue at the opening of Drury-lane theatre:

" 'Each change of many-colour'd life he drew.' "

The Doctor was taking the air at Brighton. It was quieter there, perhaps, and certainly cheaper and more hygienic. There was no need to pay a guinea a night:

"For rolling—not sleeping—in linen so damp
As struck my great toe ever since with the cramp."

Nor was there any necessity in Sussex to buy rosettes and trinkets and listen to everything about Shakespeare—and nothing of Shakespeare's composition.

There were ready purchasers for the ribbon, as well as for a special medal, engraved by Mr. Westwood of Birmingham. It was struck in three metals and carried the likeness of Shakespeare and the initials of "D. G. Steward." As Steward, Garrick carried a wand of Shakespearean mulberry, wore a special mulberry medal, and had elegant white gauntlets of formidable size.

So on Wednesday, September 6th, 1769, at the un-
comfortable hour of 5 a.m. the signal was given.
The cannon roared and those who had not been
woken by the artillery were serenaded by a party from
Drury Lane "fantastically dressed" and singing:

> "Let beauty with the sun arise
> To Shakespeare tribute pay,
> With heavenly smiles and speaking eyes
> Give lustre to the Day."

They also sang Garrick's own song: "Warwickshire
Lads," beginning:

> "Ye Warwickshire Lads and Ye Lasses,
> See what at our jubilee passes;
> Come revel away, rejoice and be glad,
> For the lad of all lads was a
> Warwickshire lad,
> Warwickshire lad,
> All be glad,
> For the lad of all lads was
> A Warwickshire lad!"

Whether the sleepy listeners did in fact "rejoice and
be glad" we do not know, but they probably were up
in time to be received by Mr. Garrick himself at the
public breakfast at nine. The revellers obtained this
for a mere shilling provided they had already sub-

scribed a guinea for the various entertainments and half a guinea for the masquerade. The noise must have been terrific, for those cannon had not been assembled for nothing. When Garrick formally received the Steward's insignia of office there was more firing and ringing of bells, while during the breakfast a band of drums and pipes performed. The next move was to the church, where Arne's "Oratorio of Judith" was rendered with the aid of "very full choruses" and the whole orchestra from Drury Lane. After this all left the church, and paraded the town, headed, needless to say, by Garrick complete with his medal and wand, while the choristers sang:

> "This is a day, a holiday! a holiday!
> Drive spleen and rancour far away;
> This is a day, a holiday! a holiday!
> Drive care and sorrow far away.
> Here Nature nurs'd her darling boy,*
> From whom all care and sorrow fly,
> Whose harp the Muses strung:
> From heart to heart let joy rebound,
> Now, now, we tread enchanted ground,
> Here Shakespeare walk'd and sung!"

So to Shakespeare's Hall for "turtle and Madeira" and a grand "public ordinary": then the Company went to dress for the Assembly. The supply of noise was

---

* Sung at the house where Shakespeare was born.

steadily maintained by Signor Angelo's fireworks and at last came the more tranquil dancing of minuets which lasted until midnight.

The Second Day was to be the Great Day. It opened with the now familiar gun-fire, bell-ringing, and serenades: also with unfamiliar quantities of rain. However, there was no flinching. The public breakfast was well attended and the entire company moved on to the Rotunda for the Jubilee's particular pleasure, the recitation by Garrick of his "Ode Upon Dedicating the Town Hall and Erecting a Statue to Shakespeare." The actor stood with wand and medal beneath the elegant statue and recited the major part of his composition of which he was so proud. The airs and choruses were sung by a choir conducted by Dr. Arne. The rain beat on the roof: outside the Avon was beginning to swell ominously: as the morning advanced the press in the Rotunda began to make itself felt. Part of a wall collapsed and several benches gave way beneath their occupants. But none smiled. All were silent, all were rapt. Boswell, who was present, described Garrick as one in ecstasy, "a mortal transformed into a demi-god," and the audience, he thought, would have murdered anyone so rash or rude as to interrupt. Even Foote was silent.

Garrick's poetic style was of an ample platitudinous kind. He proclaimed devotion with a formal rapture:

"Now swell at once the choral song,
Roll the full tide of harmony along;
Let rapture sweep the trembling strings,
And fame, expanding all her wings,
With all her trumpet-tongues proclaim
The lov'd, rever'd, immortal name!
SHAKSPEARE! SHAKSPEARE! SHAKSPEARE!
Let th'inchanting sound,
From Avon's shores rebound;
Through the air,
Let it bear
The precious freight the envious nations round!"

So on it went, with the chorus intervening to proclaim:

"Wild, frantic with pleasure,
They trip it in measure,
To bring him their treasure,
The treasure of joy!

How gay is the measure,
How sweet is the pleasure,
How great is the treasure,
The treasure of joy!"

The ode was duly and warmly acclaimed: it was followed by a discourse. Garrick, it must be remembered, was in the throes of a temporary retirement from the stage: actors are bad retirers; they will always come back. Garrick must have had within him a fair amount of pent-up exhibitionism. The Jubilee was his chance. Having demonstrated his prowess as a poet he proceeded to impress as a lecturer. His prose now seems a good deal better than his verse. It had a Ciceronian grandeur. In the manner of his age he enlarged with elegant periods on the idea of Genius looking through Nature, not upon it. He asked for opposition, if any could be found and Mr. King, a favourite comedian of the day, but scarcely known in so rural a place as Stratford, since the camera's aid to reputation was not existent, speedily entered the ring. He took off his overcoat, exposed a smart suit of blue frogged with silver, and delivered a mock-serious attack on Shakespeare which was resented and hooted by those who took it in earnest and much appreciated by the others, who understood the joke. Afterwards the irrepressible Garrick delivered a poetic epilogue and the prodigious pressure of the company caused further damage to the premises and furniture. Not even the highest in the land were immune from humiliating and painful misadventures. The Earl of Carlisle, for example, was much injured by the fall of a door.

Dinner was at three: at five glees and catches, of which Garrick was a prolific author. Nobility and gentry joined in song, unquenchable as the rain around them.

"Untouched and sacred be thy shrine,
Avonian Willy, bard Divine."

The lyrical praise worked both ways. Warwick was
rhymed with Garrick. Hymns to David of
Twickenham were as eagerly chanted as the
dithyrambs in honour of Avonian Willy.

The best was done to discharge damp fireworks
and illumine the sodden town. Through the dreary
twilight the untiring Signor Angelo sped like Lucifer
touching off his rockets, set-pieces, and revealing his
"illuminated transparencies" at the Rotunda and the
Birthplace. There was plenty of time to study the
symbolic designs thus offered to the view, for the
great Masquerade was not due till midnight. So,
for long hours, Signor Angelo continued his
unequal battle with the English climate. The
latter, one gathers, heavily defeated the Italian in
the end.

It also menaced, but could not ruin, the
Masquerade. The river was now overflowing: the
meadows were a quagmire; the Rotunda had to be
approached by duck-boards. Carriages were bogged.
It was all most unfortunate. But primed with hot
brandy and Shakespearean ardour, the nobility and
gentry faced the midnight music to the number of a
thousand. Wheler gives a vivid picture of the scene:
"Among the most distinguished of the guests were
Lady Pembroke, Mrs. Bouverie, and Mrs. Crewe,

habited as witches, who excited general admiration:
the astonishing contrast between the deformity of the
feigned, and the beauty of the real appearance, was
everywhere observed. Nor did a Shepherdess and
Dame Quickly, in the "Merry Wives of Windsor"
(personated by the two Miss Ladbrookes), pass without the universal applause of the Company. Lord
Grosvenor was magnificently dressed in an eastern
habit; but the greatest part of the nobility, and most
of the literary gentlemen, were in dominoes. Mrs.
Yates personated a *petit-maitre:* Mr. Yates, as a wag-
goner, gave much satisfaction; as did a gentleman,
from Oxford, in Lord Ogleby. Mr. Boswell, the celebrated friend of Paoli, appeared in a Corsican habit,
with pistols in his belt, and a musket at his back: in
gold letters, in the front of his cap, were the words
PAOLI, and *Viva la Liberta.* A person dressed as a
devil was inexpressibly displeasing: the three witches
however charmed the company into good humour,
the shepherdess, with Mrs. Quickly, confirmed those
agreeable sensations; and about five everybody
retired."

The whole history of English Comedy can hardly
have offered anything so curious as that Masquerade
on the sodden banks of Avon. Boswell, aflame with
Shakespearean as well as Corsican enthusiasm, not
only paraded with his musket but carried a long staff
with an Avonian swan carved on the top of it. He
then endeavoured to emulate Garrick by doing some

recitation on his own account. He had written a piece and began to declaim it:

"From the rude banks of Golo's rapid flood
    Alas, too deeply tinged with potent blood,"

so he began. But the banks of Avon were even ruder than those of Golo. The company had had enough of recitation for one day. Garrick had sufficed. Poor Boswell was shouted down.

Yet Boswell was impressed. The brilliance of the scene allured him, but its paganism struck horror to his Scottish heart. "My bosom glowed with joy," he wrote to the Scot's Magazine, "when I beheld so brilliant and numerous a company of nobility and gentry, the rich, the brave, the witty, and the fair assembled. But I could have wished that prayers had been read or a short sermon preached. It would have consecrated our Jubilee while gratefully addressing the supreme Father of all Spirits, from whom cometh every good and perfect gift."

The next day was a sad one. The weather did not mend. The Avon seemed utterly ungrateful for the compliments which had been paid to it. Numbers of trees on the Bankcroft had been obligingly cut down (by permission of the Duke of Dorset and Dionysius Brooke, Esquire) so that a better view of the sacred stream might be had by all. But the river's response was only to rise up and get in everybody's way.

Twice it had been hoped to arrange a theatrical procession to the Amphitheatre of London players representing "in proper dress" the main Shakespearean characters. There was to be a triumphal car, in which Melpomene and Thalia, with the Graces, were to be drawn by six men dressed as satyrs, the chariot and team being surrounded by choristers in full voice and bandsmen in full blast. The inevitable serenade of Shakespeare's statue was to be the high moment, and a laurel wreath would, of course, be formally set on Avonian Willy's brow. But on both occasions the rain was too severe. Garrick, who had arranged to recite his Ode a second time beside the statue, was cheated of his occasion. Probably there was less grief caused by this loss than by the damage done to Signor Angelo's fireworks.

Rain can stop an Englishman listening to an Ode, but it cannot stop him going to the races. After all, it was Race Week before it was Shakespeare week. If the rain cut the cackle, the folk might come to the 'osses. So off to Shottery they drove, where special preparations for the crowds had been made, and there the horses splashed over the miry fields in pursuit of the special Jubilee Cup, value fifty guineas. It was won by the steed entered in the name of Mr. Pratt. Many had now begun to drive away if they were lucky enough to free their coaches from the muddy ruts and boggy holes. But there was yet another night of gaiety in the Rotunda. The revels went on till four and Mrs. Garrick, who before marriage had been a professional dancer, executed a minuet "beyond description gracefully." Mr. Garrick, no doubt, had other and more serious morning thoughts.

> "The candles burn their sockets,
> The blinds let through the day,
> The young man feels his pockets
> And wonders what's to pay."

There were many who anticipated then the sad sentiments of A. E. Housman's lyric.

Poor Garrick, who had had such wretched luck with the weather, had guaranteed much of the expense and was now as much out of pocket as the Stratford caterers and landladies were in funds. Moreover, there was that tiresome brother George of his making matters worse with his confounded borrowing. A Mr. Hunt, Town Clerk of Stratford, had rashly advanced a hundred pounds to George, could not recover, and made a strong appeal to David. Hunt received a rude reply from David who offered to refund the hundred pounds *plus interest*. How much was ultimately paid, after this interchange of discourtesies, is unknown.

Meanwhile, the company had broken up and the road to London was packed with coaches. Foote, rejoicing that so many of the arrangements had been spoiled, wrote of the proceedings: "A Jubilee is a public invitation circulated and arranged by puffing. To go posting without horses to an obscure borough without representatives, governed by a Mayor and Aldermen who are no magistrates: to celebrate a poet, whose works have made him immortal, by an ode without poetry, music without melody, dinners without victuals, and lodgings without bed: a masquerade where half the people appear bare-faced, a horse race up to the knees in water, fireworks extinguished as soon as lit and a gingerbread amphitheatre which tumbled to pieces as soon as it was made." Foote's squibs, more fiery and explosive than the poor soaked toys of Signor Angelo, went echoing round the town.

Garrick's Jubilee was partly conceived in honour of Shakespeare and partly in self-esteem. He had to pay in cash and ridicule for the pleasure of appearing as Poet, Reciter, Orator, Steward and High Panjandrum. However, he managed to build a show out of his arduous endurances for Drury Lane in the autumn. There he presented a kind of musical pageant called "Jubilee," bringing in the people of Stratford, Warwickshire songs, and a grand tableau of Shakespeare's plays presented in succession with the parts performed in dumb show. There was the usual triumphal car with Mrs. Abingdon as the Comic Muse. Garrick did not, apparently, recite his Ode every evening, but he managed to squeeze it in sometimes. The Statue, which he was giving to Stratford,

was brought up to London and placed on the stage
of Drury Lane, surrounded by his players. Then
Garrick, handsomely posed in front of it, would
declaim:

"The lov'd, rever'd, immortal name,
 SHAKSPEARE! SHAKSPEARE! SHAKSPEARE!"

The Drury Lane show, strange to say, was well
received and ran through the autumn. The Statue
was returned and set in its niche on the wall of the
Stratford Town Hall. But Garrick made no more
Jubilees. He was tired and out of health. He had sore
memories of Stratford mud and Stratford streets.
There was that vexing business of his brother George,
Mr. Hunt, and the hundred pounds. So, when the
invitation came, he politely declined. His letter,
hitherto unpublished, we are able to publish through
the kindness of Mr. Wellstood, the Secretary and
"Archivist" of the Birthplace Trustees at Stratford:

Hampton, 1770

Dear Sir,

*I have been very low with my late illness and scarce
able to write my lines together. The air of this place
has turned my spirits again and restored my appetite,
tho' my legs will not yet permit me to dance an
allemande.*

I am very much flattered that you are desired to

91

consult me how I would advise our friends to celebrate the memory of our Immortal Bard yearly. The day (I think) should be on his birthday unless the day established for the grand jubilee should be thought to have marked it out more particularly for rejoicings but, on second thoughts; as the jubilee comprehends more days than one, I think the annual commemoration should be on his birthday. The manner how must be left to the gentlemen who feel the honour of being Shakespeare's townsmen and who have a proper zeal for the first genius of the World. The bells should be rung and bonfires should blaze, the ladies should dance and the gentlemen be merry and wise, viz., end the day with mirth and good fellowship. There should always be proper songs introduced at the table and joined with the hearts and voices of all the company in a feeling enthusiastic chorus—something of this kind for the lesser festival. But, my good friend, would the gentlemen do real honour and show their love to Shakespeare, let them decorate the town, the happiest and why not the handsomest in England, let your streets be well paved and kept clean, do something to the delightful meadow, allure everybody to visit the Holy-land, let it be well lighted and clean underfoot, and let it not be said, for your honour and I hope for your interest, that the town which gave birth to the first genius since the creation is the most dirty, unseemly, ill-paved wretched looking place in all Britain.

Excuse this scrawl, I can scarce hold my pen longer to tell you

I am most sincerely yours,

D. Garrick.

PS. My love and best respects to all my brethren at Stratford.

Garrick's Shakespeare pageant, which the weather prevented, received a last, belated honour at Stratford on July 9th, 1927. A pageant was then held on behalf of the Theatre Rebuilding Fund and Mr. R. Crompton Rhodes, the dramatic critic of the *Birmingham Post*, an authority on the texts and lives both of Shakespeare and Sheridan, and ever a most active spirit in all Midland dramatic festivals (since his tragically early death in 1935 these festivals have never seemed quite the same), adapted a pageant from Garrick's scheme. The Tragic Muse and the Comic Muse were impersonated by Miss Sybil Thorndike and Miss Irene Vanbrugh (who worthier?), while Mr. Lewis Casson appeared as David Garrick and read Garrick's Shakespearean Ode.

Garrick certainly deserved this long-delayed honour. He had worked very hard for "self and others." However, he was not forgotten locally. When ceremonies were resumed in 1816, in observance of the bicentenary of the poet's death, Garrick's toast as well as Shakespeare's was honoured. And still, on

93

the Gainsborough canvas, he stands in the Town Hall of Stratford, leaning against "Avonian Willy." He has every right to be there, on Shakespeare's shoulder, among the names of Bailiffs and Mayors and Worshipful Persons. For, more than any of his age, he put Stratford on the English map and served the Shakespeare Industry.

CHAPTER V

"CLUBS, BILLS, AND PARTIZANS"

"The unending seas are hardly bar
To men with such a prepossession.
We were? Why then, by God, we are!
Order! I call the Club to session."
H. BELLOC, *Dedicatory Ode*.

A FOREIGNER once mystified his English host by expressing a desire to see our *Casinosleben* of which he had heard so much. The host, an indifferent linguist, explained that our British laws bore hardly on casinos. True, we are a gaming nation. An Englishman and his money are parted the moment he can discover a bookmaker, a totalisator, or a game of cards. But the thing has to be done in certain ways. We play cards in the home, we go to race-courses, and we telephone or telegraph to our bookmakers. The frank gambling of a Casino is not for a nation so careful of appearances. It was the foreigner's turn to be baffled. All he had meant to ask about was our Club Life, which is so augustly carried on amid the leather-clad arm-chairs of London mansions.

The English have a great passion for doing things privately. "We are the secret people," as G. K.

95

Chesterton sang. We love to get together behind closed doors. Thus is our gambling carried on, thus much of our scholarship, as well as much of our revelry. The novel accepted as most typically English, *Pickwick Papers,* is about a Pickwick Club. Not long ago some clever advertisers invented a fictional body called The Mustard Club, in order to appeal to the British club-spirit for the greater consumption of Mounseer Mustard-seed. The Englishman is not very partial to eating and drinking and celebrating in public places: he loves to join up with a society, take a room and there unbend. Our democracy has its own exclusiveness. Hence all these proletarian gatherings of Buffaloes, Foresters, Ancient Brythons and all the rest: hence these banquets at which the chairman wears the oddest insignia of office: hence the middle-class assemblages of people with special ties and slogans. The institution of a club enables you to keep the other fellow out. That is a practice which the British most heartily enjoy. To combine the popping of corks with the throwing of black-balls, what bliss!

It was therefore inevitable that when Shakespeare became a British Industry and a National Institution we should find ourselves with Shakespeare Clubs, whose members combined cultural zeal with physical thirst. All our great favourites elicit this kind of support by sodality. The Shakespeare Clubs were the predecessors of the Scottish groups celebrating their

96

"Nichts wi' Burns" and of Dickensian Fellowships treading in their master's steps from tavern to tavern or shrine to shrine. But before we consider the inevitable emergence of the Shakespeare Clubs in Stratford and elsewhere, we must pause a moment to watch the progress of Bardolatry after Garrick had retired, amid cheers and some laughter, from the rain-swept meadows by the Avon.

The Garrick Festival, as we saw, produced some dubious poetry, much eloquence, and no acting, except of the kind which goes on every day in normal life. Certainly there was no acting of Shakespeare's own work. That would have been deemed shockingly out of place. But Shakespeare plays in Shakespeare's own town were soon to be acceptable, and even normal. The first authenticated series of performances of such a kind were at "The New Theatre, at the Unicorn" in Stratford and took place in the spring of 1771. This must have been a humble attachment to a tavern. There was given "The Merchant of Venice," Shylock by Mr. Kennedy, described as "this celebrated comedy taken from a real fact which occurred in Venice." There was also "Hamlet" (Mr. Booth as the Prince), and this was held to be insufficient entertainment in itself: it followed, presumably in a much-cut version, a musical show called "Padlock," "as it was performed in London with Universal Applause." The chief character in "Padlock" was Mungo the Black. The Nigger Minstrel had arrived, attendant to the Dane. The playgoers of those days liked mixed company. The wise manager always offered tragedy, and farce, "fine, confused feeding."

Another Stratford attraction of the time was "Romeo and Juliet," with "a Masquerade Proper to the Play" and an Additional Scene representing (improperly to the play) "The Funeral Procession of Juliet to the Capulet Monument, accompanied by a Solemn Dirge to which will be added a Diverting Farce, 'The Lying Valet.' " Since this was the eighteenth century, Shakespeare's plays were never acted "as writ." For example, when "The Tempest" was given at Stratford, it was a version of Dryden's version of Shakespeare's text. Miranda had a sister Dorinda and a new comic character had arrived in the person of "Mustacho the Mate." Some expense may have been spared in providing the spectacular effects, but no expense of language was spared in advertising them. "The Tempest" was "to open with a shipwreck and a Shower of Fire," and the whole to conclude with a "Beautiful View of a Calm Sea," in or on which were to be seen "Neptune and Amphitrite drawn in a Chariot of Sea-Horses." How all this was contrived with the modest theatrical premises and equipment then available in a small country town is difficult to imagine.

Stratford's theatrical life after that had intermittent bursts of Shakespearean energy. It was natural, for example, that an Infant Roscius (of that formidable mite the early nineteenth century was prolific) should spout his stuff where the Infant Shakespeare had drawn his early breath. Stratford was not honoured by the leader of these "little eyases," Master Betty. It received, however, a visit from a certain other precocious urchin, Master Grossmith of Reading. Owner of a name later on to be renowned in many forms of entertainment, Master Grossmith, at the age of seven, delighted the Warwickshire lads with his renderings of Hamlet's soliloquies and various scenes and speeches from "Richard III" and "The Merchant of Venice." That was in 1825. In 1828, at Stratford's New Shakespeare Theatre, built on the ground now known as New Place Garden and visited annually by many thousands of pilgrims in addition to being used as a dancing arena for the young on Shakespeare's Birthday, "King Lear" was played together with the farce of " 'Fortune's Frolic' by Desire of the Waterloo Club and other Benefit Societies." The specially billed attraction in this was "Royal Edgar Challenges Usurper to Mortal Combat."

It was during the early years of the nineteenth century that the general public of Stratford-on-Avon became consistently Shakespeare-conscious. Hitherto the Shakespeare Business had been limited to certain individuals like Sharp and Jordan. Possibly the inhabitants had been put to shame by a Mr. John F. M. Dovaston of Westfelton, near "Shrewsbury

99

Clock," who, in 1808, began at that place an annual
celebration of the poet's birthday. It was a private
party, confined to his own literary circle, but he
carried out his Bardic devotions for something like
nineteen years. Although little is known concerning
these early celebrations, it can be assumed that news
of them filtered through to Stratford-upon-Avon and
that, in consequence, William's townsmen were put
to shame.

The bicentenary of Shakespeare's death (1816) presented itself as a suitable opportunity for active celebrations, but even the suggestion for that Festival
came from an outsider, a Mr. Britton, a London publisher. He shares the credit for founding the present
well-known Shakespeare Club. Britton wrote to
Robert Bell Wheler in 1815 from "The Shakespearean Institute, London." He said that it was proposed to form "an Institute or Club of Gentlemen of
congenial minds and ardent attachment to the Bard
of Avon." He added: "It is also proposed to meet at
Stratford in September, 1815, and establish a Literary
Jubilee commemorative of the second Centenary of
his decease." Bell Wheler became active; the meeting
in the autumn took place and ultimately the Shakespeare Club was formed, though not for another nine
years. Things moved slowly in Stratford-upon-Avon.
It was still barely aware of the fact that, with William
Shakespeare as its great attraction, it ought to be one
of the most celebrated places in the world. Bell

Wheler became one of a committee to organise, in proper manner, the bi-centenary celebrations.

In the meantime Britton, who seems to have been something of a Pickwick in his own person, had sent Wheler a copy of a resolution passed in London. "It appearing difficult or impracticable to celebrate the day by any great public festival, as the Drury Lane Company and persons connected with that Theatre would be particularly engaged in preparing and bringing forward 'The Shakespeare Jubilee'* on that night, it was *Resolved* that the present company constitute themselves 'The Shakespeare Club.' " Thus it is seen that the Stratford Club took its name deliberately from the one formed in London. Britton enclosed a letter with his resolution. In it he stated his intention of coming to Stratford on April 23rd accompanied by some of his friends, presumably "Gentlemen of congenial minds." He "anticipated a delightful day if the weather is fine." He also threatened Stratford-on-Avon with a visit from Mr. Dovaston of Shrewsbury, and said that if the Stratford Committee would invite that Salopian, there was little doubt that he would accept the invitation and he would also "give you one or two new odes to Shakespeare." Unhappy Stratford, were Garrick's poetic efforts not enough? Mr. Britton's appreciation of Garrick's Old-School-Tie methods was noticeable in the last paragraph of his letter: *The medal I cannot*

* This was Garrick's version.

get in time, but I shall have a new seal, full face, from the Bust; the print and two small wood-cuts of full face and profile from the Bust. Britton was all energy.

He was, however, disappointed. Kemble, the actor, had intimated his interest in the proposed Jubilee. R. W. Elliston, the leading Drury Lane player, was playing at Birmingham with his Company and would willingly have given a series of performances at Stratford. But where could they be housed? Stratford at that time possessed no sufficient theatre. There was, it is true, a fit-up barn in Greenhill Street (then called Moor Town's End), but its holding capacity was very small. The Mayor and Corporation would not hear of the barn being used. They frowned on theatrical performances because, they said, the distressed state of the country following on the twenty-two years' war with France did not warrant such goings-on. The ambitious programme of Britton and Wheler was therefore much modified; the suggested Jubilee was postponed to the autumn and then never took place at all.

The Birthday passed off fairly quietly, as they say, but whether a programme consisting of music and the firing of cannon can be properly so described is another matter. There were a public breakfast at 10 a.m. which only cost 2/6, a dinner at 4 p.m. which cost 15/-, but included wine and dessert, and a Ball in the evening which began at 10 p.m. and cost a mere 7/6. Altogether it was a much less expensive and less elaborate affair than Garrick's celebration had been. All this was, however, sowing the seed for the Shakespeare Club. Shrewsbury was still busy with its Shakespearean devotions. Sheffield decided to practise similar piety and stole a march on Stratford by forming its own Shakespeare Club in 1819. This Club had a merry life of about ten years and published an account of its proceedings in 1829.

The actual beginnings of the Stratford Club are as secret as much of Shakespeare's early life. That the Club actually came into being, for Gentlemen only, in 1824 is established, but a printed account issued in 1828 states "that the Club was re-established in the former year." Mr. Wellstood, Secretary of the Birthplace Trust, says that he can find no certain evidence that the Club existed, as such, at any earlier date, unless, indeed, the committees which had carried out the previous celebrations were held to constitute a Club. On this point, however, there is some doubt.

"Mine Host of the Falcon," Mr. Ashfield, in April, 1824, gathered around him about a dozen of his cronies, admirers of Shakespeare. He gathered them to celebrate, quietly, William's birthday. There was dinner, there were speeches, and a Society was formed. They were of the class to which Shakespeare belonged, gratifying their own personal pride "in the fame of their illustrious townsman" and with periodical meetings in honour of his memory. Quickly the small band of beer-drinkers increased its membership to about 150, and within six years it had grown to nearly 400. The larger the membership the more sincere became the members—in the cultural as well as the alcoholic aspects of homage. By this time "some of the most respectable inhabitants of the town and neighbourhood" had countenanced the objects of the Club and substantially aided its exertions.

The first object of the Club was the annual celebration of the Poet's birthday as well as the carrying out of a triennial commemoration on a larger scale. 1827 and 1830 saw the larger scale of celebrations, but after that they were discontinued. Some of the early dinners must have been highly amusing. At the third dinner in 1826 a special song was written for "The gentlemen belonging to the Shakespearean Society" by a Mr. J. Bisset, of Leamington. Mr. Bisset not only wrote but sang his own composition "with great glee and reiterated plaudits." The large membership had now made it necessary for the dinners to be held in the Town Hall, and not in the dining-room of the Falcon, as at first.

It was appropriate, the members felt, that the whole town should see what was being done to honour its Bard. So in 1827, taking a leaf from Garrick's book, they dressed up as various characters in Shakespeare's plays. This business of joining processions, still maintained on the Birthday and on the Birthday Sunday in Stratford, is most dear to the English. Every year the whole commerce of Central London is impeded by a Lord Mayor's Show which ought to be twice as spectacular as it is in order to justify the amount of public nuisance which it creates. During the Whit-sun holidays in Manchester the whole city is held up by vast processions of school-children, organised according to their parents' faith: Church of England, Nonconformity, and Rome, each sect having a day of its own. Our Trade Unions are much given to the bearing of standards, and at one time their vast civilian armies with banners used to congregate frequently in places appointed for such demonstra-tions. Stratford's addiction to marching, in costume or with flowers and brass band, is part of a deep-rooted national urge for this peculiar exercise.

The Shakespeare Club's procession had reasonably good weather and was seen by thousands. The assembled company, those in costume and those in ordinary clothes, proceeded to the Birthplace where an address in blank verse was delivered, and then to the church where Shakespeare's epitaph (set to music by Dignum) was sung by amateur vocalists. Suitable homage having been done at these two places, the Company went to the New Place Garden, where the foundation-stone of Stratford's first permanent theatre was laid.

The members did not get their costumes for nothing. Mr. Palmer, of Tavistock Street, London, made £75 out of this side of the Industry. Local caterers also did well. Breakfasts, dinners, fireworks, a masquerade, and Ryan's famous Olympic Circus were all included in the three days' jollifications. The Shakespeare Club seemed to have begun its work with favourable circumstance, but it was soon to have a jolt. In this same year (1827) a rival Stratford Shakespeare Club came into existence. This was called "The Shakespearean True Blue Club,"* but it got the nickname of "The Bran and Chaff Club." Its headquarters were at the Golden Lion Hotel. One of the True Blues' first investments was a Bust of the Bard, price sixteen shillings, and another item in their accounts is to "Barnacle's Bill" for Advertising, £2 10s. od. The First Club had to announce that they had no connection with the other firm, and "this is the only Club patronised by the Corporation." "The True Blues" had a short life and a merry one. They gave a performance of "King Henry VIII" in the so-called Shakespearean Theatre, which was no more than a barn. The play was followed by comic songs and a dance specially executed by Master Rignold. After this was given a farce called "Love, Law and Physic," which later became a favourite vehicle for Charles Dickens in the display of his acting talent. On Shakespeare's Birthday, 1828, "The True Blues" had their own Shakespeare dinner at the Lion, and proved that they, too, were adepts at an Ode. Their

---

* In this connection it is worth noting that Stratford's historic neighbour, Coventry, has now two Birthplaces of its famous daughter, Ellen Terry. One is labelled "The Birthplace," the other "The Original Birthplace."

effort, instead of praising Shakespeare, damned the
other and original Club, with its Falcon and its Royal
George, discussing the Monarchy with a freedom
which would have seemed very strange a century later.

"Townsmen unite! Fear not the adverse surge
  Nor spotless broadsides from the *Royal George*
  Nor the weak compeers of such doltish things
  As vain, conceited, proud, coxcombic Kings.
  For where's the *Falcon,* prowling for a prey,
  Dare pounce the *Noble Lion* on his way?
  Go on, my Friends! Be to your colours true,
  Now, three times three to Shakespeare and *True
  Blue!*"

A few days after the "True Blue" performance of
"Henry VIII" the original Club gave a performance
of "The Merry Wives of Windsor." This was performed with due ceremony in the New Theatre,
whose foundation-stone had been laid in the previous
year. Meanwhile Processions remained popular.
Stratford had to wait till 1830 before there was a
really formidable array of Shakespearean characters.
A Captain Saunders of Stratford-on-Avon achieved
local fame (along with considerable grandiloquence
and some very old syntax) by the publication of a
satirical account of the 1829 Festivities. It is worth
quoting:

"It must appear strange, while the whole of the United Kingdom is highly drilled to the march of intellect, that the town which gave birth to Shakespeare, the pride of national understanding, should be actually surpassing all others in a tenfold ratio, nay, moving in double-quick time and in seven-leagued boots in the *pas de change* of mental power."

"This progression," continued the eloquent Captain, "has been strangely exemplified on Thursday, the 23rd inst., at the Annual Festival of the Club formed to *do honour,* as they call it, to their immortal Bard, when members and visitors to the number of 247 sat down to a three o'clock dinner, an unfashionable hour truly, but necessarily so, to allow for the early introduction of pipes and tobacco, which it is then imagined (though the immortal bard says nothing about it) give a great intellectuality. The system began to work in about an hour after a general muster, which consisted of the parish squire, two bourgeois squirets, four aldermen, seven capital burgesses, one clergyman of a country parish, four attorney's clerks, two apothecaries, one reporter (or gentleman of the Press), the rest tradesmen, artisans, players, Chelsea pensioners. . . . About this period the mixed conglomeration became metamorphosed, when the whole assemblage were found to consist of and call each other 'gentlemen.' This is one of the first steps of the march.

"The Mayor, a farmer, banker and draper, rose in the chair and gave the *healths* of the King and St. George, on which Mr. Vice-President began to stare, and protested that he long thought the Patron Saint of England had been dead, when an *Intellectual* explained that the toast meant his immortal health and the King's mortal!"

Such sarcasm did not daunt the Shakespeare Club, who were now busily occupied preparing for the 1830 Triennial commemoration of the poet's Birthday. King George IV had adopted St. George's Day as his birthday. Because of this and the fact that Shakespeare's Birthday fell on the same day, he was graciously pleased to become the patron of the Club and the proposed festivities. Henceforward the Club was to be known as the Royal Shakespearean Club, a title which has since been dropped.

Spurred on by the regal blessing the Club decided, quite properly, that the procession of 1830 should be the grandest imaginable. So did the True Blues, who also claimed the King as Patron and had a rival show in hand. Bardolatry had its familiar bad luck with the weather. It rained as it had rained on Garrick. The streets were crowded by eager sightseers who had taken up their position since the early hours of the morning. The procession, organised by the original Shakespeare Club, should have moved off at eleven o'clock, but the downpour was merciless; it looked

as though the fiasco of the Garrick Procession was to
be repeated; at twelve the rain showed signs of slack-
ening; at one it had almost stopped: the crowds still
waited patiently. At two o'clock it had ceased
altogether and the sun shone fitfully. It was
announced that the Procession would definitely set
off on its tour of Stratford not later than half-past
two. The eager waiters, who had long been drenched
to the skin but were kept reasonably warm with beer
and cheese, were at last rewarded. The grandest of
all Shakespeare processions passed before reverent and
enraptured thousands. First to greet their eyes was
the Committee on horseback, ornamented with a
Shakespearean medal. This was a brave choice on the
Committee's part, but there is no record of any
equestrian disasters. There followed

The Royal Standard of England.

Full Military Band.

St. George, on horseback in full armour, his banner
borne by his Esquire on horseback.

The banner of the Borough.

Melpomene, the Tragic Muse, in a car drawn by
four fiends, and banner. Then came characters from
eleven plays, each team with a banner. Then, to
balance Melpomene, came, with her own band,
Thalia, the Comic Muse, in a car drawn by four
Satyrs, with banner. Next came teams from six more
plays, and finally Bottom, with an ass's head, and, of
course, a banner. Behind these were more banners,

the Royal Standard of England once again, and the Banner of the Club.

As soon as the much-bannered procession had arrived at the Birthplace, according to Smith in his *History of Warwickshire*:

"the two Muses, attended by one or two gentlemen, ascended a temporary platform and proceeded to crown a bust of the Bard of Avon, with wreaths of laurel: the scene at this period was one of the most gorgeous and animating that can possibly be conceived, the line of characters all attired in the most splendid costumes, extended the whole line of the street; the windows and tops of houses were crowded with thousands of 'the last but best of God's creation.' "

It was at this point that the fitful sun sympathetically emerged, "at once banishing the misgivings of the spectators, and adding to the magnificence of the pageant." The ode, now a customary part of Bardic worship, was recited at the Birthplace by a Mr. Booth, one of the actors at the New Theatre.

The Industry made use of the garments worn in this procession. They were sold by auction in London and realised £280, much less than the original cost. The sale was not without its other humours. The *Warwickshire Advertiser* of June 19th, 1830, tells us that "Considerable merriment was excited on the

111

production of a pair of *inexpressibles* which were worn by Madame Vestris on the first night of *Hofer,* and afterwards rejected by her in consequence of being a *miss-fit.* So little gallantry, however, was manifested that they were knocked down to a *gentleman* for eight shillings." These 1830 celebrations were the last of the triennial efforts of which there had been but two earlier examples.

Meanwhile the True Blues were not sitting idle. There hangs in the hall of the Shakespeare Hotel, at Stratford, a programme of theirs which reveals the full scope of their competitive ardour in 1830. Did the other fellows make procession? They could manage something far better than that. They had two Mr. Southbys, one a droll of Drury Lane, the other a pyrotechnician from Vauxhall; they had Mr. Blackmore, the American, the record-breaking funambulist, also of Vauxhall's Royal Gardens. They could render to the day's hero proper and monumental honours. So here was the answer of True Blues to the mere Shakespeareans. Dinner at the Golden Lion was announced by a discharge of artillery. Then came a masquerade. Then all passed over to the Royal Saloon, which was erected on the Bowling Green, at the Shakespeare Inn, late part of the garden and pleasure-grounds attached to the second mulberry-tree, a scion from that of the poet's own planting. The cult of that Golden Bough was once more joyfully proclaimed.

"The Mulberry Tree is hung with wreaths of lamps,
The Mulberry Tree stands centre of the dance,
The Mulberry Tree is hymn'd with dulcet airs."

The Saloon was illumined by upwards of 4,000 variegated lamps. Mr. Southby, celebrated clown of the Theatre Royal, Drury Lane, with Harlequin, Columbine, Pantaloon, and other eminent performers from the principal London theatres, obliged by sustaining "a variety of the most grotesque characters."

After this came pyrotechny on a scale never seen since Signor Angelo's great effort. Indeed, it was announced as: "The grandest and most truly unequalled display of Fireworks ever witnessed, prepared by and under the direction of Mr. Southby, artist of The Royal Gardens, Vauxhall, London." Mr. Southby specialised in "Pyramids, Batteries, Saucissons, Mines, and Tourbillons" as his particular flames of obeisance to the Bard. During this brilliant exhibition, surrounded by fireworks of every description, Mr. Blackmore (the American), of the Royal Gardens, Vauxhall, London, was billed to perform his astonishing ascent to the enormous height of near eighty feet on the tight-rope. Then came the evening's masterpiece. This was a grand illuminated "Choragic Monument of Shakespeare, of the height of thirty feet, ornamented with every requisite device, in the centre of which was introduced a most beautiful Transparent Portrait of the Immortal Bard." And this was only the first day of the fun. There were two more to follow. The War of the Clubs meant joy indeed for those Stratfordians who preferred Romeo's self-chosen office, to "be a candle-holder and look on."

The "True Blue" effort seems, naturally enough, to have exhausted that faction. The original Shakespeare Club continued to meet and to organise the Birthday Dinners; sometimes the Club drew a blank and at other times it was successful. It was highly elated to have the distinguished American tragedian George Jones as Guest of Honour in 1836. He recited, for their benefit, a set of verses of which the following is an example:—

> "Revolving years have flitted on,
> Corroding time has done its worst;
> Pilgrim and worshipper have gone
> From Avon's shrine to shrines of dust.
> But Shakespeare lives unrivalled still,
> And unapproached by mortal mind;
> The giant of Parnassus' hill,
> The pride, the monarch of mankind,
> Great as were those of Greece and Rome,
> The glory of our island home."

Rapturous applause no doubt greeted this ode. All odes seem to have been well received in Stratford-on-Avon, with the sole exception of poor Boswell's effort.

As the years passed the Club began to hold a good

opinion of itself. The members imagined that they were now so well known that they could prevail upon the greatest of the land to accept their hospitality. In 1847 they invited the Poet Laureate, William Wordsworth. Wordsworth declined, but sent a letter advising them on the proper running of a Shakespeare Festival. *May I venture to say that, in my judgment, a Triennial Meeting would be preferable to an annual one; as it is to be apprehended that so frequent a recurrence of the celebration, though for the first few years it might be met with pride and pleasure, would, in a long course, lose its spirit.* He signed himself *Your most obliged, William Wordsworth.*

This was rather a blow to the members of the Club who had, some nine years earlier, been much written of and discussed when they started a campaign to raise funds for the restoration of the Bust over Shakespeare's grave. The Royal Family subscribed handsomely, as did other important people throughout the country. The handiwork of Malone was to be undone and undone it was. The newspapers had made much of their restoration of the Bust, and yet Wordsworth appeared to be ignorant of their existence.

Two years before the Wordsworth incident the Club had found itself in a quandary. For some reason, now obscure, it had a quarrel with the Landlord of the Falcon. He had been steward of the Club since its inception and had possibly become self-important. Anyhow, he refused to hand over the books of the Club, the banners and other belongings, so the Club moved off in a pet from the Falcon, and made either Shakespeare's Hall ((i.e., the large room in the Town Hall) or the Shakespearean Rooms (once the theatre in New Place Gardens) its scene of meeting. Eventually this trouble so sapped the Club's strength that it ceased to exist. It was revived in the eighteen-seventies, and is now known as the Shakespeare Club, having dropped the word "Royal."

For years the annual Shakespeare Birthday Dinner was in the hands of the Club, but now there is a Luncheon organised by the Borough of Stratford with a certain number of Shakespeare Club members on its Birthday Celebrations Committee. The Club, which at one time was for gentlemen only, is now open to both sexes. Its membership, surprisingly, has not increased above the 400 mark. It is this body which began, in the closing years of the last century, the ceremony of the flag-unfurling in Bridge Street on the Birthday. But nothing, we fancy, ever paid so richly strange a homage to the Bard as that "True Blue" Jamboree in and around the Royal Saloon when, in Shakespeare's honour, one Mr. Southby sustained grotesque characters, another fired all his mines, pyramids, and saucissons, while Mr. Blackmore (of America) ascended on his tight-rope eighty feet into the Avonian air. As for the "Choragic Monument" —after all, what is, or was, a choragic monument? "Choragos" was the leader of a Greek chorus, we know, and a Choragic Monument, says Chambers, is "a small temple on which were dedicated the tripods given in the Dionysian contests to the victorious chorus."

Small temple indeed! Surely, too, "Avonian Willy, Bard Divine," was now deemed to be something more than one of a troupe, however vocally triumphant. Still, how well the Choragic Monument sounds. And how well, no doubt, it looked.

CHAPTER VI

HANDS ACROSS THE SEA

"Crowns in my purse I have and goods at home,
And so am come abroad to see the world."
—*Taming of the Shrew*, I. 2.

IN political and economic circles it is generally
supposed that when nations stretch hands across
the sea it is for purposes of putting them into one
another's pockets. But in this matter of Shakespeare
that is not at all the case. American hands have
reached across the Atlantic to pour money on to
Avon's banks. Occasionally, as we saw in the first
chapter, they have had some slight recompense in a
basinful of Avon's sacred stream. But the English,
in their memorials to "Avonian Willy," as in certain
other matters, are much in America's debt and
insufficiently remember it.

Shakespeare's connection with America began with
his arrival in London and was confirmed with the
posthumous publication of the First Folio. The Earl
of Southampton was his early and adored patron.
"The love I dedicate to your lordship is without
end . . . what I have done is yours: what I have to
do is yours: being part in all I have, devoted yours."

This, from the dedication of "Lucrece," is no mere formal declaration of a literary loyalty. Again, in the preface to the First Folio, its editors, Heminge and Condell, spoke of the "most noble and incomparable pair of brethren," the Earls of Pembroke and Montgomery, as prosecuting the author with great favour. These three peers, who so favoured and championed Shakespeare, also favoured and championed the cause of American travel. Both Southampton and Pembroke were members of the Council of the Virginia Company. Pembroke was a large investor in this cause and also, with Southampton, he was a member of the Council for New England. Southampton was an unquenchable enthusiast for the exploration and colonisation of the American coast. In 1602 he had aided a Captain Gosnold, who investigated the shores of New England: in 1605 he supported the voyage of Captain Weymouth. In 1609 he became a member of the Council for Virginia. Indeed, all that party who had been under the influence of the rash but radiant Earl of Essex were rapt with glorious notions of the new Atlantis. At the same time they worked hard to prevent the new lands from becoming servile properties of the English Crown. They were the Patriot Party who insisted from the first on colonial rights and won several important charters for the citizens of the New World. Other Virginian enthusiasts, who must have known Shakespeare well, included Sir Henry Rainsford, a patient of the poet's son-in-law,

Dr. John Hall, and himself the poetry-loving squire of Clifford Chambers, a village which lies only two miles across the fields from Stratford and was much visited by Michael Drayton. Rainsford was a member of the Virginia Council. So, too, was Sir Dudley Digges, whose young brother Leonard wrote, with a deep sense of personal devotion, verses for the First Folio. All these men must have "talked America" a great deal, and Shakespeare obviously heard them. What is more, it is quite certain that he was permitted to read and use the private papers sent home by the explorers.

"The Tempest" was written in 1611. In June, 1609, "a fleet of seven good ships and two pinnaces" had left Plymouth for Virginia. A hurricane fell upon the convoy, whose chief vessel, *Sea-Venture,* carrying Sir Thomas Gates, the new Governor of Virginia, was driven on to the "dangerous and dreaded Ilands of the Bermuda," supposed to be inhabited by spirits. Gates and his party landed safely and found Bermuda not to be too vilely haunted, but an excellent place in which to winter, as many fortunate people have done since. New pinnaces were built, and they proceeded to Virginia in the summer, found the colony in a bad way, gave it what help and direction they could, and returned to England in September, 1610. Their safe arrival naturally set everybody in London talking about the wonders and opportunities as well as the dangers of travel to the New World. Shake-

speare's play "The Tempest" was therefore topical: it
was also extremely well-informed, because the poet
was privileged to use a document circulated to the
members of the Virginia Council, but not publicly
issued for another fifteen years. This was a narrative
by a William Strachey, brought home by Gates, called
"A True Declaration of the Estate of the Colonie in
Virginia." There are numbers of verbal parallels
between this and "The Tempest," which prove that
Shakespeare was sufficiently trusted by the members
of the Virginia Council to be allowed access to its
private papers. The descriptions of the storm, the
wreck, and the island have so much in common that
Shakespeare's use of Strachey's manuscript is obvious
and generally conceded.

The last play, then, which Shakespeare wrote alone,
was his salute to the "Brave New World." Not so
brave or so beautiful, it may be said, if we accept
Caliban as his first portrait of an American. But
Caliban is not his first American: that honour goes
to the enchanting Ariel, if living on the island for
twelve years in a cloven pine constituted a qualifica-
tion for Bermudan or West Indian citizenship.
Caliban, being the son of a witch from Argier by a
father unknown, scarcely counts in this argument. If
the trans-Atlantic public choose to claim Ariel as
Shakespeare's fancy of the aboriginal American and
Brave-New-Worlder, they are not to be denied. When
America erects Shakespeare memorials, either East or

West, it should bid the sculptor remember that lovely sprite. The last line of "The Tempest" contains what will surely pass as a prayer, not only for Ariel but for all those adventurers who, towards the end of Shakespeare's life, were seeking a new career of liberty across the ocean. "Be free," says Prospero, "and fare thou well."

There is another early, strong, and strange link between Shakespeare and America. Visitors to Stratford will notice in the High Street an almost oppressively antique house in a very high state of preservation. This is called Harvard House because a daughter of one of its Elizabethan owners married a Robert Harvard, of Southwark, and bore a son, John, who emigrated and founded Harvard University. At the suggestion of Miss Marie Corelli, Mr. Edward Morris, of Chicago, bought the decaying house and had it repaired to Miss Corelli's satisfaction. Mr. Morris then presented the title-deeds to Harvard University, and it was opened to the English and the touring public by the American Ambassador in 1909.

The connection is a double one. Shakespeare was a Stratford man who went to Southwark—and conquered. Robert Harvard was a Southwark man who went to Stratford—and married. His wife was Katharine Rogers, daughter of Alderman Thomas Rogers, butcher and maltster. He took her back in 1605 to live close to the Globe Theatre and to St. Saviour's, which might be described as the English

Drama's first parish church. It is unlikely that a Stratford woman would not have shown some interest in the Stratford man who had done so well for himself as writer, actor, and "sharer" in the theatrical ventures which took place so close to the Harvards' Bankside home. Little John Harvard was baptized on November 29th, 1607, in the church which became Southwark Cathedral, just before Shakespeare's brother Edmund was buried there.

Presumably, American pilgrimage to the shrine of "Avonian Willy" began during the eighteenth century, if not before. After all, Messrs. Jordan and Sharp were waiting for the faithful with a fine equipment of their crab and mulberry gew-gaws. The most illustrious of such visitors, and the first to put his impressions in a book, was Washington Irving, who was at Stratford in 1815.

Young Irving, whose father came from Orkney and his mother from Falmouth, so that British extremes may be said to have met at his conception, was given his Christian name because of a remark made by his mother that "Washington's work is ended, and the child shall be called after him." Irving's work was yet to begin. His name is now perpetuated in Stratford in two places. The American Fountain bears a quotation from his "Sketch Book": "Ten thousand honours and blessings on the Bard who has thus gilded the dull realities of life with innocent illusions." The Red Horse Hotel, where he stayed on the three occasions that he visited Stratford, has been lately renamed the Washington Irving Hotel, and visitors to the erstwhile Red Horse, when they sign their names, do so on a counter behind which is the little parlour wherein sat Washington.

In seeking material for his "Sketch Book," which was a best-seller of its day and is still much in demand, he found no place more helpful than Stratford and its neighbourhood. Perhaps here he felt that he was amongst the pre-eminent Europeans. He had often expressed a desire to travel and to mingle with the great ones. He made some ironic play with the humble idea that the great of Europe were far greater than the great of America.

He remarks amusingly in his preface: "I had read in the works of philosophers, that all animals degenerated in America, and man among the number. A great man of Europe, thought I, must, therefore, be as superior to a great man of America as a peak of the Alps to a highland of the Hudson; and in this idea I was confirmed, by observing the comparative importance and swelling magnitude of many English travellers among us, who, I was assured, were very little people in their own country. I will visit this land of wonders, thought I, and see the gigantic race from which I am degenerated." So just before the Battle of Waterloo, young Irving, who was destined later to become the American Minister Plenipotentiary in Madrid, sailed from New York.

He landed in Liverpool as the news of the victory was filtering through. This was his second visit to Europe, but his first to the land of the "great." With England in a state of jubilation he doubtless thought that the inhabitants were even greater than they thought they were.

In due course he found himself in Birmingham and later he paid Stratford his first visit. He was enchanted with the town and with the spirit of make-believe which then hovered over the Birthplace. The Sharps and Jordans had done their work thoroughly. The Bogus was everywhere about. Irving knew that he was having his leg pulled and that most of the relics which he saw were far from genuine; but he was that rarity, a pioneer with a sense of humour: his idea was to enjoy what was offered and to make the best of it. The Birthplace, in his day, was not under proper control as now, but was in charge of a garrulous old lady. He noted that "the walls of its squalid chambers are covered with names and inscriptions in every language, by pilgrims of all nations, ranks and conditions, from the prince to the peasant, and with universal homage of mankind to the great poet of nature."

The garrulous old lady, the widow Hornby, amused Irving, but he was not taken in by her old wives' tales. He was shown the shattered stock of the very matchlock with which Shakespeare shot the deer. He was shown his tobacco-box which proved that he was a rival smoker of Raleigh. (Shakespeare, by the way, not once mentions smoking or tobacco in any of his plays.) He saw the sword with which Shakespeare played Hamlet and the identical lantern with which Friar Laurence discovered Romeo and Juliet at the tomb! He also saw much of the mulberry wood "which," says Irving, "seems to have as extraordinary powers of self-multiplication as the wood of the true Cross; of which there is enough extant to build a ship of the line." All who visited the Birthplace sat in the Bardic chair, "whether this be done with the hope of imbibing any of the inspiration of the bard I am at a loss to say." So many people placed their buttocks upon it that Mrs. Hornby assured Irving that, although its seat was made of solid oak, it needed a new bottom at least once in every three years.

Here was the Shakespeare racket at its very worst, utterly uncontrolled. Innocent victims of the widow would swallow everything that she said. Irving was not as simple as all that. He made no pretence of anything but a playful species of belief. "I am always of easy faith in such matters and am very willing to be deceived, where the deceit is pleasant and costs nothing. I am therefore a ready believer in relics, legends, and local anecdotes of goblins and great men; and would advise all travellers who travel for their gratification to be the same. What is it to us, whether these stories be true or false, so long as we can persuade ourselves into a belief of them, and enjoy all the charm of the reality?"

Mrs. Hornby evidently felt that Washington Irving had swallowed everything, for she confided in him that she was a lineal descendant of the Poet. This was rather too much even for the tolerant American: but he retained an expression of bland innocence which he was immediately to regret. Having so far prevailed, Mrs. Hornby thrust into his hands a play of her own composition, which, after he had read it, "set all belief in her consanguinity at defiance."

From the Birthplace, then full of its bogus relics, he wandered to the church and was much impressed with the tomb of Shakespeare, with the churchyard, its moss-covered graves and its archway of trees which leads to the main porch. He appears to have made friends with the old sexton, whose cottage still exists on Waterside and he had many a gossip with this old codger. The sexton was also very doubtful of the veracity of many of Mrs. Hornby's statements, but this doubt was probably prompted by reasons of jealousy rather than reasons of honesty. The visitors to the Birthplace considerably outnumber those to the grave.

The sexton had been employed as a carpenter on the preparations for Garrick's jubilee. He remembered the prime mover well and described him as a "short punch man, very lively and bustling." The old man had a bosom friend (the two had been boys together) who claimed to have assisted in the cutting down of the mulberry-tree. He produced a piece of the wood from his pocket, which, said Washington Irving, was "no doubt a sovereign quickener of literary conception."

Irving's description of the church is excellent. He was so impressed with the thought that the "remains of Shakespeare were mouldering beneath my feet," that it was a long time before he could drag himself away. As he left the churchyard he plucked a branch from one of the yew-trees, "the only relic that I have brought from Stratford." Irving's *Stratford-on-Avon* is far more than a guide-book. It is an essay, finely descriptive and simple in style. It is but one chapter in a "Sketch-Book," but it is a chapter which continues to make and keep Americans interested in Stratford-upon-Avon.

The current American invasion of Stratford varies according to "prosperity" and the strength of the stock-market. The tourists like to buy little models of the Birthplace and imitations of the Sanctuary Knocker which has rested for centuries on the door of the church. That purchase will find a place on an American front door and people will come from miles round to call on its owner and use her Stratford knocker. They will retain their piece of rosemary, show it to their friends with pride, and lay stress on the fact that they walked, with this in their hand, in the Birthday procession to the church. They will "do" Stratford very thoroughly indeed. With the camera they will visit Anne's Cottage at Shottery and Mary Arden's house at Wilmcote as well as the main Stratford buildings and museums, and the pictures will be a permanent record of their visit to the shrine.

The stories of Americans "doing" Stratford in five minutes are much exaggerated. Many of them, and they number about ten per cent of a season's visitors, spend at least a week amongst the relics. They ask sensible questions, show a lively interest, and altogether are a good example to the English visitors. There are some odd examples of Americans in Stratford, but they are the exception rather than the rule. The verger at the Church tells the story of an American woman who examined with great interest the church register of Baptisms and Deaths and then turned round and said: "Say, Mr. Verger, can you seriously tell me that those are the signatures of William Shakespeare?" Again there was, not so very long ago, an American of great bulk who descended from an expensive car outside the theatre and demanded admittance within. When told that he could not go in as a rehearsal was in progress, he said: "That sure is cruel. I left London at 11 o'clock this morning—it's now 3 o'clock and I've got to be back by 7 o'clock. I can't possibly tell the folks at home that I came to Stratford and did not enter your theatre." As a consolation he was allowed to take one quick peep at a darkened interior. He was quite satisfied. Experiences like this are more than unusual; they are extremely rare. Undoubtedly they are due to an over-enthusiasm, charming in its way, which is in direct contrast to the indifference of a certain type of English person.

A few years ago an elderly and rather fatuous English woman who was visiting Stratford-on-Avon met one of the junior members of the Company. On learning of his theatrical work she displayed great interest. "Tell me, what do you *do* in the plays?" "Oh, I—er—I sing in 'As You Like It.'" "How very, very interesting. Let me see. That's the film that Elisabeth Bergner is in, is it not?" Fools there are in all walks of life and a number of them, though fortunately not enormous, are to be found walking round the Avonian Shrine.

Since Washington Irving's day America has, in her adulation of Shakespeare, built many monuments to the Poet. Her interest in him has spread across the seas. She has not been merely content to erect Shakespeare libraries, statues, theatres, etc., in her own land; she has done the same in England.

Through the munificence of Andrew Carnegie Pittsburgh has built a library in the very street in which Shakespeare was born. Stratford, on the whole, welcomed this gesture, although it met with a certain amount of formidable opposition. The leader of this was that very prickly resident of the town, Marie

Corelli. She objected very strongly to the erection of an "ugly" building in a street hallowed by Shakespeare. She objected to this "vandalism" which she said would mean the pulling down of cottages which Shakespeare had known. According to an interview given to the Press by Miss Corelli, Carnegie met her face to face in London and told her very bluntly that: "If Henley Street were as old as Christ I would pull it down," and he gave her to understand that in all probability young Shakespeare himself would have preferred an upstanding Free Library to the collapsing old houses of his friends. All of which need not be taken too seriously. Marie Corelli had imagination as well as temper. At least it shows that Carnegie, despite the vulgarism of which Marie Corelli accused him, had a wider appreciation of the man Shakespeare than did the woman Corelli.

This formidable settler in late Victorian and Edwardian Stratford hated anything American, and during her life made herself, so far as American interest was concerned, the "Foote" of her day. Foote impeded Garrick: she impeded Carnegie. Neither of the impeders had much success. The difference between these two characters is that the actor was inspired by jealousy whilst the authoress was inspired by a notion of "divine right." Shakespeare was her patron saint and nothing—at least so far as Stratford was concerned—must be done without her special blessing. She was a strange creature, a brilliant

131

creature, a creature to be reckoned with by any American who wished to help to perpetuate the name of William Shakespeare.

Miss Corelli made great capital out of the confession that Andrew Carnegie had never so much as set foot in Stratford-upon-Avon. A man who had never visited the town must have some ulterior motive in wishing to interfere in its affairs. He wanted to pull down the street and had never even bothered to look at it. The most historic street in the world! Poor Miss Corelli fought hard for the preservation of the cottages, but she lost her fight; America, through Carnegie, was graciously pleased to give Stratford a building in which to house its books, and Stratford meekly accepted what might have been resented as an insult.

The American Memorial Window in the Stratford church also caused Miss Corelli a few heart-flutters. The Window—famous for its strange design—was purchased with £250 subscribed by American visitors, and was unveiled on St. George's Day, 1896, by the Honourable Thomas Bayard, the American Ambassador. The artist made a brave effort to combine Biblical and Shakespearean interests, but cannot be said to have succeeded any too well. He attempted to adapt the Seven Ages of Man from "As You Like It" to notable biblical characters. Abraham appears as "the lean and slippered pantaloon." This can hardly be called appropriate.

The Window itself bears the inscription: "The gift of America to Shakespeare's Church." This brought forth further irony and sarcasm from Stratford's illustrious authoress. She was asked in an interview: "How about the American Window?" She quickly retorted: "It is not yet paid for. I should have ventured to try to collect the remaining sum due upon it, had the vicar been a kindly man. But the treatment I have received since I paid the larger debt due on the church restoration does not encourage me to make any further effort to assist him. All the same, I think it somewhat of a disgrace to Americans that they do not finish what their subscriptions have begun." Miss Corelli was at war with the Church as well as with America. Marie Corelli was Shakespeare's self-appointed guardian angel and nothing should be done without her especial permission. That was the impression gained by the benefactors. To consult Corelli or not to consult Corelli? That was the question. Her stubborn, buffer-like character made consultation the greater of two evils; so unconsulted she went and insulted she became.

She said that she would welcome help from Rockefeller and suggested that he might buy as much of Stratford-upon-Avon as he could, pay all its miserable municipal debts, and make it the happiest little place in the world. "Fancy all the nations worshipping at Shakespeare's shrine, and finding it as much as possible an unspoilt memory of the sixteenth century."

Rockefeller, in common with the American nation, did his best for Stratford when it came to the rebuilding of the Memorial Theatre.

Earlier American contacts with Stratford-upon-Avon were all the pleasanter for the absence of the town's illustrious novelist. Her brilliance and her aggressiveness might have prevented the erection of the American Fountain which stands opposite the White Swan Hotel in Stratford-upon-Avon. To-day it is considered by some to be a Victorian atrocity, but when it was unveiled by Henry Irving in 1887, the Jubilee Year of Queen Victoria, it was looked upon as the last word in artistic design.

To Dean Stanley must go the credit for thinking of a fountain as a suitable memorial to Shakespeare, and to George W. Childs, American philanthropist, goes the credit for carrying out the Dean's scheme. This fountain, which served both man and beast, was the sixth Shakespeare Monument ever built in England. The chronology of these is curious.

The first was the famous bust over the tomb in the Stratford church, the second was the bust in Westminster Abbey, placed in position in 1740, the third the Garrick Statue on the North Wall of the Stratford Town Hall, which played so prominent a part in the 1769 Festivities, the fourth was the huge statue which David Garrick bequeathed to the Nation and was housed, and still rests, in the British Museum, and the fifth was the statue in Leicester Square given by

Albert Grant, M.P., later Baron Grant, in 1874. The seventh monument appeared in Stratford-upon-Avon about a year after the unveiling of the Fountain, and because of its now prominent site is probably one of the most famous in England.

Visitors crossing the River Avon cannot help looking at the statue presented by Lord Ronald Gower. Shakespeare is here enthroned on high, facing towards Snitterfield, the home of his grandfather: he is surrounded by some of the great characters of his imagination: Lady Macbeth, Prince Hal in "Henry IV," Part II, trying on the crown, Falstaff and Hamlet. Anguish, youth, comedy and tragedy guard him night and day. There was a time when this important statue was in the gardens of the old Memorial Theatre. Then the poet faced the church in which he was christened and later buried. The hand-wringing Lady Macbeth then faced the theatre, and after the fire, when the building was but a shell, this tragic character could be seen from amongst the ruins, looking straight on to the chaos. She might almost have been sending up a prayer to America to help Stratford in its straits. America heard that call and its share in rebuilding the theatre was large. There was no fuss when this Gower statue was unveiled. Perhaps it was felt that the excitement which attended the unveiling of the Fountain could not be repeated at such a short interval.

At the Fountain ceremony were present the

important of both countries. Mr. Phelps, the American Minister, represented the U.S.A., whilst Henry Irving represented England. These two were supported by Mayors, Mayoresses, Civic Dignitaries and others of note. American literature was represented by a nine-versed poem from Oliver Wendell Holmes in honour of the Fountain's dedication. Holmes achieved a minor miracle in mentioning but once the name of Shakespeare. Henry Irving read the poem One who was present at this important ceremony said that it was an unforgettable few minutes whilst the great actor gave each word its full value and each line its full beauty. To us this work appears merely dreadful, as much a Victorian atrocity as the fountain which it honours. Well, here is the last verse and the reader may revel in it, if he can.

"Land of our Fathers, ocean makes us two,
   But heart to heart is true!
Proud in your towering daughter in the West,
Yet in her burning life-blood reign confest
Her mother's pulses beating in her breast.
This holy fount, whose rills from heaven descend,
Its gracious drops shall lend—
Both foreheads bathed in that baptismal dew,
And love make one the old home and the new!"

In his speech which followed the rendering of the poem, Irving said: "The simplest records of Stratford show that this is the Mecca of American pilgrims, and that the place which gave birth to Shakespeare is regarded as the fountain of the mightiest and most enduring inspiration of our mother tongue. It is not difficult to believe that amongst the strangers who write those imposing letters U.S.A. in the visitors' book in the historic house hard by, there are some whose colloquial speech still preserves many phrases which have come down from Shakespeare's time. Some idioms, which are supposed to be of American invention, can be traced back to Shakespeare. And we can imagine at the old Globe Theatre there were ignorant and unlettered men who treasured up something of Shakespeare's imagery and vivid portraiture, and carried with them across the ocean thoughts and words, 'solemn vision and bright silver dream,' which helped to nurture their transplanted stock."

After Mr. Irving's speech the water of the Fountain was turned on, a cup was filled, and for the first time "the Immortal Memory of William Shakespeare" was drunk in water. As soon as the toast had been drunk the Mayor announced to the assembled company that the water had been pronounced by authority to be clean, palatable, and good. The band then played "God Save the King" and "Hail, Columbia," whilst hearty cheers were given for the Queen, for the President of the United States, for the American Minister, for Mr. George W. Childs, the munificent donor, and for Mr. Henry Irving, the Mayor and

Lady Hodgson, and for all others concerned. By the
time the final cheer had been given it can be taken
for granted that throats were parched and that water,
however clean, palatable, and good, was not enough.
There was a procession to the Town Hall where a
large and by no means aqueous luncheon was enjoyed
by all.

The ceremony, by a happy coincidence, was held on
Jubilee Day, thus giving revellers and others a double
excuse to enjoy themselves to the brim. The
American Minister, who had kept quiet at the unveiling, made a suitable and dignified speech at the
luncheon. He said: "It is appropriately erected on
the place where the memory of Shakespeare has
extinguished all other memories, a place to which
Americans, by the pilgrimage of successive generations, have established a title as tenants in common
with Englishmen by right of possession." At the
conclusion of the Minister's oration the Mayor
announced, amid great cheering, that a telegram
from Her Majesty had just arrived: "The Queen is
much gratified by the kind and loyal expression contained in your telegram, and is pleased to hear of the
handsome gift from Mr. Childs to Stratford-upon-
Avon." Shortly afterwards the Toast of "The
Immortal Memory" was drunk in the wine of the
Rhine, while the Avon flowed quietly by, neither so
clean nor so palatable, but very good to look upon.
American interest in Shakespeare in America has

been, until recent years, more cultural than theatrical. There is a Shakespeare Association with six grades of membership: Annual Sustaining, Life, Special Life, Fellowship, and Patron. The difference between Life and Special Life may puzzle: financially it amounts to fifty dollars a year. The Association, whose President is the book-lover, Dr. Rosenbach, publishes a Quarterly Bulletin of Shakespearean Studies. Certainly the scholars of the United States have every opportunity to peruse Shakespeare at first hand, for more than half the First Folios in existence are at Washington in the extremely handsome library there built on a central and splendid site by Henry Folger, once of the Standard Oil Company. Folger spent his great wealth lavishly on Tudor books and relics, and it is a magnificent collection of which a great Shakespearean scholar and biographer, Professor Joseph Quincy Adams, is Curator. There is also in the building a model of a Tudor theatre: being wholly indoors, it is not a replica of the Globe and its proportions could be challenged. But it is an extraordinarily attractive addition to the establishment and sitting there dreamily on a warm afternoon of the fall, when modern Washington itself offers such a magnificent spectacle, one can easily imagine oneself back in Shakespeare's London and people the galleried stage with the parts of his creation and the players of his troupe. England has nothing like the Folger Library, considered as a specialised Elizabethan exhibit. There are also most valuable and important Shakespeareana in the Huntington Library in California.

In England Mr. William Poel and Mr. Robert Atkins have been lonely champions of the Platform Stage for Shakespeare. The Americans have experimented more fully with the Elizabethan Theatre. The centre of the English Village at the Chicago World's Fair was the "Old Globe Theatre," where Shakespeare's plays were acted throughout the day, almost non-stop, under the direction of Mr. B. Iden Payne, who is the present Director of the Stratford-upon-Avon Festival The plays were somewhat cut, played very simply and very fast, and proved enormously popular. This theatre was later erected at Dallas, Texas. Its opening was marked by the ceremonial sprinkling of earth and water from Stratford-upon-Avon, of which we have already written. A similar Elizabethan stage was arranged for the New York World's Fair of 1939 in a "village" called Merrie England and nineteen Shakespeare plays were to be given in "tabloid" form.

In recent years there has been a tendency to rescue Shakespeare from immolation in the studies and libraries of American scholarship and to give him the proper freedom of the stage. The somewhat limited interest in acted Shakespeare, long sustained by Booth, Daly, Hampden, and Barriemore, was keenly renewed and expanded by the duel of two Hamlets, those of Mr. John Gielgud and Mr. Leslie Howard in 1935–36, and by the enormous favour won by another English actor, Mr. Maurice Evans, who, after a season at the Old Vic, where his work had been well liked but not immoderately revered, suddenly took America by storm with his "Richard II" and, yet again, in 1938, with his "Hamlet." Further American concern with Shakespeare as an ever-living dramatist rather than as a cultural force was shown by Mr. Orson Welles's much-praised production in 1937 of "Julius Cæsar" as a study of Fascism in modern uniforms, a "stunt," no doubt, but one likely to remind Broadway that Stratford's famous Bard was a play-boy after its own hot taste for action and reality, and not a composer only of mottoes for calendars, titles for novelists, and texts for unhappy school-children to recite and annotate.

CHAPTER VII

THE BIRTHPLACE

"Here his first infant Lays sweet Shakespeare sang."

THE Poet's Birthplace in Henley Street is ever the first resort of the visitor in Stratford. About ninety thousand people pay to go in during an average year. In the Record Year of 1928, 118,000 passed the turnstile. That is about ten times the population of the town itself. The old house is so famous that it is, as we saw, simply labelled on direction-signs, "The Birthplace." The infant's name is unnecessary in Stratford. At the same time there is no definite or final proof that Master William was born at "The Birthplace," just as there is no completely final proof that he was born on "The Birthday," April 23rd. Both are guesses, and the guess about the Birthplace is, in all probability, correct. For these premises certainly were once the house of John Shakespeare, the poet's father, and since it was then unusual and perhaps wholly unknown for expecting mothers to seek expert aid and take refuge in a nursing-home, we can, with all confidence, assume that William Shakespeare addressed the world for the first time under the roof so long, and once so profitably, associated with his origin.

> "We came crying hither;
> Thou know'st, the first time that we smell the air,
> We wawl and cry."

Here, then, in all probability, young William wawled.

John Shakespeare first settled in Henley Street to reside and carry on business as a glover in or before 1552; during that year he was fined for leaving a muck-heap opposite his house. He was tenant in possession of two houses: he purchased the eastern house in 1556 and the western in 1575. Fripp, whose specialised study of Tudor Stratford made him an authority of great weight, writes:

"In Michaelmas term, 1575, Alderman Shakespeare considerably enlarged his property in Henley Street. By the purchase of the premises adjoining, described in the fine as 'two messuages' with 'two gardens' and 'two orchards,' he acquired the whole block of buildings of which his shop and residence hitherto formed the eastern wing. At the end on the west was probably a large gable corresponding to the one on the east. It was a handsome little property, of the homely substantial kind in favour in Warwickshire in the early half of the sixteenth century."*

* *Shakespeare, Man and Artist*, Vol. I, p. 72.

It is possible that John, having bought the eastern house, then rented the other section until he was rich enough to purchase both.

The Birthplace, as the modern visitor sees it, was gradually restored and repaired between 1850 and 1860. The buildings had seen much change of circumstance, much dilapidation and repair. The elements are those of a typical Warwickshire Tudor house with an oak foundation on the "ground-sill," with walls marked by narrowly spaced vertical timbers and with a square panelling of beams higher up. The back portion is supposed by Fripp to have been the section allotted to William if and when he brought Anne back to his father's house following his marriage in 1582. According to Mr. Oliver Baker, the author of *Shakespeare's Warwickshire,* there was much modernising of windows, but "on the whole the ancient contours have been preserved, and when the three gables on the front were re-edified it was stated that the original mortice-holes in the wall-plate had been found and re-used."

It is not our business to guide the reader through the museum within. We need merely say that probity and scholarship now rule where conscienceless old women once held a preposterous market and sold their eternal chips and shavings of the supposedly Bardic chair. We are dealing with the cottages before which the noblest have practised prostration. Wrote Jusserand: "This dwelling has become a place of worship for pilgrims of all nations and its walls, long used to vulgar sights, have, in our days, seen a Princess of Stuart and Plantagenet blood, destined to wear an imperial crown, fall on her knee at the threshold." Suitably impressed by the royal salaams, let us trace the cause and nature of those "vulgar sights" which intervened between the death of John Shakespeare in 1601 and the purchase of the premises by Trustees on behalf of the Nation in 1847.

William Shakespeare, who, in 1601, was owner of New Place and presumably dividing his time between there and London, inherited the Henley Street houses and permitted his married sister Joan Hart to remain in possession of one. She was still there in 1616, when he made his will, by which "he devised unto her the house with the appurtenances in Stratford wherein she dwelleth for her natural life under the yearly rent of twelve pence." Mrs. Hart was certainly living cheaply: Shakespeare was strict, we gather, in money matters, but not at the expense of a sister. The old lady flourished on his bounty, for she did not die till 1646, at the age of seventy-seven. The freehold passed to his daughter, Susanna, the wife of Dr. John Hall, and from her to her daughter, who became Lady Barnard. Lady Barnard bequeathed it to her cousin, Thomas Hart, the grandson of Mrs. Joan Hart, so that the property returned to the family and became the natural headquarters of the family business, which, as William's fame expanded, was now the founding and

developing of the Shakespeare Industry. The Harts
lived in the western house and shrewdly kept the
other part of the premises for use as an inn. It would
have been a handy arrangement for the visitors to get
Bard, Bed, and Breakfast under one roof. But there
is no evidence that they let rooms. There were
particularly sordid trade disputes, for Jordan, whose
activities as a maker of Shakespearean legends and as
a general racketeer in the growing commerce we have
already mentioned, quarrelled with the Harts and
told the world: "Even the house that for upwards of
half a century has been shown for and venerated as
the place of his nativity is a most flagrant and gross
imposition, invented purposely with a design to extort
pecuniary gratuities from the credulous and unwary,
who fired with an enthusiastic admiration and regard
for the poet's memory, are induced by the loquacious
ignorance of low-bred mercenary and illiterate people
to visit and pay for entering this paltry hut." Previously Jordan had been of an entirely different
opinion. Having published his new-found views, the
Stratford rhymer had to do something to help his
absurd assertion: he set about it, quite vainly, by trying to show that Brook House on the Waterside was
the place where Shakespeare breathed his first.

Garrick's "Jubilee" made Stratford familiar to
English tourists and the good "perambulators" would
not fail to take a turn in Stratford and, once there, in
Henley Street. The Hon. John Byng, for example,

who has left us the Torrington Diaries, paid several
visits to Stratford, and some of his manuscript is in
the Birthplace. The reigning Mrs. Hart was at that
time trading briskly in the bits and pieces of the cult
and running a Bardolaters' bazaar. Here is Byng's
record of a conversation of 1785:

"How do you, Mrs. Hart? Let me see the wonders
of your house."

"Why there, Sir, is Shakespeare's chair and I have
been often bid a good sum of money for it. It has
been carefully handed down on record by our
family; but people never thought so much of it till
after the Jubilee. And now see what pieces they
have cut from it, as well as from the old flooring
of the bed room."

Byng then bought "a Slice of Chair equal to the size
of a Tobacco Stopper." Also he "eagerly eyed the
Lower Cross Bar of the Chair, curiously wrought."
With this Mrs. Hart could not be tempted to part.
But Stratford was letting much be taken, sobeit the
visitors flocked in. Byng was one of many who
pilfered a piece of the Roman pavement then at the
head of Shakespeare's grave. Naturally the Bardic
furniture could not stand for long Mrs. Hart's policy
of "cut-and-come-again." The mulberry-tree remained
prolific, but the chair vanished. During a later visit
Byng thus recorded his examination:

"At six o'clock we entered the town of Stratford-on-Avon, rendered famous by Shakespeare; and the Jubilee. . . . The evening was cold and gloomy. I walked about the town in a Shakespearean reverie. At the house of his birth they would have tempted me in, but I said: 'Where is his old chair, that you have sold? I, now, enter not.' My words seemed to shock them; and they have discovered that they have sold the goose that laid the golden eggs.

"Had they been makers of Italian policy, they had always kept an old chair ready to succeed the one sold; or rather, kept the old one, and parted with the substitute. I look'd into the mulberry shop; where the goods are most wretchedly executed; and then to the old book-seller's; and had I time and spirit I wou'd hunt his garret; (tho' well sifted) for he formerly bought the library from the house within Shakespeare resided."

The "mulberry-shop" was, of course, Thomas Sharp's, of whose shocking fertility mention has already been made. The "old book-seller" was either Walford or Keating, both of whom lived in High Street. The puzzle of Shakespeare's books remains unsolved, for there is no other record of a local bookseller having acquired the library from New Place. The traffic in chairs, however, was by no means wound up. Should Stratford run dry of curios, Shottery could become a fountain of refreshment. In 1793, there was on sale at Hewland Farm, now preserved as Anne Hathaway's cottage, the chair on which William had sat with Anne on his knee. It was bought, as we have seen, by William Ireland.

According to William Smith, the author of *A New and Complete History of the County of Warwick* (a gentleman apparently somewhat prophetic, since he described the events of 1830 in Stratford while his publisher marked the volume as an issue of 1829), the Harts sold out in 1806. In 1829 (or 1830)

> "The premises originally occupied as one dwelling, are now divided into two habitations; the one part being used as a butcher's shop, and the other as a public house, known by the sign of the Swan and Maidenhead. The outer walls of the whole were divided into pannels by strong pieces of timber; but a brick front has been substituted in that part of the building now used as a public house or inn; the ancient form is yet preserved in the other half, or butcher's premises. The rooms are plain, somewhat gloomy, and of limited proportions; yet such a building may be readily supposed the abode of a trader of no contemptible description in the sixteenth century."

"The Swan" may have been Leda's friend. Others think it a compliment to Shakespeare, "Sweet Swan of Avon," whilst the "Maidenhead," some say, stood

for Queen Elizabeth, who was his Queen, "fair vestal
thronèd by the west." The Inn sign was a wooden
one and was, unfortunately, pulled down in 1808 by
some local sons of Belial, members of the Warwickshire Yeomanry, who, in their liquor, said that "as
the only Maidenhead left in the town was a wooden
one, they would destroy it." As it is thought that
the house became an Inn in Shakespeare's life, this
drunken jest of the licentious soldiery and the petty
rape which followed it might have robbed the Birthplace of one of its most interesting relics; but the sign
was saved from ruin and is now on view.

When the Birthplace was sold by the Harts, it was
very dilapidated and there was therefore great difficulty in finding a purchaser. The Harts had, by now,
lost most of their money and their poverty did not
allow them to keep the place in decent repair. It fell
into other hands, hands of one who in a half-crafty,
half-crazy kind of way realised that there was much
money to be made out of this Shakespeare business.

This next tenant was a widow, a Mrs. Hornby, a
determined but unskilful hoaxer, who fully justified,
for tourists, the historic advice to "bevare of vidders."
Washington Irving, who claimed that he was not
taken in by the old lady, described her as possessing
"a red frosty face, lighted up by a cold blue anxious
eye, and garnished with artificial locks of flaxen hair,
curling from under an exceeding dirty cap. She was
peculiarly assiduous in exhibiting the relics with

which this, like all other celebrated shrines, abounds."
For many years Mrs. Hornby profitably showed the
house and the relics to the credulous. Her tales
mounted with the years. She claimed descent from
Shakespeare; she averred that she herself, inspired by
her home, wrote wonderful plays*; the more she
talked, the more she expected to be tipped. She was
eventually de-throned by a rival widow named Court.

Mrs. Hornby had occupied the butcher's shop.
Mrs. Court took the "Swan and Maidenhead" and
decided that she would have tenancy of the other
house as well, since she owned both. So the two houses
in Henley Street once again belonged to one tenant.
Mrs. Court commercialised the house as Mrs. Hornby
had done, but she had to do without the "relics." The
Widow Hornby had removed these to another house
across the road. We are told that "these rival
dowagers parted on envious terms, they were constantly to be seen at their doors abusing each other
and their respective visitors, and frequently with so
much acerbity as to disgust and even deter the latter
from entering either dwelling."

> "What, Birthplace here! and relics there?
> Abuse from each! Ye brawling blowses!
> Each picks my pocket, 'tis not fair,
> A stranger's curse on both your houses!"

* She published two, *The Battle of Waterloo* and *The Broken Vow*,
also some *Extemporary Verses Written in Shakespeare's Birthplace.*
All were printed locally. London seems to have haughtily ignored
her muse.

The author of this rather feeble commination is unknown. It can be presumed that his sentiments were common to visitors infuriated by the squalid rivalry of the huckster-harridans.

Eventually, in 1823, the "war" had got to such a pitch that the one street could not hold both the widows. Mrs. Hornby packed her outfit of bogus relics and found herself another house in Wood Street; later she moved to Bridge Street, and shortly afterwards to 23, High Street, where the stuff remained for about fifty years in charge of her granddaughter, Mrs. Arabella Jones. After two other Stratford "resting-places" the collection was moved to King's Thorpe in Northamptonshire, where it was kept by Mr. Thomas Hornby, a nephew of Arabella. On the death of Thomas it went to the auction-rooms of Messrs. Christie, Manson and Woods, and found various purchasers. A piece of mulberry-tree fetched £2 12s. od., and so the collection, mostly trash, was at last dispersed. Just before Mrs. Court took up her residence in "The Swan and Maidenhead" the following notice appeared in a window:—

"WILLIAM SHAKESPEARE WAS BORN IN THIS HOUSE.
N.B. A horse and taxed cart to let."

Mr. R. B. Wheler, in his short history of the Birthplace, strongly disputes the genuine quality of its contents at the beginning of the nineteenth century. He gives us some further light on the new Warwickshire industry of manufacturing Bardic Chairs. "In this lowly dwelling," he says, "some antiquated lumber was formerly imposed upon the world as its original furniture at the period of Shakespeare, to none of which the least authenticity belonged. In the moment of unsuspected enthusiasm, persons of easy faith in such matters too implicitly relied upon its originality: for it is well known that the furniture of this house has undergone more alterations than the building itself, and that it has, of late years at least, changed with every tenant. The chair for which the Princess Czartoryska in 1790 gave twenty guineas is as spurious as that which immediately supplied its place. It was, however, conveyed to the continent with a certificate of its authenticity; and Mr. Burnet, in his *View of the Present State of Poland*, page 257, mentions the formality of its production in the salon of the Princess, who had amassed an extensive collection of curiosities of various descriptions, among which this despicable chair, in a green case, was carefully preserved." Washington Irving, in his *Sketch Book*, mentions the number of Poetic Seats, and says: "It is worthy of notice also, in the history of this extraordinary chair, that it partakes something of the volatile nature of the Santa Casa of Loretto, or the flying chair of the Arabian enchanter; for although sold some few years since to a northern princess, yet, strange to tell, it has found its way back again to the old chimney corner."

The Princess arrived, with her twenty guineas, before Mrs. Hornby's time. One of Mrs. Hornby's lines of business was the Autograph: she thus seems to have pioneered in a commerce or hobby more popular than ever to-day. Here, too, was infinite swindling. Her visitors' books contained many signatures of notable people who did not visit her. The signature of the Prince Regent appeared in the book; so did that of the Duke of Wellington. "Fictitious names are abundantly inserted in that and in all other albums; and Mrs. Hornby, who endeavoured to impose on all, was in this respect imposed on by others." (R. B. Wheler.)

In May, 1822, the following, printed on a little card, was distributed throughout Stratford-on-Avon: "Mrs. Court respectfully invites the nobility and gentry visiting Stratford-upon-Avon to gratify their own laudable curiosity, and honour her by inspecting the house in which the Immortal Poet of Nature was born." This publicity campaign on the part of the widow in possession might have had some say in deciding the widow across the way to move her "Shakespeareana." She was already quarrelling about the rent. In 1823, Mrs. Hornby moved and took her astonishing "collection" with her.

In our chapter on "The Golden Bough" we drew on William Howitt's account of his visit to Stratford in the eighteen-thirties. The Birthplace scandal was then at its worst. Everybody who went to Henley Street scribbled his name on the walls. Mrs. Hornby's collection of "relics" was on view at Mr. Reason's house, opposite the Town Hall. As one item was bought and disappeared, a new one popped up to fill its place. There were abundant chunks, needless to say, of the authentic and unquenchable mulberry-tree and of the no less authentic and unquenchable Bidford crab-tree. Of course, there was a Poet's Chair. This one had been given to Shakespeare by the Earl of Southampton and carried the Earl's Arms; better still, there was Little Hamnet's Chair, supposedly the beloved perch of the poet's son, who died in early boyhood. There was a portrait of Shakespeare in the character of Petruchio, alleged to have been painted by his nephew, William Shakespeare Hart. There were pieces of the Bard's own bed—none of your "second-best" article. There was the sword with which he had performed in "Hamlet" and which the Prince Regent had wanted so much to buy in 1815, saying "he knew very well the family that gave it to Shakespeare." There could not, in any single case, be the slightest evidence to justify the claim. But the market was ready. The fish gathered with open mouths and Mary Hornby, her heirs and assigns, had determined, of their charity, that it was cruel to leave them hungry. Fed they should be, and fed they were.

Best of all, perhaps, was a piece of the matchlock

wherewith Shakespeare shot the deer in Sir Thomas Lucy's park. As this story of the poaching has now been completely discredited, Lucy having neither park nor deer at the time, the provision of the poacher's actual weapon showed the degree of readiness in invention to which the Shakespeare Industry was attaining in the early part of the nineteenth century. The time was, however, drawing near when the Birthplace Racket was felt to be a scandal beyond endurance. But this did not happen during the lifetime of either of the Widows. The nation had to wait till Mrs. Court died before the two buildings were put into the public market. The story of the purchase is an interesting one. The nation was becoming conscious of the fact that Shakespeare's Birthplace ought to be under strict control.

Stratford began to take action in the matter. Then there was a London Committee appointed to run the Stratford scheme. In this Charles Dickens was prominent.

Dickens was an indefatigable amateur actor and could, which is rare in amateur actors, rely upon attracting "big houses." He had among his colleagues such eminent Victorians as Leech, Cruikshank, Douglas Jerrold, Mark Lemon, and G. H. Lewes. Their first object had been to raise money for the relief of Leigh Hunt's old age: they then proceeded, in their eager philanthropy, to the aid of the dramatist Sheridan Knowles, the idea being to buy Shakespeare's

THE BIRTHPLACE, 1846

Birthplace and endow a curatorship for Knowles. Dickens was immensely enthusiastic, and no less than nine plays were prepared. He always enjoyed having Ben Jonson's "The Alchemist" on the programme, since he greatly fancied himself in the part of Sir Epicure Mammon. Forster describes this performance, somewhat equivocally, as being "as good as anything he had done." Other dramatists favoured were Beaumont and Fletcher, Goldsmith, Jerrold, and Bulwer Lytton. It suddenly occurred to them that, since saving Shakespeare's Birthplace was one object of their endeavours, they might actually include one of Shakespeare's plays. So "The Merry Wives of Windsor" was rehearsed with a farce to follow called "Love, Law, and Physick," chosen because it offered Dickens one of his favourite roles.

In "The Merry Wives" he played Justice Shallow, an astonishing contrast with Sir Epicure Mammon: but evidently the modern vice of "typecasting" did not exist then. Dame Quickly was played by Mrs. Cowden Clarke, a devoted Bardolatress and compiler of the well-known Shakespeare Concordance. The productions were an enormous success. There were single presentations at Manchester, Liverpool, and Edinburgh and double ones at Birmingham, Glasgow, and London (The Haymarket). The sums taken seem vast. How many modern managers would expect a house of £467 for a single night at Liverpool? London, although Queen Victoria and Prince Albert attended, only produced £319 for two shows. The total gross receipts were £2,551 for nine performances. Sheridan Knowles must have rubbed his hands and certainly Dickens was happy. Here is Forster's picture of this exuberant giant who could find time among all his writing (he was just finishing "Dombey and Son") for so much energetic by-play:

> "In the enjoyment as in the labour he was first. His animal spirits, unresting and supreme, were the attraction of rehearsal at morning, and of the stage at night. At the quiet early dinner, and the more jovial unrestrained supper, where all engaged were assembled daily, his was the brightest face, the lightest step, the pleasantest word. There seemed to be no need for rest to that wonderful vitality."

The money remaining, after expenses had been paid, was offered to Stratford. But Stratford had, very properly, as Forster said, turned proud and resolved to do its own work of preservation. So Knowles got some money without having to do the curator's work and Dickens could proceed to other cares and causes. Stratford and London still had a committee working together, and finally it was a joint offer of £3,000, which bought the Birthplace on behalf of the nation. In this transaction London was represented by two notable antiquaries, Thomas Amyot and Peter Cunningham, and Stratford by its mayor, Dr. Thomson, and a Mr. Sheldon.

BIGGER AND BETTER—THE BIRTHPLACE TO-DAY
(Reconstructed according to an etching dated 1788)

"The extraordinary interest manifested throughout the country by the announcement of the sale of Shakespeare's House at Stratford-upon-Avon" prompted the *Illustrated London News* to compile a special full-length Shakespeare article, illustrated on the spot by Mr. E. Duncan. The paper's representative found the Birthplace in wretched state. Here is part of his report:

> "Of what it was in 1574, no notion can be gathered from what it is in 1847. There is something, indeed, most painful in the contrast of its present wretchedness, and our idea of its condition as the comfortable home of Shakespeare's parents. The low, crazy frontage—the crippled hatch—the filthy remnant of a butcher's shamble, with its ghastly hook—on the outside; and the squalid forlornness of the rooms within, convey together such a sense of utter desolation as merges all those feelings of respect and awe which such a relic should inspire. Let us hope the result of Thursday's sale has saved this interesting property from further desecration."

He visited Shottery, which then had a pleasant rustic tavern called "The Shakespeare Inn." It is described as "fringed with Ophelian pansies." Anne Hathaway's cottage seems to have been in far better condition then than was the Birthplace.

"Thursday's Sale," at which the Birthplace was successfully transferred by Mr. Robins, the auctioneer, to the Stratford and London Shakespeare Committee for £3,000, had its humours. "A person interposed and called upon Mr. Robins to prove that the house he was about to sell was the identical one in which the Poet was born." Here was scepticism indeed! Subversive blasphemy even! What would become of the Industry if talk like that were to go on? Mr. Robins firmly appealed to Tradition (Cheers). He said they must take it as a matter of course. He wished that those who were sceptical on the point would stay away. After this rebuke to the irreverent, the proceedings went forward smoothly. The actual sale evoked "immense cheering," and Mr. Robins said he had never witnessed scenes of such extraordinary enthusiasm. The "person," no doubt, had either resolved obediently to stay away or been ejected by that time. In any case, he would scarcely have remained to bid for the subsequent sale of Shakespeare Relics, such as the ancient spectacle-case and "small carving of Shakespeare's Monument," stated to be from the True, the inexhaustible Mulberry Tree of New Place.

There was plenty of trouble to come.

In 1856, John Shakespeare, Esq., of Worthington, Leicestershire (who claimed to be a collateral descendant of the poet), bequeathed to the Trustees a sum of £2,500 for the general purposes of the fund, and an annuity of £60 for a custodian. In 1861, the Court of Chancery set aside this deed of gift, and the committee who had undertaken repairs and improvements on the faith of this legacy, were brought into considerable difficulties.

The Trustees had bought the Birthplace entirely empty. Then their first task was to repair the houses so that they were made weather-proof without losing their original Tudor aspect; to charge a sufficient sum for admittance so that the buildings could henceforward be kept in a proper state of repair; to have sufficient money to be able to buy veritable pieces of "Shakespeareana" whenever they came into the market and also to pay a well-informed Curator who was unlikely to be taken in by the numerous traders in dubious antiques. The Museum only came into existence a dozen years after the purchase, when the repairs were completed.

That the Birthplace came under such control was excellent. The public was now fully protected from deceit and robbery. Moreover, a genuine Shakespeare Museum was thereby created. No false claims are permitted, however much some visitors like to see the Poet's pen and all the rest of it. The administration is now most scrupulous in its treatment of "relics". The Trustees are naturally anxious to receive gifts, and a glance through their catalogue will show that at least ninety per cent of the numerous items on show have either been presented or bequeathed. A few have been lent and the remainder have been acquired by purchase.

A walk round the Birthplace Museum is not just a stroll among the dust and ashes of fame, the dull business that museum-tramping may become. If you must have a Poet's chair, there is one, with more atmosphere of midnight ale than midnight oil. It comes from the Falcon Inn at "Drunken Bidford," and is the seat "in which the Poet is said to have sat when he held his Club Meetings here." The Trustees, with complete honesty, leave the club and its sittings open to doubt; the Hornbys and Courts would have asserted it as a certain fact. There is an interesting old document, covering the year when John Shakespeare was Bailiff of Stratford, which gives the amount of money paid to the strolling players. This document makes it quite clear that Shakespeare's father gave the actors an official welcome. The boy was only five years old at the time, but he would, if he were present, have acquired vivid impressions of his first contact with the theatre. There are two documents which offer positive proof that John Shakespeare lived in the Birthplace. There is also the priceless piece of parchment whereby William Underhill, Gent., assures to William Shakespeare a messuage (i.e., New Place), two barns and two gardens for £60.

Shakespeare's London is not neglected in the Museum. There is a record of Shakespeare's Blackfriars estate. There is a letter addressed from London by Richard Quyney to his "Loveinge good Frend and contreymann mr. Wm. Shackespere," in which he asks for a loan of £30. This is the only article in the Museum which, it is known, was touched by the hands of the Poet. It is not known whether Shakespeare showed himself a "Loveinge good Frend," but in all probability he did, as the letter came into the hands of the Trustees through the Stratford Corporation: no doubt it had been filed in the way of public business, for Quyney did work for the Corporation. There are splendidly preserved copies of the First, Second, Third and Fourth Folios. Copies of these will also be found in the Memorial Theatre Library. An interesting reminder of the Shakespeare Industry in Germany are three photographs of the so-called "Darmstadt Death-Mask of Shakespeare." This mask is said to have been formerly in the Kesselstadt collection dispersed at Mainz in 1843 and purchased by Ludwig Becker, of Darmstadt, in 1847, and to be now in the possession of his representatives at Darmstadt. The inscription "Anno Domino 1616" is on the edge. All it needs, says the cynic, is the proven signature "William Shakespeare" to make it genuine.

There are numerous books on view with which Shakespeare's work shows him to have been familiar. Also there are the well-known tributes of Francis Meres and of England's Parnassus, in which Shakespeare is quoted ninety-five times. Seven other authors, however, are given even greater prominence:

Spenser, Drayton, William Warner, Samuel Daniel, Sir John Harington, Joshua Sylvester and Thomas Lodge. Among the literary tributes is the striking one of Michael Drayton, who certainly stayed much at Clifford Chambers near-by and may have been at a "merry meeting" before Shakespeare's death.

"And be it said of thee,
Shakespeare thou hadst as smooth a Comicke vaine,
Fitting the socke, and in thy naturall braine,
As strong conception, and as Cleere a rage,
As any one that trafiqu'd with the stage."

The flamboyant figure of Sir William Davenant has its place in the Museum. He, some allege, changed his name to D'Avenant in order to establish a link with the River Avon! He was a vain man and attempted to make capital out of the Shakespeare Industry by claiming that he was Shakespeare's bastard. His father was an Oxford innkeeper and the Inn to this day proudly claims, on all its advertising matter, that it is the Inn where Shakespeare stayed. Davenant, to give him his right spelling, wrote a poem in 1638 "In remembrance of William Shakespeare." It is not a good poem, but its picture of the Banks of the Avon ("each Flower hangs there the pensive Head") charmingly forecasts a meeting of the Governors of the Memorial Theatre in grave deliberation. Aubrey was not the first biographical writer to notice Shakespeare. We are reminded at the Birthplace that this honour goes to Thomas Fuller, who was eight years old when Shakespeare died. "Many were the wit-combates betwixt him and Ben. Jonson, which two I behold like a Spanish great galleon and an English man of war; Master Johnson (like the former) was built far higher in learning, solid but slow in his performances. Shake-spear, with the English-man of war, lesser in bulk, but lighter in sailing, could turn with all tides, tack about and take advantage of all winds, by the quickness of his wit and invention. . . . He died Anno Domino 1616, and was buried at Stratford-upon-Avon, the Town of his Nativity." This pretty simile, likening Ben and Will to the Spanish Armada and our own fleet, engaged in a sea fight then uppermost in the minds of man, was published in 1662. Aubrey's *Brief Lives* were mainly written during the next twenty years.

From 1847 to 1891 the Birthplace was administered by a committee formed under a Deed of Trust. It was then incorporated by Act of Parliament and formally invested with New Place. This had actually been independently purchased by public subscription as a National Memorial, together with Nash's House and the garden, in 1862. The Act of Parliament allowed the Birthplace Trustees to make other purchases, and within one year of the Act coming into force they had acquired Anne Hathaway's Cottage; this also is preserved as a Museum. In 1930 Mary Arden's House at Wilmcote came into the possession of the Trustees.

The official Birthplace Catalogue, in itself a fine book of reference, informs us that "Two cottages adjoining the Birthplace garden on its eastern boundary, which were, during Shakespeare's lifetime, in the occupation of the Hornby family, were presented to the Trustees by Mr. Andrew Carnegie in 1903, and have since been used as the offices of the Trust." Although Carnegie had threatened to pull some cottages down to build his Library, he was not the vandal that Marie Corelli imagined he was. He never did pull them down, and the Public Library is actually a Tudor building.

In 1862 the New Place Estate, which had had such a strange, eventful history in the hands of the Cloptons, Underhill, Shakespeare and his descendants, again the Cloptons, and then the destructive Gastrell, became, as we saw, another Shakespeare Memorial. Nash's House is now a museum showing exhibits of local history and archæology from the earliest times, while the beautifully kept garden is specially given over to flowers mentioned by the poet. Although Anne Hathaway's Cottage at Shottery is a mile out of the town, it appears to be a recognised Beauty Spot and a much-approved Site of Historic Interest in the opinion of the modern tourist. In 1937, while the Birthplace was attracting 85,122 visitors, Anne's home scored no less than 80,800, and many thousands more must have looked over the fence without going in. Wilmcote is three and a half miles away, and Bardolaters seem to be free of a mother-fixation. Only 6,398 paid for a look at the Arden home. Anne's has the greatest lure.

Anne Hathaway's Cottage may or may not be Anne Hathaway's Cottage. Anne, when one looks into her affairs, turns out to be as dark a lady as ever won fair sonnet. There were Hathaways at Shottery: there were Hathaways in Gloucestershire. There were Hathaways all over the place. Certainly Shakespeare married a Hathaway, and, if we cannot find an appropriate Anne, we can find an Agnes in the records, and the name Agnes was sometimes deemed to be interchangeable with Anne, like our Robert and Bob. We know that Hewland Farm, now proclaimed by authority to be Anne Hathaway's Cottage, was thus shown in the eighteenth century, and that the sale of Shakespearean chairs flourished as briskly there as elsewhere. The house is undoubtedly a genuine antique, its setting against an orchard is a fair one, it is certainly on the Hathaway lands; so why be difficult? Why not assume that, when William would a-wooing go, hither he came?

At any rate, the Cottage has been a tremendous asset to the Industry. Its rusticity stirs the sentiments. It suggests the meadows painted with delight, the lyric note, the wood-notes wild. It attracts nearly four times as many visitors as Nash's House* and nearly

---

* The major garden, beyond the site of New Place, is open to the public free and no record can be kept of the number of visitors.

possesses the lure of the Birthplace itself and the Birthplace is in the town and handy for the Theatre and the Church. It figures on countless calendars and Christmas cards, for the reason that it resembles the general notion of Ye Olde Countrie Cottage. It is difficult to believe that much effective courting took place on anything so hard and so uncoaxing as the narrow-seated, straight-backed settle in the kitchen. But some dalliance on that severe perch was no doubt the prelude to walks in the meadows, one of which tender excursions in August, 1582, must have been responsible for the conception of Susanna Shakespeare and the necessary marriage three months later. Such reversal of the proper order of events was, and still is, by no means unusual in rustic life. You may buy in Stratford stationers' shops post-cards of the Courtship at Shottery. Anne, in cap, ruff, and apron, is on the settle, demurely fingering the flowers which Will has brought her. Will is gazing into her eyes sideways, from a high arm-chair. He is handling a book and has been reading to her: now he is thinking, perhaps, more of deeds than of words. With his fine moustache and imperial, he looks a mature fellow for his eighteen years, and Anne looks young for her twenty-six. Both have an air of spotless innocence: it is difficult, on this showing, to decide which led which up the garden.

So Shottery will always be a favourite place of visitation. The Industry, it is true, has at times revealed some of its more grotesque aspects in the immediate neighbourhood. But, while the village of Shottery has been much spoiled, the Cottage itself, with its garden and orchard, is most agreeable to look at and to look over, and the Trust is a careful guardian. Here or hereabouts was the Birthplace of William Shakespeare's early passion; the place where he wooed and won (or was wooed and lost) will always be as sympathetic to the tourist's fancy as the house in Henley Street, where first he wawled and cried.

CHAPTER VIII

TO HAVE AND TO HOLD

"What a devil dost thou in Warwickshire?"
—*I Henry IV*, II, 2.

THE Wars of the Roses are, in the eyes of the true Stratfordians, not to be compared with the bloodless war which raged between Stratford-upon-Avon and London during the years 1861 and 1864. Each side scored points and, at times, the battle seemed to be an evenly matched contest. It was a ding-dong affair with the first few rounds going to London; then came a change of luck and Stratford slowly but surely overtook the capital in its fight to ensure that Shakespeare's home town should be, for ever, the headquarters of a great Industry.

It was not an easy matter to convince the world that the Tercentenary of the birth of Shakespeare should be nationally celebrated in the town which claimed that honour. It appeared to be a walk-over so far as London was concerned, for the great City apparently had every advantage over its country rival. Stratford had no actors and no theatre worth the mention. It also appeared to have no persons who were adept at organising anything on a really grand scale. But it had one great advantage over the opponent. It could show the world where Shakespeare was born, where he walked, where his wife lived, where he went to school, and, above all, where he got his inspiration. Stratford-upon-Avon could thus take pride in presenting London, and the world at large, with the greatest poet and dramatist of all time. London, on the other hand, claimed to have the actors, the theatres, the men of organising ability, the men of letters plus an excellent transport system. A festival held within its boundaries would be easily reached. Stratford also had a transport system; it was not so up-to-date as that of London, but it was sufficiently up to date to ensure that all could, if they so desired, make the journey to the little town on the Avon. Had there been no railway invented then it seems almost certain that Stratford would have lost the contest outright. As it was, capital was made out of the latest invention and advertisements for the Tercentenary Festival laid great stress on the railway facilities.

The idea of a Tercentenary Festival emanated from Stratford and was quickly seized upon by London. Why should Stratford want to make this important event national? London was the proper place for such a celebration. Was it not here that he learnt to act, wrote his plays, and earned his money? Stratford's retort was that Shakespeare always returned home whenever he had the opportunity, that many of his plays were based on Warwickshire, and that if it had not been for the strolling players who visited his town in his boyhood, there would have been no dramatist to honour. Stratford formed a committee as long as three years before the actual celebration. London did likewise. Stratford arranged for representatives to visit various provincial towns and ask for help. When they got to Birmingham they found that London had beaten them by a day. The London Committee was leaving no stone unturned to ensure that they could exploit this great opportunity. The trained organisers of the big City were leaving nothing to chance, and always appeared to be one move ahead of their small town rivals, until it was suggested that the Stratford celebrations should be international. London had not thought of that!

The local committee decided, rather late in the day, that every town in the world was to be circularised so that every enlightened foreigner could have the opportunity of paying homage to the Bard. "Italians would come in their tens, Frenchmen their hundreds, Germans their thousands, and Americans their hundreds of thousands." For what object? To pay homage in a practical manner. To devote money towards a scholarship which could only be earned at Shakespeare's school and to devote money towards the cost of a Monumental Memorial as well as to the Festival Fund. The public had these three choices. The Monumental Memorial Fund proved the most popular with the Festival Fund a close second. The Scholarship Fund did not attract the popular fancy, and whilst subscriptions to this were fairly numerous they were easily outnumbered by those who wanted to see something for their money. The Corporation of Stratford-on-Avon, however, showed complete impartiality by subscribing £50 to each of the three worthy objects.

Others showed their feelings by the amount they gave. Mr. E. F. Flower, who was Mayor of Stratford-upon-Avon and one of the moving spirits of the whole glorious adventure, had publicly decried the erection of a Monument. In fact, so heated did debate on this point become that he resigned his seat as Chairman of the Committee and undertook the secondary position of Vice-Chairman. Despite his strong stand on the Monumental question, he appears to have relented at the last moment, for we find that he gave £50 towards the Monument, £50 towards the scholarship and only £5 towards the Festival Fund. Perhaps it was only as Mayor that he objected, whilst as Mr. Flower he approved, for he said: "He was Mayor of the town, and wanted to serve the townspeople, but he was also one of the Tercentenary Committee, and he must obey the order of the public meeting. He felt himself bound by what that meeting did. It would be painful to himself and to many others to disregard the expressions of the public meeting of the town, but it would be impossible for them to dis-

regard the instructions received from a public meeting which had been already held, and in which the
town took part."

His position was certainly a difficult one, and undoubtedly his honesty of purpose was as well appreciated as is that of the present Flower generation who
have served Shakespeare and Stratford-upon-Avon so
well. Mr. Flower was, at all events, a pillar of strength
on the Committee. He thought nothing of making
long journeys to Manchester, Glasgow, Edinburgh
and other places to appeal for their support for the
Stratford project. He usually got that support. Like
his grandson, he worked so hard and instilled such
confidence into those with whom he came into contact
that one wonders whether the Committee would have
achieved very much without his able leadership.

Lack of leadership was London's weakness. Great
expectations were expected from London, but nothing
very much happened. True, the list of Vice-Presi-
dents got longer and longer, which meant that the
funds got bigger and bigger, but imposing names and
more imposing figures did not impress the public.
People began to feel that they were being put upon,
and consequently showed signs of impatience. They
wanted to see a practical project. Stratford had
offered something practical, and this fact put it several
points ahead in the battle for the Industry. Its well-
planned programme looked exceedingly attractive.
In order to announce its ideas Stratford had the

effrontery to enter the enemies' field and steal some of their best actors as well as some of the scenery from the principal London theatres. It looked something like a grand game of "French and English" without any marauders on the leaderless side. Stratford even went so far as to open a London office.

Had it been suggested that London should open an office in Stratford, the capital might have achieved a little more than it did. The newspapers began to hear about the activities of the Stratford pirates and some of them gave them unexpected encouragement. The *Daily Telegraph,* the *Daily News,* the *Star* and *The Times* all came out with pro-Stratford leading articles. They praised the efforts of the little country gentlemen. They told their readers that the provinces were solidly for Stratford, and in almost as many words they said their sympathies, if they had any in the matter, were definitely on the side of the town which gave us Shakespeare, "both as a matter of necessity and from a sense of justice." This was a bitter pill for London and gave the Avonites unbounded encouragement to forge ahead with their idealistic plans. *The Times* went so far as to rap the London Committee well on the knuckles and told its members that their best policy was to form themselves into an auxiliary committee to the one at Stratford or, if they were unable to do this, the next best thing would be to disband. They were told that the country towns had often assisted London and that it would be a graceful gesture if, this time, London would assist a country town.

Stratford was now gaining points right and left from London. Where were the trained London organisers? Apparently nowhere. Listen to *The Times:* "There is no doubt that this Committee has been badly managed, that its executive has not been wisely chosen, and that it has lost, if it ever possessed, the public confidence." All these big shots were fired at the London Committee on the same day, and the fact that they were not aimed by Stratford but by London itself caused even greater havoc than otherwise would have been the case. Stratford felt that it now had a clear field and could proceed with less caution than previously. Lack of caution was very nearly the undoing of the whole affair, and only by some judicious wriggling did the Tercentenary Festival not become the laughing-stock of the world.

Mr. Flower and his colleagues were certainly knowledgeable men and not the country bumpkins some Londoners would have had us believe. When they said they were going to build a temporary theatre, they meant it, and went the right way about it, but they did not realise what troubles they were going to have when it came to making arrangements with well-known actors and actresses. How they must have regretted the decision to present plays during this Festival! How they must have wished that they had another Garrick to help them in their quandaries!

They had said that they would out-Garrick the Garrick Festival, and that they could have done if they had not thought of a theatre and the acting of plays. The townsfolk, who had heard of the glories of the first Festival and those of later years, had imagined, in the first place, that they would be allowed to dress up and parade the streets in a grand procession. Their disappointment was great when they heard that it was not the intention of the Committee to stage a procession at all. Instead it *was* the intention of the Committee to let the townspeople see Shakespeare's characters come to life in a theatre in his native place. Trouble had started in Stratford, but the Committee stood firm. They had been chosen to see this thing through, and no outside influence was going to make them deviate from their course. Had they not slain the London dragon? They had dealt with that menace so capably that a little trouble in their own camp was just a mere nothing— something to be ignored.

Fate, however, in the shape of a Mr. Ginnett, who owned a large number of horses and capable riders, rode into the arena and the populace, as a result, were not deprived of their grand procession. They were permitted to "process" on two separate days but, be it noted, during the second week of the Festival, and not during the first. Such common straight-from-the-heart festivities would, in the eyes of the nobility and gentry, have completely spoilt the whole affair.

The first week was a feast of Shakespeare snobbishness. Contemporary reports admit that the prices were so extraordinarily high as to prohibit the townsfolk from taking any part whatever in the proceedings. If they had five shillings to spare they could enjoy the doubtful pleasure of watching the quantity eaten by the Quality during the Banquet held on Shakespeare's Birthday; but five shillings, in those days, went almost as far as a pound does to-day, and it is extremely unlikely that many of the real populace took advantage of this hunger-making spectacle. The prices of admission to the plays were also almost prohibitive during the first week, but in the second week inferior actors, with correspondingly inferior prices, acted the plays of the Warwickshire poet for the benefit of the Warwickshire people. It should not be imagined that the plays were badly produced for this popular week; they were merely cast without such distinguished names as were the productions of the Snob Week. Shakespeare, we know, liked to be known as "Gent.," but no doubt he would have resented the celebration of his Tercentenary with such an atmosphere of class distinction, based on ability to pay.

We have already hinted at the troubles which the Committee had over the question of London actors. The first blow was Samuel Phelps's blunt refusal to take part in any of the plays. A tactless Committee who knew nothing of the strange vagaries of actors, of their petty jealousies, of their likes and dislikes, had invited M. Fechter—a famous French actor who had created a London sensation with his "Hamlet"— to play this part at Stratford. M. Fechter had accepted and, in consequence, Mr. Phelps found that his nose was more than put out of joint. He was the most important English actor; he had done more to popularise Shakespeare's plays than any living actor, and "Hamlet" was one of his great and most successful parts. But the Committee had told him he could play what roles he liked and at the same time had invited this Frenchman to appear in the very role which he, himself, would have chosen for presentation on the Stratford stage. When Phelps's decision had been communicated to the Stratford Committee there was almost an uproar, followed by the publication of some score of letters which had passed between Phelps and Mr. E. F. Flower. The letters, in the light of to-day, seem to be almost puerile, but, obviously the molehill of the twentieth century was, with the close vision of 1864, a mountain of terrific height.

The Phelps storm eventually blew over and the Festival, minus this great actor, seemed to be well set. M. Fechter would, of course, appear, and so would the gracious actress, Helen Faucit. With this comfortable thought the arrangements went forward well. Then Fechter backed out of his contract. He had heard, unofficially, that the Committee had soundly censured one of its members for inviting him before definite arrangements had been made for Mr. Phelps. Fechter took this as an insult and refused to appear. Again scores of letters were published and the Committee were in an even worse predicament. They had advertised the Frenchman's appearance . . . they had booked many seats on the strength of his name . . . they had carried out structural alterations to the temporary theatre to suit the whim of the great Fechter, and now he announced that he would not play at Stratford. He was begged to change his mind, but refused.

The Festival must take place without his valuable assistance. The London Committee must have enjoyed the discomfort of their Stratford rivals. This fight for the Industry was fast going in favour of those who felt that Southwark was the proper place to do honour to our National Poet. Even if their efforts had failed, even if they had been thoroughly chastised by their own newspapers, it would amuse them to see Stratford fail as a direct outcome of inexperience in the matter of organising actors and actresses and, more important, of understanding their various idiosyncrasies. Stratford was learning, in pain, that the art of the theatre and the tactful handling of temperaments go together. Stratford believed that it had one very good card to play and that there was no possible chance of that one failing them. Helen Faucit would, of course, keep her word and appear as Rosalind, but even Helen

Faucit decided to let them down. The third of their aces had failed to take a trick. The Committee, however, did not quarrel with Miss Faucit—perhaps they were weary of this incessant confusion or perhaps they felt that, if they treated the matter with the consummate tact which had been so lacking previously, the lady might change her mind and still appear in "As You Like It." Although she did not appear she did help the enterprise financially and gave it her blessing. In all probability her decision was influenced by Phelps. A certain amount of hurried rearrangements had to be effected and as a result of these many setbacks it was not possible to give a Shakespeare play till the Fourth Day, when The Haymarket Company appeared in "Twelfth Night" with a distinguished cast.

The Festival opened on April 23rd, the Birthday, and was chiefly remarkable, in the light of present-day events, because it had a foretaste of the arrival of the now numerous foreign representatives. A German Delegation travelled specially to Stratford to tell the Committee how they admired Shakespeare and begged Stratford to accept an address from them which concluded in the following terms:

"Hail to the memory of William Shakespeare!
Hail to the town of Stratford-upon-Avon!
Hail to the people of England!"

The address, which was most beautifully illuminated, bore the name of Goethe's House. Thus a pretty compliment was paid to the Shakespeare Industry by the then equally important Goethe Industry. Since this initial ceremony Shakespeare and Goethe have exchanged Birthday greetings—war years excepted. Russia was also prominent in paying its respects to Stratford-upon-Avon, but it did not go to the trouble and expense incurred by the Germans. Russia was content to send a couple of telegrams, one of which read: "The Imperial University of Moscow, recognising the great influence of Shakespeare on the Russian literature and stage, this day publicly celebrates the three hundredth anniversary of the birthday of the great genius, and hereby congratulates his countrymen on the occasion."

Russia, it seems, had made its own arrangements to celebrate the Tercentenary and can thus readily be forgiven for not sending delegates to Stratford-upon-Avon. One wonders whether those two great countries, Russia and Germany, realised what seeds they were sowing. Not many years after it was to become "the thing" for the ambassadors of all countries to come themselves, or send representatives, to the little town on the banks of the Avon. These Germans were but pioneers of the great St. George's Day trek to Warwickshire. There were no flags for them to pull—as there are to-day—but the Birthplace was there, with a smaller visitation than it has at present; Anne Hathaway's Cottage stood unspoiled by the smells of petrol fumes—is there ever a moment any summer day when there is not a motor-coach with a load of worshippers outside Anne's simple and serene garden? The School was much as it is to-day. The Church rose just as gracefully on the side of the river. In fact, there was nearly as much to interest those German delegates as there is now. They doubtless visited the plays in the Wooden Theatre, enjoyed the Banquet which cost the considerable sum of one guinea, and may even have wondered at the curious English custom of staring. For never could it have been better exemplified than by those, who themselves, we hope, well-primed, were peering at the eaters and drinkers. Perhaps the heavy spectacle of other men's meat was mitigated by the many brilliant utterances of the day.

The Birthday speeches of the Tercentenary read so exceedingly well—much better than do some of the more recent eulogies delivered since the war—that the Stratford Committee had every good reason to compliment themselves on the organisation of *that* part of their Festival. The Banquet, which apparently lasted several hours, was immediately followed by a fireworks display and the rising of two large fire-balloons. One of these was marked "Stratford" and is reported to have gone up with good effect. The fate of the other, which might have been called London, is not recorded. The grand

183

climax of the pyrotechnic display was an illuminated portrait of William Shakespeare, but apparently there were, then, no fireworks without smoke, for we are told that: "The brilliancy of the finale was sadly marred by the density of the fumes." It is interesting to note that this show was an effort to imitate the grand display which should have taken place during the Garrick Festival.

There is no need to specify the pieces which were performed during this auspicious Festival, but it can be said that the plays offered, during both weeks, gave general satisfaction. The artists who appeared during the "Snob" week gave their entire services, less their travelling expenses, whilst those who played for the benefit of the "common people" received the common persons' salary. One sad little story connected with this Festival was the arrival in the town of Wombwell's Menagerie. Mr. Wombwell had thought that Stratford would be so full that he would be sure to do well. The human lions, however, were too strong competition for those of the circus. Cackle was more popular than 'osses. So he folded his tents and left about twenty-four hours after his arrival. One imagines that reverence for Shakespeare was not his strongest emotion. The Stratford Committee were also gloomy, for the number of visitors was far below their optimistic expectations. In all probability there were not enough snobs in Warwickshire—or the rest of England, for that matter—to make the first week pay. Their sadness may have given way to happiness when they saw their ordinary townsfolk enjoying themselves so immensely, "processing" in the streets and filling the theatre at popular prices. It seems that the people's Festival really was a success, just as it is nowadays; for not by any stretch of imagination can the Festivals now be considered as "Snob" affairs.

The men of Stratford in 1864 were, it seems, a simple lot. There is a story about a policeman who was shepherding the procession of those dressed up as Shakespeare's characters. He noticed that the impersonator of Mad Edgar (Tom's-a-cold) was behaving in a mildly erratic manner and making no effort to keep in step. Edgar was called to order and no doubt an American visitor decided, for the first time, that our police are wonderful.

After all, the worshippers were not, and are not now, professed scholars. Their zeal is more than their knowledge. Hunter, in his highly interesting record of the Tercentenary Festival, confesses, with a charming innocence, his lack of Shakespearean knowledge in the following words: "His works, I am thankful to say, are growing more popular daily; and one great result of the late celebration will be to increase the number of their readers, and, let me hope, the patrons also of the theatres at which they shall be worthily performed. For my own part, my knowledge of them is but limited and superficial. There is employment for the leisure of my life in reading and studying them, and at last I shall probably feel with Newton, 'I have only been playing with pebbles on the strand, whilst before me lay the unexplored ocean.' But from what I do know of his works, I can say with all due reverence, blessed be God for Shakespeare." That at least was honest confession, and it was honesty of purpose that seems to have been the light which led the Stratford Committee to such a successful—in the artistic and organising sense—conclusion of their Festival. By holding to their course they defeated the London Shakespeareans and gave Stratford a festive fortnight which will for ever live in the annals of the town. They organised a Festival, a school scholarship, and the erection of a Monumental Memorial—or didn't they? Nobody to this day knows what happened to that projected Monumental Memorial.

Meanwhile the local Puritans, active in Shakespeare's own time, were again aroused and alert. A zealot who signed himself "Yours in the Lord, Wm. F. Kerr" tried to prevent the new worship and the "terrible influence" which all this play-acting might have. As a counter-stroke he sent for "a good large preaching-tent" and abundant tracts from London. "This is no party movement," he wrote, "but simply evangelising in a dark and benighted and almost, I might say, Idolatrous place as regards Shakespeare." Even tent and tracts were of small avail. St. William always goes on winning.

CHAPTER IX

HANDS UPON THE BARD

"Bacon-fed Knaves. . . . On, Bacons, on. . . . Ye are grand-jurors, are ye? We'll jury ye, i' faith. . . . It would be argument for a week."—*Henry IV*, II, 5.

NO great Industry escapes litigation. Disputes about discoveries, innovations, expansions, rights, and patents of all kinds are as costly as they are common. Patent lawyers rarely die poor. The Shakespeare Industry has had, and is still having, its battles of this kind, for the Bardic Patent has been much challenged. Where there is so much honour, jealousy and rivalry are likely to accumulate. These tussles do not come into court, as a rule, but are conducted in the libraries and studies of the anti-Stratfordian parties. These, while disagreeing as to who really did write Shakespeare's plays, are fully convinced that our Avonian Willie did not. They are agreed that he was an illiterate actor, coming of illiterate stock in a crass Midland town. Once a butcher's boy and a calf-killing youngster, he could never have acquired the knowledge to write plays which communicate a wide knowledge of court-life, of foreign travel and, most especially, of legal practice and terminology. The plays, we are told, were fathered on to the Stratford player by some nobleman who could not put his signature directly (he could do so by hint or in cipher) to work intended for the common stages. Such an act would have been fatal to his status and to his career at court.

The game of Grab has been applied to the Bard from many angles. Catholics and Protestants have fought bitterly for his soul. Welshmen and Midlanders have contended for his blood. In the autumn of 1938 an East Anglian scholar proved beyond doubt that Shakespeare came from his own eastern shires. A Cambridge sage has demonstrated that Shakespeare was not really a Stratfordian: he may have been born by the Avon, but he spent his boyhood at the other end of Warwickshire. To the German he is Aryan and "Unser." There is sufficient evidence, according to the standards acceptable to so many Shakespearean theorists, to prove Shakespeare a Scot or an Irishman, a specialist in French history or a pre-Harveyan authority on the circulation of the blood.

Those who make no positive claims but merely announce that the fellow wrote none of the works attaching to his name, are only part of a general raid upon Shakespeare's gigantic reputation. Everybody with a cause or a camp wants Shakespeare in his section of the tented field. Some, like Sir George Greenwood, have argued only that the Stratford lout was incapable of writing at all, much less of writing for all time. They have not proceeded in every case to name the face behind the Droeshout mask, the hand behind the Folio. For these agnosticism sufficed. On the other hand, many others have gone bravely forward to nominate the real author of Shakespeare's works. Sir Francis Bacon, afterwards Lord Verulam, was first favourite for a long time. Edward de Vere, 17th Earl of Oxford, has been strongly supported in recent years. But these are not all.

In 1931 Dr. Gilbert Slater, a well-known historian and economist, published a book called *Seven Shakespeares* in order to prove that the Immortal Bard was only conceivable as a Group Movement. In his exact words:

"the Shakespeare Plays came from a group of writers, closely connected with one another and with the Elizabethan Court. This was the theory advanced by Miss Delia Bacon in 1857, and suggested by other writers even earlier; it was the theory maintained by Sir George Greenwood in a series of books remarkable for width and accuracy of learning, and lucidity and acuteness of reasoning. Sir George Greenwood however is almost unique in his persistent refusal ever to specify even a single member of the supposed group; and the group theory has been pushed into the background by the partisan enthusiasm of the discoverers of 'true Shakespeares,' among whom the Baconians have distinguished themselves by pushing their advocacy of their candidate to the wildest extremes."

Dr. Slater's Seven Against William are Francis Bacon, William Stanley Earl of Derby*, Christopher Marlowe, Roger Manners Earl of Rutland, Edward de Vere Earl of Oxford, the Countess of Pembroke, and Sir Walter Raleigh. It is odd that Shakespeare's particular friend and patron, the Earl of Southampton, should not figure in so inclusive a list. Mr. Walter Thomson, who has ingeniously argued in his book, *The Sonnets of Shakespeare and Southampton,* that the latter's hand is to be found in some of the sonnets, also believes that Southampton contributed not a little to the comedies. Dr. Slater confidently portioned out the poet's scattered limbs. "There is striking evidence for at least the part authorship of 'Richard II' and 'Richard III' by Bacon, of 'Love's Labour's Lost' by Derby, and of 'Hamlet' by Oxford." To the lady member he allotted large sections of "As You Like It," "Twelfth Night" and "Much Ado"— a compliment indeed! Since the Countess lived at Wilton beside the Wiltshire Avon, she was the Sweet Swan of Avon alluded to by Ben Jonson. Raleigh was her especial colleague in the comedies and had much to do, as an explorer, with "The Tempest." It never occurred to Dr. Slater that there is such a thing

* Derby gets special consideration in a volume by Mr. R. M. Lucas called *Shakespeare's Vital Secret.*

as unity of style and that, at least in all but his earliest work, the author, whoever he was, signed himself uniquely in almost every line.

The anti-Stratfordian suspicions began much earlier than many suspect. Of course, the champions of Bacon and de Vere would say that plenty of people knew the truth at the time, but remained tactfully mum. What we are concerned with is the public affirmation of doubt as to the author's identity. Curiously enough, the first attack of this kind and the first open* attribution of Shakespeare's work to Bacon came from Shakespeare's own county. It was a vicar of Barton-on-the-Heath, a Warwickshire village lying a little to the north of Stratford, who, during the eighteenth century, first announced that the Stratford man was only the mask in front of Francis Bacon's personality.

Previously it had been held that the honour of being the first to dissipate the Shakespeare Myth went to America through the hand of Joseph C. Hart, U.S. Consul at Santa Cruz, who, in 1848, had stripped the Stratford man of his unearned glory in a book unlikely to be deemed heretical by those who merely glanced at the cover, since it was innocently called *The Romance of Yachting*. But, in an article pub-

---

* We say "open," because Baconians insist that the secret was continuously hinted at from the publication of Hall's *Satires* in 1597 and that subsequent lives and commentaries are full of allusions to the great truth. A detailed history of the early Baconian hints was compiled by Mr. Bertram G. Theobald and appeared in *Baconiana*, January 1935.

lished in *The Times Literary Supplement* in 1932, Professor Allardyce Nicoll, drawing upon a little book bequeathed to the University of London by that ardent Baconian, Sir Edwin Durning-Lawrence, exposed a far earlier origin for the Baconian Theory. It appears that in February, 1805, a Mr. James Corton Cowell made a confession to the Ipswich Philosophical Society, avowing himself to be "in a strange pass" and a renegade from the Stratford faith. He had been visited by a New Light, which radiated from the rectory of Barton-on-the-Heath, where the Rev. James Wilmot, D.D., combined a cure of souls with a zealous devotion to the works of Bacon whom, as early as 1785, he proclaimed to be the real Shakespeare. Wilmot had various excitements in his life, actual or alleged. His niece, Olivia Serres, asserted that the rector had secretly married the sister of Stanislaus, King of Poland, that she was the child of that marriage, and that she had married, also secretly, the Duke of Cumberland. This sounds like the basis of a plot for one of Shakespeare's more romantic dramas, or—as Wilmot would have said—one of Bacon's.

When Mr. Cowell reviewed Shakespeare by the Rev. Wilmot's "New Light" and proclaimed the result to Ipswich, nobody seems to have paid him the elementary compliment of listening with favour or of losing a temper. The matter lapsed, until the consular yachtsman Hart began the attack, and then Miss

Delia Bacon arrived, another American, and the first Amazon in this war. Miss Bacon's own name was doubtless an incitement to be unorthodox: the odd thing is that she received her conversion from the true faith in that faith's particular temple. Mr. L. Clarke Davis, in his history of "The Memorial Fountain to Shakespeare," says, of poor Delia, with a certain lack of charity in his manner as well as of grace in his prose-style:

"The case of Miss Delia Bacon is most pathetic, although I believe it was not her Baconian theory which made her so unhappy. She was a woman of singular talent, coming from one of the most big-brained families of New England. An early disappointment had made her feel the need of an eccentric enthusiasm, and by the kind and very unusual permission of the Vicar of Stratford she was allowed to pass whole nights in the church wherein the bones were laid, which he forbade strangers to remove, but not to keep their vigils by. Although Miss Bacon was hallucinated, her 'Philosophy of Shakespeare's Plays,' introduced by Hawthorne, elicited the praise of Ralph Waldo Emerson. Her special vagary was that Shakespeare had not been Shakespeare and that Francis Bacon was the real Shakespeare, and so the idol of her mind was destroyed by her own imagination. As I said, she was not alone in this ridiculous theory, but it is sad to think of the lonely, enthusiastic woman worshipping night and day at the shrine of a god whom she would end by disbelieving altogether. Yet Samuel Taylor Coleridge was not much wiser when he said, 'Does God inspire an idiot?' "

The allusion to Bacon is not quite accurate. Delia, like Dr. Slater later on, was a Groupist. Her Shakespeare Gang included not only Bacon, but Raleigh, Lord Paget, Lord Buckhurst, and the Earl of Oxford. Delia's Stratford nocturnes were not in vain. The flood of anti-Stratfordian argument began.

The next move was to discover the hidden hand. How else than by search for a cipher? The Baconians have always maintained that their theory stands firm and can be fully justified without recourse to such cryptography: the latter, if wisely handled, could be a powerful ally to the ordinary arguments. The American Baconians were first in the contest as cipherers. Ignatius Donnelly, Orville Owen, and Mrs. Elizabeth Wells Gallup raced into the field with ideas respectively of "The Great Cryptogram," "The Word Cipher," and "The Biliteral Cipher," through which the secret truth could be found. It is not denied that both Francis Bacon and his brother Anthony understood and used ciphering as part of their work for the Government.

Lawyers have been very active on the Baconian

side, stressing particularly the immense amount of accurate legal knowledge which the plays contain. Early in that quarter of the field was Judge Nathaniel Holmes, a brother of Oliver Wendell Holmes. Lord Chancellors, Lord Chief Justices, Queen's and King's Counsel, Senators, and reverend seniors of all legal kinds have avowed that Shakespeare's understanding of courts, procedure, and terminology was of a completeness only to be expected in a lawyer of rare learning and experience, such an one, for example, as Bacon. What these wise men have failed to realise is this: If a play or poem correct in its legal terms and metaphors could only be written by a lawyer, then, by that argument, a play or a poem which reveals intimate knowledge of shepherds and their lingo could only have been written by a farmer's boy.

One instance may here be quoted. In the famous speech in which Queen Gertrude describes Ophelia's death by drowning, a death, incidentally, somewhat reminiscent of an event in Shakespeare's boyhood, the accidental drowning of Katharine Hamlet, spinster of Tiddington, in the Avon, and the sitting thereon of a "crowner's quest," the Queen displays some knowledge of English botany: stranger still, she holds up exciting and terrible news in order to drag in a smutty piece of shepherd's fun which might have gone well in a Warwickshire tavern, but which is simply absurd on the lips of a Danish Queen. As drama it is obviously deplorable. Why on earth should a mourning woman stop at this, of all moments, to bring in bawdy allusions? Here is the passage:

"There is a willow grows aslant a brook,
  That shows his hoar leaves in the glassy stream;
  There with fantastic garlands did she come
  Of crow-flowers, nettles, daisies, and long purples
  That liberal shepherds give a grosser name,
  But our cold maids do dead men's fingers call
      them."

It is conceivable that a man who had in boyhood listened to the "liberal shepherds" of Stratford might so far spoil the dramatic urgency of a speech in order to hint at gross names. But why on earth should a great lawyer write this kind of thing? It is surely easier to imagine Shakespeare acquiring his legal knowledge by a youthful year or two in a lawyer's office than to visualise Bacon immersed in the bawdier aspects of rural botany and picking up his quips in the market-merry jesting of "liberal shepherds."

The point is raised merely to show how dangerous is any argument as to authorship based on a display of special knowledge. We do not propose to argue the case for or against the Baconians. Those who are interested can apply to the Bacon Society, whose headquarters are at Canonbury Tower, Islington, a Tudor house once owned by Bacon, and a pleasing decoration of a London suburb which has beauty and

history round every corner. The literature on the
subject is enormous. The ladies, Mrs. Gallup in
America and Mrs. Pott in England, have been as
active as the men and, though the American Baconian
Society has somewhat dwindled, the English
champions of Verulam are very active. It was a distinguished member of this group, Mr. Roderick
Eagle, who, in 1938, persuaded the Dean of Westminster to permit a search into Edmund Spenser's
tomb. In the 1625 Edition of Camden's Annals Mr.
Eagle had noticed an entry for the year 1598 concerning Spenser's burial. "He was buried at Westminster,
near Chawcer, at the charges of the Earle of Essex,
all Poets carrying his body to Church, and casting
dolefull Verses, and Pens too, into his grave." As
Shakespeare was then an acknowledged poet, surely
his doleful verses and his pen might be in the tomb.
The pen might be like all the other pens, but surely
the verses would be signed and this would give us
Shakespeare's handwriting beyond a doubt—and
might that not complete the identification with
Bacon? Unfortunately the search proved barren.
Spenser's tomb could not be certainly identified, and
there was a certain natural nervousness about ran-
sacking all and sundry sepulchres.

The anti-Stratfordians have a double task. First
they must get rid of Shakespeare; then they must
establish the identity of the Real Author. (Some, as
we have seen, deem the first sufficient and decline

the second labour.) The arguments against Shakespeare allude to his illiterate home, but Fripp has
shown that signing with a mark, which was John
Shakespeare's habit, was not incompatible with
ability to write. Shakespeare's will, it is claimed, is
not that of an author. There is no allusion in it to
books and papers. There is no proof that he ever
went to school. All that we can discover of his later
life points to him as a keen business man and shrewd
investor, a hoarder of malt, a dealer in real estate,
involved in some odd marriage-broking in the Bellot-
Mountjoy case, and so forth. Considering the man's
boyhood, so polished and urbane a poem as "Venus
and Adonis" could never have been the first heir of
his invention, as he called it. In any attempted
biography of Shakespeare there must, since the certain facts are few, be a great deal of "perhaps" and
"no doubt." With this the anti-Stratfordians make
great play. Then there is the fact that the stiff
Droeshout portrait can be taken to suggest a mask
stuck on a pole rather than a human neck and face,
and that the poet's doublet seems to have two left
arms. The history of the Bust in Stratford Church,
which differed strangely when Dugdale reproduced
it in 1656 from its present aspect, with its literary
suggestion, is another counter. The Dugdale Bust has
no pen and paper and suggests no author but only a
countryman holding tightly to his stomach a sack of
wool or bag of malt or hops. Where the definitely

proven facts are scanty, it is not at all difficult to compose a case for the existence of a Shakespeare Mystery: on the other hand, it is certainly hard to escape the impression that Ben Jonson believed in the actor-author and that there was a fairly general faith in his own time that the honey-tongued Shakespeare was an authentic creator and not a dealer in supplied articles. The Baconians have plenty of explanations ready: but the least persuasive part of their case is their handling of the Folio.

On the positive side Baconians can justly claim that their hero was over and over again described as a poet. His friend Tobie Matthew wrote to him: "The most prodigious wit that ever I knew, of my nation and this side the sea, is of your Lordship's name, though he here be known by another." Aubrey called Bacon "a good poet, but concealed, as appears by his letters." Stow included Bacon among our "modern and excellent poets," and Davies of Hereford talked of "his Muse." There are many posthumous allusions to his muse, even to his buskin. It is natural to suppose from all this that Bacon wrote much verse and some drama, especially in his years of small employment. His essay "Of Masques and Triumphs" reveals a great interest in showmanship. To admit all this does not, of course, link Bacon's secret writing with the poems and plays known as Shakespeare's. There the cipherers intervene. Then again we are reminded of the Northumberland Manuscript, discovered at Northumberland House, Strand, in 1867. This folio, probably of the late 1590's, contains some essays and speeches of Bacon and has a scribbled title-page mentioning "Richard II," "Richard III," and linking the names of Bacon and Shakespeare. Also it includes the word *"honorificabilitudine,"* an obvious reference to the *"Honorificabilitudinitatibus"* of "Love's Labour's Lost" (v. 1. 144), a word with which the cipherers have naturally been busy. Durning-Lawrence finds there *"Hi Ludi F. Baconis nati tuiti orbi,"* which means: "These plays, F. Bacon's children, are saved for the world."

At this point we can leave what some of the less courteous Stratfordians would call the "Bacon knaves," for the argument will last a week and longer. Courtesy has not been a prominent virtue on either side. One of the curiosities of the whole business has been the rage of some anti-Stratfordians against poor Will, whom they oddly hope to put still lower by using the spelling Shaksper or Shagsper and by irrelevant sneers at the insanitary state of Stratford's streets. (Was London or Bacon's St. Albans any better?) That fiery controversialist, Sir Edward Durning-Lawrence, thinks that "this child of illiterate parents and father of an illiterate child was himself so illiterate that he was never able to write so much as his own name." There are many sneers at an actor who could not read. (But if he could not read, how did he con his parts?) Durning-Lawrence further abused Will as a miser and a drunkard, although those two ways of life rarely go together. Mark Twain called the Stratfordians, or "Shakesperoids," thugs, bangalores, troglodytes, herumfrodites, blatherskites, buccaneers, bandoleers, and muscovites. Even our good John Bright, turning from corn laws to principles of poetry, observed that anybody believing William of Stratford to be the author of "Hamlet" or "Lear" was a fool. The Stratfordians, in their turn, have often been somewhat too personal in their retorts, especially in the case of the Oxfordians. The cause of Oxford was first taken up by a Mr. Looney. Is it credible that debate between supposed scholars should be interspersed with jests on that gentleman's name? There are times when the would-be sages qualify for the lowest seat on the lowest form of a Narkover Academy. For those who wish to engage in battle on Stratford's behalf we counsel attention to the two men's style of thought and of expression. Does, for example, the attitude to death most common in Shakespeare's plays coincide with the attitude to death in Bacon's Essays? And why is it that Shakespeare has a vocabulary almost twice as large as Bacon's?

The Oxford Movement, which allots the authorship to Edward de Vere, 17th Earl of Oxford, is much more recent. It seems to have a particular appeal for the Naval and Military mind. After Mr. Looney had led off in 1920 with "Shakespeare Identified," he was followed into print by an Admiral, a Colonel, a Major and a Captain. But the most industrious and ingenious supporter of Oxford has been Mr. Percy Allen, a mere civilian, but as tough for his man, de Vere, as any who ever swore allegiance to their Verulam.

Edward de Vere was born in 1550 and became, on his father's death, a ward of the great Lord Burghley. His uncle was Golding, the translator of Ovid. He was educated privately and at Cambridge (St. John's), admitted to Gray's Inn, married Anne Cecil, Burghley's daughter, was favoured by the Queen, travelled,* returned to Court, followed the arts, wrote verse and comedy, had the poet-dramatist Lyly for his secretary and manager of his team of boy-players. He then lived somewhat secretly from 1586 to his death in 1604. During that time he had a royal grant of £1,000 a year from the Secret Service Fund (a large sum in those days) and it has been suggested that it was part of his job to use the theatre as a platform and put on historical dramas which stressed the necessity for national unity and patriotic co-operation with the Crown. Since he died in 1604, the Shakespeare plays which emerge thereafter must have been lying in cold storage and "released," as they say of films, from time to time.

---

* Aubrey has little to say of de Vere, except that he travelled much and at great cost. The cause for this long absence abroad he attributes to an unhappy flatulence while in the Queen's presence. This anecdote of the wind which blew a courtier into exile happens to be as old as the Arabian Nights.

The Oxfordians share the negative case with all other anti-Stratfordians and are as resolute as any to see no chance of great creative ability in the Stratford rustic with his broad Midland accent and ignorance of the courtly world. (Why a broad accent should stop a man writing is hard to see: it might have stopped him acting, but the anti-Stratfordians all accept "Shagsper" as an actor.) It has been shown time and again that poverty, rough accents, and hungry boyhoods are just as likely to stimulate genius as to crush it. The greatest writers have often been self-schooled. The anti-Stratfordians astonishingly underrate the power of a quick lad to pick up new points of view and acquire more elegant ways of living. The boy who has just left school can develop at enormous speed in the larger and more liberal life of a University or of a professional career, if he will use his leisure well. However, it seems to be little use arguing this point or citing the numerous examples of the self-taught literary genius. On the positive side the Oxfordians, like the Baconians, can do their ciphering or find hidden signatures. Edward de Vere signed himself E. Ver, or Ver, and in Sonnet 76 we can read:

"Why write I still all one, E. Ver the same,
And keep invention in a noted weeds,
That E. Very word doth almost tell my name,
Showing their birth and where they did proceed?"

They can find all the events of Oxford's life mirrored in the plays, which 'is not strange, since, thanks to Shakespeare's universality of genius, anybody can find his own friends and fortunes and even himself closely portrayed in one of the three dozen plays with a large number of widely varied and brilliantly drawn characters in each. Those who wish to pursue the Oxford claim can do so in the works of Mr. Looney, Admiral Holland, Major Montagu Douglas, Colonel B. R. Ward, Captain B. M. Ward, Dr. Gerald Rendall, and Mr. Percy Allen. They will meet plenty of serious and ingenious argument. What they will not find is the tenable suggestion in the literary remains of de Vere that he was capable of writing in the least like the supposedly illiterate, rustic actor, drunkard, miser, and general Stratford "bum," William Shakespeare or, if they prefer it, Shagsper. Oxford's poem on Women is just the kind of thing which any ingenious Tudor graduate of the arts could turn out, while some of his verse is pitiful stuff. It is difficult to believe that the author of such lines as

"Sitting alone upon my thoughts in melancholy
    mood
In sight of sea, and at my back an ancient hoary
    wood,
I saw a fair young lady come her secret fears to
    wail,
Clad all in colour of a nun, and covered with a
    veil"

would turn from this to the composition of such lyric loveliness as makes Shakespearean comedy supreme in narrative passages as in its snatches of song. The anti-Stratfordians often reveal quite extraordinary ingenuity in their manipulation of facts. One and all they seem to us strangely insensitive in all matters of style. And style, after all, is the man. It would be safer to allot "Shakespeare" to an author of whom no word remains than to any man with whose way of thought and use of word Shakespeare can be compared. If it be true that, as a master of English the author of the plays, poems, and sonnets is matchless, a belief fairly generally held, it is surely dangerous to start matching his lines and finding a fit with other compositions of the period. If our Avonian Willie was indeed soul of the age, wonder of the stage, out-doing insolent Greece or haughty Rome, Immortal Bard, out-topping knowledge, owner of the boundless, cloudless human view, then surely it is rash to confound him with a man like Oxford whose preserved work reveals no more than the competence of a well-schooled littérateur and not always that. Bacon, being intellectually the more remarkable, may be a slightly better candidate, but whether Bacon could have created the Shakespearean clowns is a matter for extreme doubt. In our opinion neither Bacon nor Oxford nor any of the Group Movement could have touched Bottom.

What has been the motive for all this activity?

After all, nobody gives a lifetime to proving that Ben Jonson's plays were really written by James I. Partly the cause has been Shakespeare's own pre-eminence. There is, we believe, in the history of the arts, no case of one so far outstripping his colleagues as Shakespeare has outstripped all in the combined use of metaphor, word, and rhythm, quite apart from dramatic values, in which, just possibly, he might have to stand some challenge. This colossal sovereignty naturally excites people and, coupled with the fact that we know little for certain about Shakespeare the Man ("the last word must be nescience," wrote the greatest living Stratfordian authority, Sir Edmund Chambers, concerning the Bard's life and personality), the sovereignty leads us on to the sniffing of mysteries. Once admit a Shakespeare Mystery and you have done more to interest many detective-minded people than you would have done by providing them with the best conceivable performances of the best of Shakespeare's plays.

Yes, the problem acts as a pull. The identity of the Bard flickers hauntingly before the public eye and incites a genuine curiosity. It is idle to pretend there is no riddle when so many, remaining Stratfordian, have confessed their difficulty in equating the poet's life with his work. Then strangely, but almost certainly, a form of snobbishness begins to work. Of course, this is not true of all or even of most anti-Stratfordians, but in some it is impossible not to sense a species of resentment that colossal sovereignty, the grand pre-eminence with its amazing monument, should be enjoyed by a tradesman's lad, perhaps, as Aubrey thought, a calf-killing butcher-boy. That England, Tudor England, Gloriana's pride, should have led the world and lead it still is splendid. But one of the Shakespeares . . . well, really. No Public School, no University. Can it be true? Surely a Lord Chancellor, a knight of the blood, or a de Vere might have been the man. But this jumped-up son of a small-town glover and fleece-merchant! That he should have outsung the courtly singers and become the symbol of the English genius all across the world is a trifle hard. Why do we pay up thumping fees for these Etons and Magdalens and all the rest if they cannot stop us being represented by such plebeians as Shakespeare of old and later on by Dickens, Hardy, Wells, and Shaw?

One of the most astonishing features of the whole campaign for annexing Shakespeare has been the curious desire to promote that genius not only to the House of Lords but even into the Royal Family. It has been freely suggested that the poet's mother was Queen Elizabeth herself. The idea, it is true, is not to provide him with a virgin birth. The Virgin Queen, fair vestal, was supposed by some to have been less pure than her repute: she was loved, it is suggested, by Lord Leicester, thus conceiving the marvellous infant who was to become Francis Bacon-

Shakespeare. Some Oxfordians believe that the actor "Shagsper" was the son of Queen Elizabeth and de Vere and that the true poet was fathering his works upon his natural son. Why people should credit such assertions is hard to discover: but, once you start to speculate on the Shakespeare Mystery, one thing does very queerly lead to another and the translation of the butcher-boy from Henley Street into a Palace bastard has been made with avidity and confidence by those determined not to let Stratford have the honour of being home-town to a genius.

Except on such a ground it is most difficult to explain the jeers at illiterate "Shagsper" or "Shaxpur" in his dungy Stratford. (In the long run your Londoner contemns a yokel as a New Yorker sniffs at the man from Missouri.) Then another great strength of the heretics has been the sense of a mission. They are rescuers. They are righting a great injustice. They are unmasking a base pretender and exalting the man who truly achieved greatness by exposing the wretch who only had greatness thrust upon him. The sense of a moral crusade enters in, keys up the combatant spirit, and stirs a bitter animosity against the complacent defenders of the wrongful sovereign. Pretenders, claimants to the throne, are apt to wear haloes before they wear crowns. So Francis Bacon and Edward de Vere begin to acquire the romantic value of a Bonnie Prince Charlie. Bacon excites sympathy in double kind, because it is felt by his champions that he not only lacks the proper and colossal praise due for being "Shakespeare" in addition to his mighty self, but has also, in their opinion, been grossly and shamefully abused by prejudiced historians, such as Macaulay, who exaggerated his offences against probity through total misunderstanding of the tradition and common practice of the time.

So it is with high ethical enthusiasm that Bacon is first of all scoured clean of his judicial misdemeanours and then raised, amid a shower of laurels, to the monument so wrongly usurped by the rough and rustic William of Stratford. Justice at last is being done. That is the mood.

Once that feeling begins to be strongly manifest, conspiracy-mania begins to peep round the corner. The anti-Stratfordians are a passionate minority and passionate minorities inevitably start to compensate themselves with fantasies of the outer world's cold wickedness and active malice. It soon becomes apparent to them that William's defenders are a shifty, dishonest lot, covering the gaps in their case with every kind of contemptible *camouflage*. So the polemical temper is inflamed and the late Sir Sidney Lee, who certainly did Shakespeare much harm in popular sympathy by reducing him to a very dull dog, became, simply in his role of Stratfordian Pontiff, a target for the keenest animosity and most furious derision. Let us frankly acknowledge the authentic intellectual curiosity and the meritorious desire to do justice which have animated the efforts to get behind the supposed mask and see "Shakespeare" plain. At the same time, the eagerness has been in some cases so extreme as to make otherwise sensible men adopt some senseless arguments and to read into a trivial fact or coincidence the most fantastical interpretations. The psychology of heresy was never more interesting than in the case of the anti-Stratfordians. The oddness begins among the orthodox: the burning passion of Bardolatry has kindled the no less ardent counter-passion for exposing the Stratford Oaf.

And suppose they could do it? Suppose some document turns up which irrefutably proves the author of Shakespeare's plays and poems to have been Bacon or Oxford or one of the Group. What of the Industry? Stratford has its other crafts, the brewing, the light metal-work, the canning of fruit. It would remain, to some limited extent, a visitable Beauty Spot for Midland motorists, Stratford-on-petrol as well as on Avon. But the theatre would be closed, the Birthplace would linger on as a curio for sniffing, smiling cynics, the church would no longer be able to charge an entrance fee, and three-quarters of the hotels and lodgings would be shuttered and deserted. Presumably, if Bacon were the victorious name, there would be a great stir of new life in the Cathedral City of St. Albans and old Verulamium would not only be proud of its Francis, Lord Verulam, but find great profit in him too. A mighty theatre would rise, perhaps hard by the Roman amphitheatre which is one of the town's historic possessions, and the motor-coaches would come roaring up from London, stopping at Canonbury Tower, with the Bardolatrous loads who once went farther afield, to find their joy at Stratford and at Shottery. If de Vere were the winner, the new shrine would have to be in one of London's north-easterly suburbs, hard by the unromantic Mare Street, Hackney, since it was thither that Oxford retired, as was believed, to do his writing in the pleasant solitudes of Essex. There it might be difficult to make "tourism" a delight and to arouse the Festival spirit. But the job would have to be done. Meanwhile, in many industries small changes would be briskly made. Calendars and laundries and garages and businesses of all kinds which have taken Shakespearean names, slogans and trade-marks would have to assume, at once, another loyalty. Publishers would have, at some cost, to scrap millions of covers and alter millions of titles. Shakespearean actors, should Bacon be the new Bard, would have to endure everlasting jokes about "Ham." Fortunately we are fairly vague as to Shakespeare's actual appearance and Bacon, with his pointed beard, was not vastly dissimilar in aspect. So many of the pictures, statues, and busts, in museums, outside garages, serving as commercial emblems or as knick-knacks on the villa's mantelshelf, might remain with just a scratching of the name, if name there be. This would save trouble.

That day has not yet come. But it is not for want of working. Crusaders for a king dethroned do not lightly abandon their campaign.

CHAPTER X

MUCH ADO ABOUT SOMETHING

"In Festival Terms."
—*Much Ado About Nothing*, V, 1.

WE now come to another Monumental Memorial which did materialise and which is still, though in a different form, after sixty years, serving its great and useful purpose. Its erection was the culmination of the Garrick Festival, the Lesser Festivals, to borrow Garrick's own phrase (presumably less important because he was not present), and the Tercentenary Festival which saw Shakespeare's plays first included in the Stratford celebrations.

The seriousness with which that 1864 effort was carried out, the fact that it was not used as a means to advertise any one person—except the Bard—and the more important fact that Shakespeare's own lines were acted, surely marked it as an even more important festivity than that original orgy of exhibitionism in 1769. Garrick's Jubilee, although tremendously important, must take second place—and thus can be called "lesser" than the Festival recorded in the last

213

chapter. That Tercentenary Festival set Mr. Charles
Edward Flower thinking. He had seen his father,
Mr. E. F. Flower, working night and day in the
interests of Shakespearean celebrations. He had seen
him negotiate the arrangements for the building of a
temporary theatre; he had, himself, helped the 1864
Festival financially; he must have longed, even then,
to erect a permanent theatre which could rise as a
truly National Memorial. The time, however, was
not ripe. In any case he was a busy man and could
not devote the time necessary to such a scheme. But
he thought about it and, when he had more leisure,
he set about his dream with amazing energy.

It was his idea; he was the prime mover. He
formed a Committee of distinguished persons, some
distinguished nationally and some merely important
people in their own little world of Stratford-upon-
Avon. Great and small worked well together, but the
result of their activities was to bring about a renewal
of hostilities between the Warwickshire country town
and the capital. London, as represented by its newspapers, let the Tercentenary battle be won by Stratford-upon-Avon, but it was not yielding another inch
in this new affair. Celebrating the three-hundredth
anniversary of the birth of Shakespeare and building
a temporary theatre in his own town was one thing,
but to let Stratford achieve the building of a permanent National Theatre was quite another matter
and London—again represented by its newspapers—

was determined to do all in its power to stop this "great impertinence."

The old arguments were raked up. Shakespeare did nearly all his work in London; he made his name in London and in London should be built the National Memorial Theatre dedicated to his name. Let it be noted that Stratford made no effort to stop London from building its Shakespeare theatre. The antagonism was so entirely one-sided that it had little or no effect; in fact, it only helped to spur the Stratfordians on to the completion of their task. Mr. Flower's Committee, or Governors, as they were called, showed the way his mind worked. In no circumstances was it to be entirely local and he found in the enemies' camp a few friends who were willing to subscribe to the project and who were glad to have their names associated with the great new scheme. Drury Lane, the Haymarket, and Adelphi Theatres were all represented on the Board, as were also a few London actors including Barry Sullivan, whose work was to prove of such high value. America was represented by her famous actor, Edwin Booth, whose brother shot Abraham Lincoln. The notoriety of the assassination was naturally not the passport which placed him on this select Committee. He was there because of his deep interest in Shakespeare, Stratford-on-Avon and the "rights" of the cause, and perhaps he felt that even if he could not organise an American National Theatre he could, at least, help this other and more important scheme. Nearly all the other members were Stratfordians, including four Flowers. How that Committee worked, how it turned the other cheek when London offered insult after insult, how brilliantly it was led would, in itself, make too long a story.

It would have been a simple matter for Mr. Flower and his confederates to have lost their tempers with London and thus to have reduced the one-sided argument to the level of a petty squabble. Flower remained above that sort of thing. He had but one object in view and that was to see a theatre, worthy of Shakespeare, rise on the side of the Avon and to see the plays of his great townsman performed annually each birthday on its stage. There was no ulterior motive and no wish to make money. As it happens he could not have done so had he wished and neither could any of the other Governors.

That is what London could not understand. Why should somebody be willing to build a theatre, knowing that it must lose money and yet be perfectly willing to put his hand in his pocket whenever cash was required? Such self-sacrifice was beyond the comprehension of the London business people. They thought there must be a "catch" somewhere. Had they known their Flower they would have realised that he was a man with a set purpose and determined to spend his wealth in the cause of Shakespeare. The seed had been planted by Garrick in 1769; it had slowly grown throughout the years. Flower had seen it blossom in 1864 and he realised that, if nothing was done about it, it would wither away and be forgotten. Hence his purpose and his determination. He resolved that all the gallant work of the past generations should now bear fruit. He knew, however, that if he gave all the money there would be a certain amount of risk that Stratford would not appreciate what was being done for it. Accordingly, he issued a National Appeal for funds in order to build a theatre which was to cost in the region of £21,000. America, which—as England sometimes inadequately remembers—was largely responsible for building the present Memorial Theatre, was early in sending help. A Miss Kate Field raised and despatched 2,500 dollars and campaigned for more, arranging that a subscription of 25 dollars entitled the donor to an engraving of the Gainsborough portrait of Garrick. The same Miss Field was also busy in London, where in May, 1878, she organised and addressed a special entertainment at the Gaiety Theatre ("What spirit breathes in Flower and Field," was the comment of a Stratford rhymer). This was indeed a remarkable occasion because a species of "broadcast" from Stratford to London was actually used. There was a telephonic transmission of music from the poet's birthplace in Stratford to the Gaiety Theatre in London. That would seem little enough now when, as Caliban said, "the isle is full of noises,"

But for 1878 it was tremendous pioneering. Once more "sleepy Stratford" seemed to be extremely wide awake.

Even so, England paid very scant attention to the call, subscribing the amazingly small sum of £1,000. This was a bitter disappointment indeed, but Stratford was not going to be beaten, and, headed by Mr. Flower, it found the required further £20,000. The greater part of this came from the Flower purse. Flower also made a magnificent gesture by presenting the Governors with the land on which to build the theatre. London laughed when it heard the result of the National Appeal, but the mood changed when the result of the Stratford Appeal became known. When the capital found that the theatre was to be built, at all costs, it started to ask a number of impertinent questions. The friendly Press of 1864 became a dangerous enemy in 1877 when the Foundation Stone was laid. But Stratford did the only sensible thing and ignored the many gibes.

How, it was asked, was Stratford to get an audience? It is one thing to build a theatre but another to fill it. It was said that Stratford was a long way off the beaten track and that, because of the lack of an audience, it would be certain to fail. The same arguments are to-day being used by the opponents of the National Theatre at South Kensington. Almost word for word the same bitter war is being waged again, but this time it is not a one-sided affair.

But Stratford is behaving just as it did in 1877 and keeping a logical detachment. If London wants a National Theatre, well and good: let it arise. It will not affect Stratford, which now has a theatre which has a special local justification as well as an international appeal. London felt, in those days, that there must be some reason, other than altruistic, which was prompting this Flower and his colleagues to persist in their wild scheme. What could it be? Then it decided that it was for the sole purpose of "puffing up a few local nobodies!" That shows how puerile the arguments had become.

Unable to stop Stratford doing what it had every intention of doing, London made itself look more than undignified by hurling ridiculous names at a cultured and dignified Committee. How wise was Mr. Flower to let London wear itself out, by keeping a silence which was not broken till a few hours before the theatre was opened. Even then the one shot fired in the direction of the south was delivered with characteristic dignity. He said: "A new line of criticism has been taken up by some who say we are presumptuous in undertaking it. They say we do not represent literature, science, scholarship, clergy or law; they say we are not inhabitants of that great metropolis which ought to monopolise such great works; they say, in fact, we are a set of Respectable Nobodies! All I can say is that, the 'Nobodies,' having waited three hundred years for the 'Somebodies' to do something, surely blame ought not to attach to us; rather let criticism be given to those great social and literary 'Somebodies' who have done nothing. I fear the case is that many of the great 'Somebodies' would have been willing enough to join our ranks, except that we desired to admit those only who were willing and able to give some real assistance. We don't want names only. How many similar projects have been started, with long lists of Committees, patrons and presidents—great and illustrious names, and names only—which have collapsed because the real hard-working element was overwhelmed by the ornamental superstructure? We have not forestalled others; we have simply taken up the work because others have not done so. I am sure that the members of this association would have been most delighted if they could have shifted the responsibility of the work, not to say the expense, to other shoulders. But this I will say—that the Memorial being established, we may depend upon the local enthusiasm which has been so much despised to ensure its being carried on usefully and honourably; that future inhabitants of Stratford will be no less alive than we ourselves to its credit and responsibility. It is quite true we are nobodies. We know that, and therefore do not despair because we cannot accomplish great things at a single effort. We shall be ready to go on quietly and patiently with our work, knowing that we do so in a true spirit of love and reverence for the great man for whose memory we do it."

A few hours after this dignified protest had been fired at the lethargic Londoners the curtain rose on a play at Stratford's own permanent Shakespeare Memorial Theatre and it was, incidentally, the first time that one of Shakespeare's plays had been acted in Stratford on his Birthday. Flower had Garrick's vile luck with the climate. April 23, 1879 was a miserably wet day. The weather was as sullen as London. For all that, Stratford was gaily dressed in the spirit of triumph. The streets were beflagged—not as they are to-day with the emblems of all nations, but with bunting, Union Jacks and a few foreign flags. Despite the appalling downpour there was a pretence of gaiety in the air; there were pomp and ceremony in the town and races in the meadows; the Theatre, the dream of one man, was to open its doors. The Governors were in the town wearing their best; the locals were on holiday; it was a great occasion. A serious occasion. Not too serious, however, to forbid the "Nobodies" to have a little joke at their own expense in the choice of play. After all the speech-making in the town and in the theatre, after all the hubbub of excitement in the crowded auditorium, when the house-lights faded and the gas-footlights had been lit, the curtain rose on "Much Ado About Nothing." The theatre itself had taken two years to build. It was three years since the design of Messrs.

Dodgshun and Unsworth had been approved by the judges in the competition of architects which had been organised. There had been a great deal of trouble with the foundations, as the site bordered so closely on the river, and a Wolverhampton firm was called in to see that the theatre was indeed built on man's best imitation of a rock. There were a Library and a Picture Gallery as well as a theatre. These remain, and from them the present-day visitor can guess what the 1879 theatre looked like and why there were even cries of relief and congratulations, including those of Mr. Bernard Shaw, when the edifice went up in flames in 1925. Edifice, surely, is a just word.

It is difficult, in any case, to find a word to summarise the mixture of timbered, red-brick, and baronial gewgaw which Messrs. Dodgshun and Unsworth had so triumphantly favoured. Those who dislike the present theatre and make rude remarks about a jam-factory can say that we are in no position to deride the taste of 1877. We may perhaps put it this way: that in no decade was English Architecture further removed from the taste of to-day than it was in the eighteen-seventies. Expert as well as public opinion then liked its art, to put it vulgarly, "with knobs on," and the Governors of the new theatre had to accept their experts' verdict. No doubt they approved it, too. Subsequent judgment deemed the style of the building feeble, fussy, and better suited to be the residence of a medievally-minded modern German in the Black Forest than an expression of Stratford life and a tribute to its greatest son. "Of the Memorial Theatre itself—that is of its outside—" wrote C. E. Montague, in *Dramatic Values* (1911)— "charity will say little. How the vision both of its form and its colour came to afflict a single mind— however, as fire from Heaven has not yet smitten it, let not man judge."

The fire did smite, fourteen years later. But charity will say no more.

To revert to "Much Ado About Nothing." The critics who were prepared to attack the Stratford acting were unable to do so. They were not even able to say that Stratford was employing third-rate actors, for the artists who played in that first Dramatic Festival in the permanent theatre were giving their services; at least their chief was giving his and had also made himself responsible for his brother artists. He had also subscribed one hundred guineas towards the Memorial Theatre Fund. It was a grand gesture from a London actor, Barry Sullivan, whose name Mr. Bernard Shaw chose to honour when endowing a seat in the proposed National Theatre in London.

The "Beatrice" to his "Benedick" was the much-esteemed Helen Faucit, who had been unable to see her way to appear in the Tercentenary Festival. Her reasons for not playing in 1864 were much the same as were those of Samuel Phelps. She felt she had been slighted, but she did, as we said in the last chapter, help the Festival financially. Evidently her interest in Stratford had been maintained, for she came out of her retirement to give this, her last, performance—for the benefit of the new theatre.

Naturally Mrs. Fowler had done the conventional thing and loaded Miss Faucit's room with many bouquets. Sullivan happened to pass the room, saw the flowers through the open door, and demanded whence they came. When he heard that they had been presented by the wife of the chief Founder of the Theatre, he demanded, forthwith, that his room be similarly decorated. Memories of temperamental actors of a past Festival no doubt were quickly brought to mind, and it can be safely assumed that Mr. Sullivan's request for "floral tributes" was met with "roses, roses, all the way."

Miss Faucit's acting appears to have been beyond reproach, and the very fact that she was playing in that first performance barred the critics from hurling any more London thunderbolts at the now almost deliriously happy band of Governors. Sullivan was also much praised, but they did make an effort to have a few sallies at his expense, especially when he played Hamlet. The *Daily Telegraph*, which later proved such a friend to the Memorial Theatre after its disastrous fire, said of the performance given on the second night: "Solecisms were permitted of so

224

glaring a nature as to make poor Shakespeare turn
in his adjacent grave. Mr. Barry Sullivan enacted
"Hamlet" in a fashion accepted by such as disbelieve
entirely in the address to the players. He was vigorously applauded by the citizens of Stratford and their
wives and daughters, but when the dramatic school
is founded (this was one of the original aims of the
Governors) there will probably be a rule to suppress
such fanciful readings as: 'I know a hawk from a
heron—pshaw!' "

The London critic has always given praise to Stratford acting whenever that praise was due, and he has,
likewise, never been backward in expressing his disappointment when he has felt that publication of his
thoughts was fully justified. This tilt at Sullivan was
no more ill-intended than was the recent criticism of
"The Merry Wives of Windsor," which was headed
"The Sad Wives of Stratford." Some Stratfordians
took exception to the *Telegraph's* comments on the
Sullivan "Hamlet," but the majority ignored them.
Stratford is not easily rattled. Its habit is to make up
its own mind and go quietly on.

Barry Sullivan was so delighted by the triumph of
his first Festival that he returned the following year
to give Stratford even more encouragement. Again
he gave his services and that of his actors. The
practical help which he accorded cannot be too
strongly stressed. He probably realised that the
second year in the Memorial Theatre, if the Strat-

ford theatre-going habit was to become a real thing, would need to be as good as the first year. Stratford, in those days, did not devote its entire Festival to Shakespeare. Bardolatry might say "Yes," but box-office said "No." The Poet had, perforce, to share his Festivals with lesser dramatic lights. Both "The Lady of Lyons" and "The Gamester" were included in the 1880 programme. This last-named play appears to have been very poorly received, and we are told that this so annoyed Sullivan—it was considered to contain one of his best parts—that he never really forgave Stratford. He never returned to play there, but as a Governor of the Theatre he continued to take a great and helpful interest in its adventures.

There can be little doubt that it was through Sullivan's interest and influence that Edward Compton, the father of Fay Compton and Compton MacKenzie, took over, though quite a young man, the Festival plays for the following year (1881). Edward Compton played the part of Don John in that historic first performance of "Much Ado About Nothing," whilst his father, Henry Compton, had been an actor in the Tercentenary Festival. It was, therefore, not as a stranger that he came to Stratford, but rather as one who knew about Stratford and of the great traditions which were beginning to surround its theatre. At the conclusion of the Festival there was a special benefit performance for Compton, and when the curtain had rung down on the play of the evening, "London

Assurance" (Shakespeare was not yet in complete control), he recited this amusing speech:—

"Though last not least" I place your good ex-Mayor
"He's borne his faculties so meek, hath been
So clear in his great office," as you've seen,
That Shakespeare's words alone form fitting dower,
"Nay, he's a Flower, in faith a very Flower".
Through his good work, folks say when they come
    down,
"Shall we go see the reliques of this town?"
At home too, welcome soundeth in his words,
"Let them want nothing that my house affords";
Many might follow Desdemona's plan,
"And wish that Heav'n had made" them "such a
    man".
To me you've taken kindly, be it said,
"With all my imperfections on my head":
"A poor player", working with main and might,
Your smiles have made my heavy work seem light,
"The labour we delight in physics pain".
"Stay but a little, I will come again".
And now, before we let the curtain fall,
From "my heart's core" a "kind good night to all!"
"Parting is such sweet sorrow" that I fear
"I shall say Good Night till it be—Next Year."

Just as Shakespeare was well served by Sullivan for a couple of years, so was he served by Compton, who

227

making good the promise expressed in his original rhyme, came to Stratford to conduct the fourth consecutive Festival. In these days the Festivals ran a very short time, a week, ten days, a fortnight at the most, the theatre being closed during most of the time in between Festivals. The Compton Festival was noteworthy for one improvement instituted after 1879. Now the entire celebrations were devoted to plays. The first Dramatic Festival in the theatre had a concert sandwiched in on the Friday night. It was a distinguished affair conducted by the famous Sir Julius Benedict. The cast included a number of names, but none so well known as that of "William Shakespeare," who, unstarred, found himself surrounded on the bill by Madame Antoinette Sterling and Mr. W. H. Cummings.

The early work of Mr. Flower, the gratuitous services of Barry Sullivan, and the cementing of the tradition by Mr. Compton served their purpose well and assured the new Memorial Theatre of fairly general approval. But approval does not mean profit. It was not till the year 1925 that the Governors were able to show a balance on the right side. It was a success at first undreamt of and unimagined. In order to fill the theatre the locals had to be loyal and they entered into the spirit of the thing with constant good will. The fame of the building, of the actors, of the standard of production, of the generosity of one man and his town had not yet filtered through to the world beyond a few miles of Stratford-upon-Avon. Trains were few and Stratford was (and is) on a branch line, roads were not very good, carriages were still of the two-horse-power variety, and so, naturally, the audiences were mainly composed of residents who lived near-by. A majority of the 1880 Shakespeare lovers would walk to the theatre, perhaps several miles, and then face the long trudge back. Others might be seen arriving on their old bone-shakers, propping them up against the wall, and claiming them again after the performance. Then there was the joy of sitting on the gallery steps, watching the actors arrive, picking out this one and that, rushing into the gallery, scrambling for the front row and watching, from a great height, the plays of William Shakespeare, Man of Stratford.

Although plays were now a regular feature of Stratford's life, it was only in the spring that they were seen, and there must have been many residents who looked forward with keen anticipation to the dramatic opportunities offered them for a few days round about St. George's Day. The actors had come to town and business would begin to look up. But visitors were not very numerous. Stratford had hoped that myriads of people would come to enjoy its Festivals.

Every year could not be a Garrick Festival, or a Tercentenary Festival, or even a year of such import as 1879. The spring season must be allowed to grow slowly. Perhaps, as time went on, it would attract more attention. Changes and inventions might make a difference. This new bicycle with wheels of equal size might bring a few more people to Stratford; you never knew, and the improved carriages on the railway might encourage people to travel towards their little town on Shakespeare's Birthday. Certainly good plays were available, but would there be an audience who, before the play started, might wander round the little streets and buy a few Shakespearean knick-knacks to take home? So the Industry was stirring. The astonishing building set up by Messrs. Dodgshun and Unsworth was surely, said 1880, very beautiful. Would it not also be a magnet and summon up Shakespeare customers from near and far?

CHAPTER XI

BANKSIDE AND "OLD VIC"

"In the South suburbs, by the Elephant."
—*Twelfth Night*, III, 3.

O F Shakespeare's London very little remains: fire swept his own Stratford, but fortunately missed much. London was not so lucky. The Great Fire of 1666 almost obliterated the City, while Southwark was largely destroyed by another fire ten years later. Plaques have been affixed to buildings here and there which happen to be on sites which have Shakespearean connections: the buildings themselves are, of course, more or less modern and usually of no interest. Perhaps the most astonishing of these is in Bell Alley, off Carter Lane. Here a tablet marks the position of the Bell Inn whence Richard Quyney, of Stratford-upon-Avon, wrote the letter to his "loveinge good Frend and Countryman Mr. Wm. Shackespeare" suggesting that a loan of thirty pounds would be agreeable and convenient. The letter was discovered by Malone at Stratford at the end of the eighteenth century. (According to Mr. Kent's handy little book, *London For Shakespeare Lovers*, Quyney lived in Bucklersbury, where he practised as a grocer-druggist,

231

a profession which was much followed in that quarter.) Surely the giddiest pinnacle of fame has indeed been reached when posterity will commemorate the site of a vanished tavern, not because Shakespeare wrote a poem or play there, but because somebody thence despatched to him a begging letter! That tablet in Bell Alley is a fragment indeed of the Amazing Monument. The entire Shakespeare Industry has nothing more curious to show than this solemn identification of a site (not a building) where so trivial an event occurred.

The perambulating Bardolater naturally turns to Southwark, the Bankside of ever-living romance and reputation. Here Shakespeare lived, here Shakespeare worked, here his colleagues and his brother Edmund, the actor who died in 1607, were buried and remembered. Of his own Southwark there is virtually nothing left. It has become a marketing and warehousing centre with wharfs to the waterside, noisy, rather gloomy, almost wholly forgetful of its past. In Elizabethan times the river was gay with wherries bringing the young bloods from the Inns of Court and the noblemen's houses of the Strand or North Bank to the bear-pits and stews and theatres for which Southwark was renowned. Or else over old London Bridge they came by foot: the river ran swiftly then and there were dangerous eddies round the bridge's water-mills, of which even gallants were afraid. Wrote Aubrey: "I have heard old Major Cosh say that Sir W. Raleigh did not care to go on the Thames in a Wherry boate: he would rather goe round about over London bridg." Raleigh would cross the Atlantic in a vessel no larger than a modern fishing-boat and explore uncharted seas and kingdoms in his search for El Dorado: but the Thames watermen were apparently too much for his nerves. If Shakespeare walked daily across London Bridge when he was lodging with the Mountjoys in Silver Street in 1604, he had plentiful view of the rotting heads of the wretches decapitated for treason. These horrid relics were hung there on poles for the admonition of the public and the benefit of the region kites.

Arriving on the Southwark shore he may have called for refreshment at the tavern of St. George. Inns were especially numerous on the Bankside because travellers, arriving at night after the City gates were closed, had to put up in the suburbs. Here, close to the Bridge, is now a part of the last of the galleried taverns of the town which still abounded in Southwark in Dickens's day. The lines in "King John" (Act II, Scene 2),

"Saint George, that swinged the dragon, and e'er since
Sits on his horse-back at mine hostess' door,"

are generally supposed to refer to the original George Inn of Southwark and its sign. But that building was destroyed in the fire of 1676. The present house probably dates from just after that year. The Great Northern Railway, seeking accommodation for vans, bought it in 1870 and destroyed two-thirds of it nineteen years later. It became uncanonised and lost the "St." in its title: but the new inn-sign goes back to England's champion and his unnatural foe. The whole of this tavern, a charming and jovial relic of old London's hospitality, very nearly disappeared in 1937. The railway company wanted to be rid of a structure which was now declared dangerous and in need of extensive and expensive repairs. However, the National Trust became its protective owners and the firm of Flower, active as ever where anything with Shakespearean associations could be saved, undertook the reconstruction, maintenance, and management of the house. In its old function of inn and dining-room it now flourishes once more.

So Stratford has come to the rescue of the wealthy capital in the task of preserving its heritage of good and ancient things. If there were such a thing as London pride, it would surely be pricked by this occurrence. At the George it is customary now to hang out the old ale-garland on the tavern's pole at Christmas. This pleasant revival of the traditional English way of announcing a new brew or a special holiday also reminds one of Shakespeare. In one of the noblest passages which he ever composed, Cleopatra's lament for Antony—Shakespeare wrote:

"The crown o' the earth doth melt.—My lord!
O, wither'd is the garland of the war,
The soldiers' pole is faln: young boys and girls
Are level now with men; the odds is gone,
And there is nothing left remarkable
Beneath the visiting moon."

The metaphor of pole and garland must surely have sprung from this then familiar spectacle of tavern-decoration. When an Elizabethan army was a-field, the sutlers would hang out pole and garland to indicate the beer-tent. They must have been familiar and beloved spectacles to Pistol Bardolph and their kind. To renew the ale-garland on the Bankside is most apt. For hereabouts were spoken first those lines of memorable loveliness.

The pilgrim, having drunk a glass of Stratford ale at the George, will doubtless proceed to Southwark Cathedral, known to Shakespeare as St. Saviour's and, in fact, the Tudor and Jacobean drama's parish church. "Philip Masenger, stranger" (Massinger to us), was buried here in 1639 and has a memorial window. John Fletcher, Shakespeare's colleague and successor as writer to the King's Men, was also buried here: his frequent collaborator, Beaumont, went up higher and lies at Westminster. The manager Henslowe and Shakespeare's brother Edmund also found burial in Southwark. The exact sites of these graves are unknown. The Cathedral has a big modern

and unimpressive Shakespeare Memorial, unveiled in
1912. The Bard, in alabaster, is reclining in heraldic
glory with a Bankside background, accompanied by
the Muse of Poetry, and the Dove of Inspiration. The
Dove seems to have passed by H. W. McCarthy, the
sculptor of this monument. American visitors will be
especially interested by a memorial window to John
Harvard, who was baptized there in 1607.

The next move will be to the river-bank. Authentic
but unexciting links with Shakespeare's London are
here available. We traverse the site of the Bishop of
Winchester's Palace. (The Bishop owned the land
hereabouts and profited by the rents of sin: the ladies
of the numerous local brothels were known as Winchester Geese, and Pandarus, at the close of "Troilus
and Cressida," alludes to their "hold-door trade.")
There is a piece of Gothic archway left in what is
now Pickford's warehouse and a section of the original
palace brickwork is said to be visible where Clink
Street joins Stoney Street. The Clink was the famous
local prison, and the name has survived in Cockney
slang. Reaching the riverside we probably pass the
site of the "great Globe itself," but there is no certainty about that. There is a tablet, announcing the
Globe's original perch, set on the wall of Barclay and
Perkins' Brewery, but scholars dispute the exact position. There is nothing here for a Shakespeare Industry to sell. It is simply the drab panorama of South
London commerce, and unimpressive at that. The

one flower in this wilderness of brick and stone and
grubby passage-way is the tiny but enchanting
Cardinal Cap House which, with its midget garden
beside Cardinal Cap Alley, looks over the water to
one of London's noblest prospects, where

> "Afloat upon ethereal tides
> St. Paul's above the City rides,"

and round it gleam the spires of the Wren churches,
those "madrigals in stone," as Henley called them.
Behind us here is the site of the Paris Garden, the
famous arena for the baiting of bulls and bears. Rose
Alley nominally reminds us of Henslowe's Rose
Theatre. A certain sinister canyon amid the warehouse buildings, dark and leading nowhere in
particular, used to be called, for fairly obvious
reasons, Love Lane. Now the London County
Council has turned ethical and cultural, and named
it after John Fletcher. Shakespeare would have
smiled.

No, Southwark has little to offer save vanished
glories. On Shakespeare's Birthday local Thespians
perform episodes from the plays on a wagon in the
court-yard of the George and beside the brewery wall,
which announces the site of the Globe. It is a small
matter, but sincere. The greater ceremonial revels
will be at the "Old Vic," also on the southern shore
of the river, but a mile or so to the west. Here, on

Birthday night, to a delirious public, famous Shakespearean scenes are played by as many of the "Old
Vic's" favourite actors and actresses, past as well as
present, as are free to help. The "Vic" is now the
Shakespeare Temple of the capital, and has been so
for nearly a quarter of a century. Its previous history
showed a strange assortment of ideals—and the lack
of them.

People who run theatres are of all sorts: the
innocent who have blundered in, the slick, the
pompous, the sincere, the fanatic, the snob, but very
rarely are they pious maiden ladies, wearing academic
robes. One London playhouse was thus commanded
and that house became so important that, when the
fanciers of a National Theatre asked for alms and
attention, the "Old Vic" was thrown in their earnest
and aspiring faces as the existing equivalent. The
ruler of the "Vic"—Empressario, may we call her?—
was, until November, 1937, Lilian Baylis, C.H., LL.D.
(Birmingham), Hon., M.A. (Oxon), Hon., which
being interpreted means that the said Lilian, in addition to knowing the exact profit on a hundred cups of
coffee and forty-two ham-rolls, was a Companion of
Honour of Great Britain, an Honorary Doctor of
Laws of the University of Birmingham and Honorary
Master (or Mistress) of Arts of the University of
Oxford.

In order to understand the late Miss Baylis you
have to understand several peculiarly English things,

such as the dual notion of the theatre as "an Abode of Vice" and the notion of the Drama as "Good for the People." Conflicting notions, of course, but since every book about the Heart of England tells the world that the English have a genius for compromise, there is no reason why they should not hold violently opposite opinions about everything—as indeed they do. The Mother of Modern Democracy, which still sustains, with full medieval panoply, a House of Lords, is surely able to believe simultaneously that the drama is both a low companion and a high art. Hence the British State appoints a Lord Chamberlain (an office held elsewhere and aforetime by Polonius) to act as censor over this unruly crowd of mummers, still deeming them, as did the Puritans of the sixteenth century, to be rogues and vagabonds in essence, dealing in lies, libels, and "feelthy peectures." At the same time Authority was so pleased to see Miss Baylis begging alms and getting people to work extremely hard for extremely little in order to exalt this same art of the theatre that it festooned her name with honorific letters, which, the cynic may observe, is a singularly cheap way out, far cheaper, certainly, than giving her grants-in-aid and slabs of hard cash.

This "Old Vic," being on the south of the river, is in the Shakespearean tradition, if not on the Shakespearean spot, for the old Bankside, where stood the Globe, Rose and Swan Theatres of Elizabethan London, is a mile or so to the east, facing London

Bridge. The "Old Vic" happened as the result of
Rennie's light and graceful Waterloo Bridge, which
was built to celebrate the Belgian battle of that name
and made the Surrey shore more easily reached. Since
London now cares little for light and grace, it has
just destroyed the bridge, but the theatre, thanks to
Miss Baylis and others, is more strongly founded. But
in its early days it was only intermittently a Shakespeare House. The two Patent Theatres, Drury Lane
and Covent Garden, had, until 1843, a monopoly of
the straight drama, and Shakespeare could only be
played outside them if mangled or burlesqued or
turned into a musical entertainment. There were,
however, all sorts of evasion of this tyrannical edict.
Edmund Kean was one who played Shakespeare at
the "Vic," drawing fifty pounds a night for himself
and also the boos and hisses of the mob who were
out to cry up Cobham, his Iago. But it must not be
thought that, because the names of "Old Vic" and
Shakespeare are now more or less inseparable, it was
always a Shakespeare house.

The opening of Waterloo Bridge after the final
defeat of "Boney" in 1815 opened up also the
Lambeth Marshes, and people began to build on this
swampy, thief-infested spot. So was erected the
Coburg Theatre, named after that Prince of Coburg
who married the Prince Regent's daughter and was
expected to be the father of an English King or
Queen. (Failure in that direction let in Victoria

Regina, of whom we have lately seen and heard so much.) The Coburg began augustly:

"this first stone was laid on September 14th, 1816, by His Royal Highness the Prince of Saxe-Coburg and Her Royal Highness the Princess Charlotte of Wales and by Their Serene and Royal Highnesses' proxy, Alderman Goodbehere."

Goodbehere could hardly be better. Miss Baylis, indeed, might have assumed so perfect a name by deed-poll. For she lived up to it all her life.

Well, before long all was ready. Said the bills:

"The above elegant Theatre WILL OPEN THIS EVENING, May 11th, with an appropriate Address by Mr. Munro. After which a new melo-dramatic spectacle, called TRIAL BY BATTLE; or, Heaven defend the Right. After which, a grand Asiatic ballet, called ALZORA AND NERINE; or, The Fairy Gift. To conclude with a new and splendid harlequinade, called MIDNIGHT REVELRY; or, Harlequin and Comus.

Lower Boxes 4s. Upper Boxes 3s. Pit 2s.
Gallery 1s.

Doors to be opened at half-past five, to begin at half-past six. Half-price at half-past eight.

Places to be taken of Mr. Grub at the box-office, from 10 till 4."

Mr. Grub, whose name is almost as suitable as Mr. Goodbehere's, did well for a while, but not for long. The Coburg's history was full of ups and downs, the downs predominating. It had local rivals, the area was rough and full of foot-pads, the two Patent Theatres of Central London monopolised the classical drama, and there was a scarcity of new authors. To cut the story short, the Coburg became the Royal Victoria Hall, the R.V.H. became known as the "Vic," the "Vic" as the "Old Vic." Under any name it was once a pretty rough house, in which crude melo-dramas and vaudeville were offered, with abundant liquor, to the cruder inhabitants of the Surrey Shore, to whom such pieces as "Sixteen Years of a Drunkard's Life" were indeed an intimate and domestic theme. As early as 1820, Hazlitt, looking in at the Coburg, deemed it full of Jew-boys, mountebanks, pickpockets, and prostitutes. There were Shakespearean interludes and doubtless that "Mr. Glavormelly," mentioned in Dickens's *Nicholas Nickleby* as making a great hit at the Coburg, offered an uplifting programme. But, on the whole, the tone went steadily down.

Shakespeare, from the eighteen-forties onward, found his true temple in North London at Sadler's Wells Theatre on the slopes of Islington. The apostle of Bardolatry here was Phelps, a fine vigorous actor and passionate Shakespearean who made an important return to Shakespeare's actual texts. When the "Old Vic" Governors rebuilt and reopened Sadler's Wells in 1931, they were endeavouring to restore a great tradition. Their effort only partially succeeded. They did not want Shakespeare in North London, because North London had forgotten Phelps long ago, had no sense of tradition, and was bored by Shakespeare. It responded, however, to opera and ballet and Sadler's Wells has built up a first-class ballet of its own since then and presents opera in a manner scarcely to be imagined by those who think that cheap seats mean cheap results.

Meanwhile an ardent social reformer called Miss Emma Cons was endeavouring to improve the housing of the London Poor. In Mr. John Booth's history of the theatre a quoted letter states:

On Monday mornings, when she collected her rents, black eyes were numerous. On inquiring the reason of this Monday carnage, she found that the men frequented music-halls on Saturday nights and drank intoxicating liquors the whole time as they listened to comic songs and foolery. They rolled home at midnight and beat their wives and little ones. . . . The conclusion was obvious; if the local crop of black eyes was to be extirpated, something must be done with the music-hall, and especially with the music-hall's drink.

Miss Cons had already been countering the saloon with her Coffee Palace Association, which offered

good coffee and victuals as the poor man's alternative
to "liquor, love and fights." She resolved to clean up
these music-halls. Why not start with the "Old Vic,"
which was known to the godly as "a licensed pit of
darkness"? So Emma started her Coffee Music-Halls,
and among her helpers was Arthur Sullivan, the composer of hymn-tunes as well as of light operatic music,
but now better known everywhere in the latter
function. In 1880 the "Old Vic" gave up its liquor
licence and served a mixed meal of tea, coffee, buns,
and vaudeville. So it went on. The cultural ladder
was re-established and slowly climbed. There were
concerts of "good music." There was rather
elementary opera. There were lectures. So successful were the latter that the music-hall became the
mother of a college, Morley College, which shared the
premises and gave evening classes to the well-intentioned and ambitious artisan. Many colleges have in
their time founded little theatres. No other theatre,
we fancy, certainly no other music-hall, has founded
a little college.

Miss Cons died in 1912. She was succeeded in
management by her niece, Lilian Baylis, who had
already been working with her for fourteen years.
Lilian's father had been a baritone and her mother a
contralto vocalist and pianist. As a girl she had
studied the violin and managed to live on her bow:
she had toured South Africa, taught music, and
organised a woman's orchestra in "Joyful Jo'burg"

244

while still quite young. So she knew something of the world when she came back to manage the "Vic" for her aunt at a salary of a pound a week. When the aunt died, she took over control and responsibility.

There had been no Shakespeare at the "Vic" until Miss Baylis was persuaded to begin. Within ten years from this start in 1914 every play in the First Folio had been performed, and a patron who attended in the fourpenny gallery could have seen the whole thirty-six for a matter of twelve shillings, less than the price of one stall in the West End. Among her chief aids at first were the crusading spirit and tireless energy of Ben Greet, Sybil Thorndike, and others who relished a struggle against odds. If the "Old Vic" had ceased to be a lively bar, at least it was now a cultural bargain-basement.

As early as 1921 the "Old Vic" company was giving invitation performances in European capitals. In 1937 it was asked to play "Hamlet" at Elsinore and consented. The old house has withstood the bad seasons and financial crises which come to every theatrical enterprise in time; it has, since the great seasons there of John Gielgud (1929–31), of Charles Laughton and Flora Robson (1933–34) and of Laurence Olivier and others (1936–37), advanced steadily in repute and prosperity. In recent years the tendency has been to play less Shakespeare and more of what may be called the modern classics; Ibsen, Shaw, Wilde, Chekhov, and James Bridie have been in the bill. And still, despite advancing years and bouts of ill-health, there would sit in the stage-box on first-nights and later would speak from the stage itself (in academic cap and gown), Lilian Baylis, C.H., LL.D., M.A. Oxon (Hon.). Certainly she could always be found in the offices by day, probably counting the pence so that the pounds would look after themselves.

To Lilian Baylis the "Old Vic" was simply a bit of heaven on earth. "I so believe," she told the world by radio, "that the theatre is our greatest power for good or evil, that I pray my earnestness may give me words in which to express this faith and to hold your attention." I am sure it did. She was Culture's Missioner. She was much addicted to prayer. There is a story told that, when things were difficult, she was found on her knees saying: "Please, God, send me good actors and send them cheap. It is a credible story. For years she always had to skimp things and to suspend the masterpiece, as it were, from a shoe-string. She had the essential piety of the English bourgeois. It is said that, when she heard Mr. Charles Laughton muttering "Oh God!" at some unhappy rehearsal, she asked him reprovingly whether that was an oath or a prayer. But you may say that the English bourgeois have never shown much interest in the arts. Well, Miss Baylis's mother was once a Miss Cons, and Cons was once Konss. Perhaps that explains.

But, essentially, Lilian Baylis was Lilian Goodbehere. She had a Cause and a flame and a flare. She never hesitated to ask favours because she conceived it to be everyone's first duty in life to help the "Vic." At a smart luncheon she could get up and ask for money from the hard-boiled "socialites," and with her untutored eloquence of faith and zeal she made their hearts throb for Shakespeare and popular culture and things like that, which they really hated and despised. Possibly even their purses were opened. She wore a scholar's gown without owning exact scholarship. She would probably have done poorly in an examination on the text and implications of a Shakespearean play. But she had a flair for the theatre and knew there was something tremendous there. She also knew, which many clever people do not, how to commend it to the public. That is to say she had a sharp instinct for knowing what players would please her patrons. So she whacked Bard and buns across at them, as the managers of the bad old days served beer and gin. One thinks of the mighty poetry coming up, as it were, through the old beer-engines and being absorbed by the eager "Old Vic" "fans" in the cheap seats, which remain really cheap on the whole, despite a tendency to charge more and collect a richer public in the stalls. At times the Mayfair "lovelies" have been known to leave *les dancings* in the West End to sip culture *chez Baylis*.

Many who had to work with Lilian Baylis said that

she was obstinate and difficult. I do not doubt that she was. So is everybody in the theatre. She was a jealous goddess of the "Vic" and a taskmistress, herself both ruler and slave of her beloved institution. But she kept the show going and growing where others might only have bickered and prattled. If it were not for Lilian Baylis, the young players would not have had work over which to grumble. The "Old Vic" was her contribution to heaven and to earth. She never rested and she was always looking for money to enlarge, to secure, and to improve her kingdom. She inherited a derelict "rough-house," which had become a coffee-concert hall, and she left it a famous theatre. People smiled at the odd little Empressario, with her fires of faith, her queer face, her spluttering speeches, her closeness in money matters, and her vanities of cap and gown. But there was this important fact: In her own commanding way she ruled a theatre which did credit to the town.

To many the "Old Vic" is not enough for London's Shakespearean devotions. Some strive for a National Theatre: others, even more ambitiously, would sweep away a portion of the commercial ugliness and squalor of contemporary Southwark and build for Shakespeare on the grand scale. It is quite a sound idea that Shakespeare should be honoured in London, where he worked as a theatre-man, as well as in Stratford, whence he came as a recruit and returned in affluence. (The divines of the two temples need not be nervous of competing for inadequate support. The worshippers abound.) This is the view of the Globe-Mermaid Association of England and America, which intends to rebuild the Globe Theatre close to its original site, together with a replica of the Mermaid Tavern and an Elizabethan Library and Museum.

Names of weight support this programme. The Marquess of Lothian is President of the Association, and General Smuts brings to it an overseas blessing. That there should be available in London a stage and auditorium similar to that for which Shakespeare composed is excellent, since often plays can only be fully understood by the light of the conditions for which they were written. It really is astounding that, considering the size and range of the Shakespeare Industry, there is no working model of his Globe Theatre in the country.* By providing a remedy for this the Association would serve us well. Of the new "Mermaid" one may be a trifle apprehensive. Its proposed attendants in Tudor costume serving "Elizabethan fare" suggest too much Mine Hoste in his Olde Oake Barre, handing out sickly potions of sack amid loud cries of: "Hither, varlet," and "Hey, Nonny." Why, in any case, revive the Mermaid on the South Bank? The famous tavern was in Bread Street and north of the river. The Association held a big Shake-

* The Tudor Platform Stage has been used with striking results for occasional performances in London by the late William Poel at the Holborn Empire, and by Mr. Robert Atkins at the Blackfriars Ring.

speare Festival in London at the end of June, 1938, paying especial attention to Tudor dance, music, and social ritual.

We cannot fairly leave the London scene without mentioning the Open Air Theatre in Queen Mary's Garden, at the corner of Regent's Park, which Mr. Sydney Carroll founded in 1933. He has since carried on every summer, despite some fairly stalwart efforts on the part of the British Climate to impede him. The programmes have included Shaw, Aristophanes, Milton, and James Bridie, but Shakespeare is the dramatist-in-chief, and four out of five plays presented here are usually his. The stage, on a grass plateau backed by trees and bushes, is as broad as it is beautiful, and the auditorium is enormous. If "The Dream," London's open-air favourite, is being played on a warm Saturday night at mid-summer, as many as four thousand can, and occasionally do, attend one performance. But the circumstances are not always so propitious and there is often a brisk business in the hiring of rugs. There is a tent-theatre for shelter in wet weather, but naturally a showery morning or afternoon is apt to be discouraging and to keep audiences away. Owing to the size of the arena there has to be mechanical amplification of voices, which some people find unpleasant. The effect of the microphones varies much according to the position of your seat. On a fine, still, dark night, when the director of operations, Mr. Robert Atkins, can make the best use of artificial light playing upon the foliage and the players, a play which contains a large element of masque and dancing—say "The Dream" or Milton's "Comus"—can be exquisitely framed and enchanting both to watch and hear. There is no doubt that Mr. Carroll and his colleagues and supporters have added richly to the amenities of summer-time in London as well as developing a deck-chair department in that almost limitless emporium, the Shakespeare Industry.

CHAPTER XII

CHILDREN'S HOUR

"Golden Lads and Girls."
—*Cymbeline*, IV, 2.

THE Shakespeare Industry's great discovery during the latter half of the nineteenth century was the value of the child. Shakespeare was now culture: children, of course, needed Culture: children, or their parents, could, and should, pay for Culture. Shakespeare also was the National Bard, almost St. William by now. Children needed St. William with his praise of the English in-arms, of this other Eden, demi-Paradise. Thousands at half-price, or even quarter-price, are just as good as hundreds at whole price, far better if the whole-price hundreds do not turn up at all. There is no escape for the children. If authority intends them to go to the theatre, then either they go or the theatre comes to them and the money is forthcoming and most welcome. What could a Business Manager like better? The children, as a rule, though they must find certain passages meaningless and boring, do, on the whole, make a good audience: unlike the adults and the dramatic critics they have not had to put up with the Gobbos and Grave-diggers scores of times. They are easy and natural laughers and do not applaud from a sense of duty.

It is acknowledged in the acting profession in England that it is useless to take Shakespeare on tour unless you can rope in the schools. The method is to find out what are "the set books," i.e., the plays appointed by the various educational authorities as "Eng. Lit." for examination purposes, and then include them in the repertory, especially for matinée performances. Thus a company "on the road" with Shakespeare will probably do better business in the afternoons than at night. The afternoon audience is mainly conscript: the night one consists mainly of volunteers. Britain believes in the voluntary system for her army: not for Shakespeare. It has been argued by Mr. Bernard Shaw, among others, that this system is abominable, an outrage alike on the poet and the pupils. By associating drama and lessons, the classics and the class-room, it simply creates Shakespeare-haters. Therefore nobody under eighteen should be taken to a Shakespeare performance. Others argue that the thing does not work out that way at all: the children, for the most part, have a thoroughly good time and are not in the least deterred. Anyhow, even listening to the booming and bellicose barons in one of the "Histories" is better than being in school and explaining what an argosy is. Stratford-upon-Avon is assisted by the carefully cultivated presence every year

of 30,000 of what Thisbe called the "brisky juvenals."
They are by no means resentful. They probably get a
long ride in a motor-coach and picnic meals. Even
without benefit of a good tuck-in the Bard appears to
be endurable.

Not long ago at Stratford a complete class of girls
from a High School celebrated the end of term by
paying for expensive seats at a performance of
"Romeo and Juliet," buying large boxes of choco-
lates as well as numerous photographs of their
favourite actors. When asked what induced them to
celebrate in this fashion, they said that: "It was
such fun being able to see the play and know
that they would not have to write an essay on it
afterwards."

It must be remembered that, almost until the end
of the nineteenth century, the Theatre was still
regarded as a House of Sin by the majority of British
educational authorities. It was only after strenuous
campaigning, for example, that Oxford under-
graduates were permitted to form a Dramatic Society
and act Shakespeare and Greek Plays in a public
theatre. To the Old Guard the whole venture was
deeply suspect. It was widely assumed that acting and
immorality go together, and that the stripling Hamlets
of the Isis were taking a downward and a primrose
path.

How did this long-standing hatred of the theatre
begin to melt in the Senior Common-room and in the

breasts of those pastors and masters who governed the curriculum and recreation of the young? Partly it was the work of "cormorant, devouring Time," which eats up mental pride and prejudice as well as youth and beauty. Partly it was the work of two remarkable actors, working in different ways to put Shakespeare on the school-room map and—no less important—in the very good books of the Business Manager. Bringing Shakespeare to school and school to Shakespeare, Ben Greet and Frank Benson made the Bard live for the young and also yield a living for the actor.

Greet was the son of a Naval Captain and was intended for the Navy himself, but he became a schoolmaster before he took to the stage. Benson was a Public School and University man (Winchester and New College), fine athlete, and altogether well qualified to be regarded as a Sahib and to be wrapped in a very large number of those school, college, and club colours which are the emblems—in so many British eyes—of a well-spent youth.

Frank Benson also became, in certain roles, an excellent as well as most vehement actor. Mr. James Agate, play-going at the "Old Vic," recognised in his diaries "the smell of schoolboys *en masse,* transporting me to the Benson matinées." He also said that "Benson impressed me more than any other English actor I ever saw, except Irving." The critical authority is here illustrious, but probably so high an estimate would not be general. What mattered very much, when Benson started on his own in 1883, was his status as a Fine Young English Gentleman. If the work of making the stage respectable and even a vessel of educational grace, work being carried on so augustly by Irving in London, was to be carried farther afield, here was the man to do it. Shakespeare had been promoted to high cultural honours by many of the learned. But, after all, said the godly, he did delight in smutty jokes. Some of his plots were far from uplifting: his vocabulary was frankly lurid. Most regrettable. But was he not the National Bard? Ah, yes. For those of riper years. But not for children. It was all very difficult. But suppose a man came along who was a Perfect Gentleman, a man who had run in the Athletic Sports for Oxford, a man who recruited gentlemanly actors and set them to play cricket and hockey as well as Shakespeare, might not William the Outspoken be more easily acceptable as St. William the National Hero and ornament of school curricula? Besides, the plays would be carefully selected and the texts cut. And the cricket would be first-class.

Benson's life-work was nearly all Shakespearean. Greet had a wider stage-life, and at one time had twenty-three companies on the road, playing all manner of drama. But Shakespeare was his passion. In those terribly difficult years, 1914 to 1917, he produced twenty-seven Shakespeare plays at the "Old Vic" and, when the Open Air Theatre was opened in Regent's Park in 1933, he was properly appointed to office as Master of the Greensward: this involved him in telling the audience about the play and whether it was going to rain in the next hour or two. As a rule, he knew more about the former than the latter mystery.

Not only did Ben Greet use Shakespeare for schooling actors: he was a prime mover in taking Shakespeare to the schools. With his singular persuasive charm he made those responsible see that the only way to teach Shakespeare properly was to let the pupils see the plays acted. The answer was that it would seriously disjoint the programme of the day if *all* the school were taken to a theatre. That objection was soon overruled by Greet, who said that he would be only too willing to bring a company of actors to the spot. So, much in that manner, Greet built up a regular touring system of big schools, little schools, schools in towns, schools in the country, schools for the deaf, schools for the dumb, schools for the blind; in fact, every conceivable kind of school became, in the course of time, a playing centre for the Ben Greet Shakespearean Company. If the school possessed a good garden or playing-field and the weather were fine, then the performance was given in the open air; if it were wet the play was given in the school hall. For actors, accustomed to ordinary theatres, it was all very difficult. Lack of adequate lighting, a small stage (sometimes no stage at all), very little scenery and an audience unused to the theatre—raw material in every sense of the word—were of little or no help in creating the conventional illusions and effects.

The actors had to make a direct impression and had nobody but Shakespeare to help them. Greet's Company arrived, like the Players at Elsinore. There were none of the structural conveniences of the Shakespeare Memorial Theatre, the "Old Vic," or any other specially constructed playhouse; but they did have Shakespeare as an ally. His plays lived in those schools for two reasons. They were vigorously acted in very much the same simple manner that the author had in mind. Their young audience probably did not appreciate the difficulties, but they were impressed. They were certainly not frightened, as many less fortunate were, by the dreary method of teaching by the text-book. It is this once juvenile audience, trained and encouraged by Ben Greet, that contributes largely to the adult audiences to-day.

Many more were trained and encouraged by Frank Benson. There can be no question that Benson, apart from Irving (under whom he learnt the rudiments of his job), is one of the greatest personalities that the English theatre has known in the last eighty years. As a teacher he was supreme. At least fifty per cent of the senior actors of the first rank in England and some also in America were Benson-trained.

Benson can claim to be the first manager to tour Shakespeare's plays to provincial theatres according to the curriculum set in the schools. He made it his

job to find out what plays were being taught in the
way of Literature in order to bring the lesson to life
and to give dramatic literature its proper quality of
acted drama. He wrote to the schools, weeks before
his visit, and asked how many children they would be
sending to a particular performance. If, as sometimes
happened, it could not be arranged for the school to
visit the theatre, then he took his entire company to
the school. There is a common belief, which is quite
inaccurate, that Benson systematically toured schools.
He did not, but he *did* systematically bring the
"school" plays to the towns and he did manage to
get the juvenile audience to the theatre. It is doubtful whether Benson, himself, visited more than a
dozen schools a year, but some of those which he did
visit provided him with curious occurrences.

In particular there was a famous visit to the
Cheltenham College for Ladies. Some fifty years ago
the headmistress of Cheltenham invited Benson and
his company to give a performance of "The Merchant
of Venice." They were at the time fulfilling a week's
engagement at the Cheltenham Opera House. After
Benson and his team had arrived at the school he
was told, by the headmistress, that only on one condition could the play be given. The part of "Jessica"
must be omitted! Benson protested and asked the
reason for this strange request. The headmistress
replied: "I don't want the idea of elopement to be
put into my girls' heads." Benson might well have

marched his troupe away again. But he did not. He argued. Jessica was allowed an inch of life, so Shylock appeared almost without a daughter. No costumes were allowed. The men wore dinner-jackets and the women evening dress. There could be no make-up. So young men, by the aid of squeaky voices and awkward stoops, made heroic efforts to convince the young ladies of Cheltenham of their great age. This was a head-mistress's production with a vengeance, for she had insisted that there must be a complete segregation of the sexes. The women of the cast had to enter and leave on the right and the men on the left. The entire audience, of several hundred, contained one male, the Vicar, who sat in the middle of the front row. This story offers a striking example of the indignities suffered by Shakespeare in our schools in the past century and also of what Ben Greet and Benson were combating in their big effort to make Shakespeare a "live" subject for the future generation. It was their aim to stop the dry-rot—the reading of the plays in a dull manner, the impression that Shakespeare was a museum piece, and that he was a subject to be forgotten as soon as school hours were over.

Stratford-upon-Avon and Benson are naturally much connected. Greet's first visit to the Stratford Theatre was in 1895; Benson was established there long before that. How he became associated with Stratford-upon-Avon is an odd story. After he left Oxford he got a job with Irving at "The Lyceum," where he was given the part of "Paris," though, as he himself says, he would much rather have played "Romeo." A few months later he went into the country, on the advice of his "Chief," and joined a touring Company. The Company had for business manager a scamp who suddenly disappeared with all the money. The actors, Benson included, were wondering what to do about this sudden turn of misfortune when Benson received a letter from his father. The letter was a reply to a Benson appeal, and gave the young man assurance that he could, if he cared, take on the financial responsibility of the Company. He told the rest who received the news with incredulity. But, however incredulous they were, they soon got down to business and, as a result, the Benson Company was born.

Two years later Benson was playing at the Leamington Theatre and, anxious to get control, if only for one year, of the Stratford Festival, he had written to Mr. Flower and invited him to come over to see one of the performances. Leamington is only ten miles away from Stratford, and obviously it would have been discourteous of Mr. Flower if he had not accepted the invitation. He and his wife set off one night, in a carriage and pair, to see a performance of "Macbeth." And what a performance!

It is common knowledge that ill-luck follows in the wake of this play. The 1938 Festival at Stratford opened with "Macbeth." An old man was knocked down in the car-park, by his own car, and fractured both his legs. On another occasion in the same season Miss Phyllis Neilson-Terry, on her way to Stratford to play "Lady Macbeth," crashed her car into a shop window and sustained nasty head bruises. On another "Macbeth" day, Gyles Isham, the "MacDuff" of the production, fell off his horse and was out of the bill for days on end. It will also be remembered that Lilian Baylis, the foster-nurse of Shakespeare in the Waterloo Road, died on the eve of a "Macbeth" production.

The particular "Macbeth" at Leamington is best dealt with by Sir Frank Benson in his delightful *My Memoirs*. He says: "Much was hoped by me from this performance, not only as a preparation for 'Macbeth' on a large scale at Reading, but as possibly bringing about an engagement for the Memorial performance at Stratford-upon-Avon. Unfortunately, as sometimes happens when one is particularly anxious all should go right, on that night everything went wrong. Weir, who usually gave an impressive mystical rendering of the First Witch, had in the afternoon gossiped with convivial friends over five healths five fathoms deep. He came down to the footlights in a friendly, cheery way, beamed vacuously at the audience, and then, in a confidential whisper, informed them that 'The cat has mewed three times.' I think I never realised the difference

between prose and poetry so acutely as I did when
missing the witchery of:—

> " 'Thrice the brinded cat hath mewed,
> Thrice; and once the hedge pig whin'd
> Harper cries?—'tis time, 'tis time!'

and in place of this invocation merely came, in the
manner of the latest racing tip, the friendly information concerning pussy recorded above.

"To make matters worse, Herbert Ross, who was
blessed—or cursed—with a keen sense of humour,
fastened the cauldron to Weir, so that in the fourth
act the First Witch found himself pursued all over
the stage by a bowl of liquid fire and sulphurous
fumes. To the intense delight of Ross, the poor man
kept appealing to him as to whether he had 'got 'em'
or not.

"I was proud of my new business in having a small
tea-bell sounded as a signal from Lady Macbeth that
it was time for the murder to be accomplished. Unfortunately, as I was preparing for my great exit, the
man in the flies thought the bell was the signal for
lowering the curtain, and down it came in the middle
of the scene.

"A faint hope still remained to redeem these mis-
haps by the spirited acting of the guilty couple after
the murder. I, who was inclined, as we have seen, to
make muscular activity do duty for mental percep-

tion, used to pick up Lady Macbeth with my left arm, carrying her off the stage on my left shoulder, whilst I kept at bay with my right sword-arm the infuriated thanes. On this particular night I brushed my fair partner against one of the wings. 'Hope I did not hurt you?' I murmured, as I hurried past the stage box, in which Mr. and Mrs. Charles Flower sat. 'No, dear, I am all right,' replied Lady Macbeth. The next moment this friendly assurance was suddenly changed, as she was banged against an archway, into: 'Damn you, you clumsy devil, you have broken my back!' All this in tones plainly audible to the august persons in the box."

Mr. and Mrs. Flower were naturally annoyed and left the Leamington Theatre before the end of the performance. Young Benson followed them in despair to Stratford the next morning. He had a long chat with Mr. Flower, stayed to lunch, and somehow managed to persuade him that this performance was really very far below the usual Benson standard. He must have been a very capable pleader. For the outcome of Benson's visit was an invitation to take charge of the Stratford Festival for 1886.

The very fact that he controlled the Festival for nearly thirty consecutive years shows how well he justified the Flowers' confidence. He began at Stratford as a young man in the mid-twenties and left there after he had passed his fifty-eighth birthday. He won great and genuine affection. When Benson arrived at the station the whole town turned out to give him a welcome. There was no need for him to look for a carriage to take him to his hotel. One was waiting for him. No horses were in the shafts: young people were all rivals for the honour of pulling him through the streets.

The Festival, during the Benson days, grew in length from a few weeks to a few more weeks. It grew from a Spring Festival to a Summer Festival. The Company arrived for the Birthday Celebrations, played for a fortnight or three weeks, went away again, and came in the summer to find just as grand a reception awaiting them. Stratford-on-Avon was looked upon by the Benson Company as a happy change. It must have been a great holiday for them to play there after the smoke and grime of the various industrial centres. In a big northern town the Company would be almost unnoticed, except for their prowess in the athletic field, whereas at Stratford they were fêted.

Malvern, to-day, has an atmosphere very much like the Stratford of Benson's day. The Festival has begun, the actors have come to town, the thing must be a success and everybody must be happy. Now the actors have become an institution; they are accepted as part of the town and no particular preparations are made to entertain them, for which, no doubt, they are extremely grateful.

Benson did many courageous things in the name of

Shakespeare. He produced every play in the Folio except "Titus Andronicus" and "Troilus and Cressida." He put on "The Merry Wives of Windsor" when it was much out of favour. He created theatrical history by producing an uncut version of "Hamlet." In living memory there was nobody in England who had ever seen the complete version of this play. For once an audience knew what happened to Hamlet when he went to England. This uncut version was the cause of a great deal of Press controversy and did much to popularise Benson and his Company. Actually it was at the first performance not quite uncut. Benson had overlooked a young actor who completely forgot a couple of important speeches, and so upset Benson's good intention as well as the author's.

A journey to America was made in 1913, when H. B. Irving took Benson's place at Stratford. Irving, unlike Benson, experimented with a badly cut version of "Hamlet." This caused one dramatic critic to suggest that the title should be changed to "Incomplete quotations from the tragedy of 'Hamlet'." This much-criticised work suffered from the cutting of the grave-yard scene. It was a triumph for Benson when he was invited to visit the States. He was following in the footsteps of Sir Henry Irving. He was taking Shakespeare to our American cousins. Irving's Company was one of London actors, whilst Benson's had the added attraction of coming from Shakespeare's home town.

Some of Benson's American notices caused a great deal of amusement in the Company. America was far less accustomed to Shakespeare than it is now, and many of the responses were very odd. "Humour three hundred years old, but funny," was typical of the Press reception accorded to them. Others read: " 'Merry Wives of Windsor' gives audience laughing cramps," "That Stratford troupe certainly can play Richard," "This husband knows how," "Wife-taming pleasant diversion," "Falstaff gets gay with the Windsor Dames," and the one that caused the greatest amusement was: "Smothers the kids while Mother weeps; or Richard Plantagenet slays youngsters in order to reach the throne, and is thrown through the double cross."

The work that Benson did in the cause of the Shakespeare Industry is incalculable. He put poetry right with the middle classes. In England that is not so difficult: in England you can put anything right with the right-thinking man, even religion, if you mix it up with cricket and physical fitness and a healthy outlook on life. He strongly believed that players should play games. The well-known story of Benson wiring to his agent to "Send a good fast bowler to play Laertes" is typical of the man. He urged his actors to play cricket, hockey and football. He encouraged them to swim, to run, to walk. He once said: "Give me an actor who is fit—really fit—and I'll make a *great* actor of him." There is a story told of

Oscar Asche that when he joined the Company he told Benson that he had come over with the Australians; so he had, but only on the boat! That, with Benson, was a sign of grace. O. B. Clarence, Randle Ayrton, Henry Ainley, Sir Cedric Hardwicke, H. R. Hignett, H. O. Nicholson and Murray Carrington are but a few of those who trained under Benson both as Shakespearean actors and as Bensonian athletes. In the Shakespearean arena they all gained notable fame and developed as first-class actors, thanks to their own abilities and the more than lucky chance that a young man called Benson once found himself in charge of a company which had been left without a manager.

The work which Benson did for Shakespeare was recognised by H.M. King George V when he knighted him, in 1916, at Drury Lane Theatre. (Philip Ben Greet became Sir Philip in 1929.) That was a tremendous honour for any actor and it was accentuated in Benson's case by the fact that he was knighted in the theatre. At that performance (of "Julius Cæsar") he was surrounded on the stage by all the famous actors and actresses of the time, and the vast majority of them were of his schooling. After the Crown, the Town. Stratford-upon-Avon recognised the worth of Benson's achievements, some years before the knighthood, by giving him the freedom of the Borough. He shared that with Garrick, the only other actor to be so honoured. But Benson's reception in Stratford, immediately after the touching scene in Drury Lane

Theatre, exceeded in warmth any previous "home-coming."

So the lads and lasses have proved golden to the Industry. Or at least the silver and coppers have rolled in. Many a Shakespeare Company has blessed the schools. Do the scholars bless Shakespeare? One sees them packed in the "Old Vic" on winter after-noons or reclining in Regent's Park deck-chairs on summer ones. Some obviously are relishing the experience: others seem to be sleepy, bored, puzzled, wanting the strange noise to stop. No doubt the majority vote would be in favour. In 1936 the Eng-lish Schools Theatre Society—giving preference to Shakespeare's plays—was formed and matinées of required plays put on in the West End with really first-rate casts. The young spectators have been put on to try their hands at dramatic criticism, and some of their efforts are most incisive. Fortunately the actors do not see these observations, which can be very saucy in dispraise.

CHAPTER XIII

OUT OF THE FLAMES

"Now a new House has risen: it is given
Not by one citizen or state: it stands
Given to us by many hundred hands
American and British: nay, each race
Upon this earth has helped to build this place.
Lovers of Shakespeare everywhere have striven,
Every man gave it out of all earth's lands."
—JOHN MASEFIELD.

THE year 1925 was of crucial importance for the Shakespeare Industry in Stratford. The three outstanding events were the granting of a Royal Charter to the Memorial Theatre in Stratford which made H.M. King George V its Patron, a privilege enjoyed alone by this theatre, the making of a profit (as well of renown) for the first time in its forty-six years of life, and an appeal by George Bernard Shaw for an altogether new building. Mr. Shaw, when he made his appeal, was proposing the Toast of the Immortal Memory at the Birthday Luncheon of the Shakespeare Club in Stratford. It was an amusing occasion, the one-time Hammer of Bardolatry now rampant at Bardolatry's high table. He said very little about Shakespeare—anyhow, he may be deemed to have finished that off in his critical days—but he did say a great deal about the theatre.

He said that he could not discuss something that did not exist, and therefore was not going to mention the ventilation. He thought that a theatre which suffered from floods, as this one did, ought to be pulled down and another built in its place. He thought that it was about time for a General Appeal for funds to erect a really fine theatre in memory of William Shakespeare.

Mr. Shaw's words carried weight. He was speaking not only as our chief dramatist, but also as a Governor of the Theatre. There is little doubt that many of his Fellow-Governors were not in sympathy with his mood, but that was not going to worry Mr. Shaw. He had been a trenchant critic of plays in the past: why not of a playhouse now? He looked at the theatre without prejudice and said what many people had thought for years. It was time the "Victorian atrocity," "the unsightly edifice," was replaced by something bigger, more modern, better-looking, and more useful.

The ways of the world had altered much since Mr. C. E. Flower had seen his theatre rise. Electric light had taken the place of gas; transport had improved a hundred per cent; thousands of people in place of hundreds were now visiting Stratford, and they should be shown a theatre meriting a world-reputation and not only worthy of Stratford-upon-Avon as it was in the eighteen-seventies. Many of the London newspapers, showing a very different attitude to their old one, gave Mr. Shaw their support. Stratford, they agreed, ought to have a theatre which was the finest in the world. Forty-six years had made a great difference. Traditions had sprung up around the theatre. Great actors of the day had learned their job at Stratford; players of the front rank had been happy to perform on its stage; Frank Benson had created a special atmosphere which endeared the theatre and the town to the ever-increasing number of visitors. None the less, there was a general and growing feeling, expressed by Mr. Shaw, that a beloved atrocity might give way to something not atrocious and yet loved none the less.

Within a year Chance solved the problem. Accident committed to the flames what criticism had not yet succeeded in committing to the house-breakers. On a breezy spring afternoon of 1926, Saturday, March 6th, the Memorial Theatre was discovered to be on fire. Nobody ever discovered the cause. Nobody could in time discover a remedy or prevent immense destruction. Fire-brigades came racing from all over Warwickshire. Soon hoses innumerable were being played on the flames which threatened, at any minute, to bring the hideous baronial tower crashing on to the roof of the Library and Museum, where were kept so many treasures of Shakespeare and his day. These had to be saved. Volunteers were called for and quickly responded. A human chain was made across the road from the interior of the Museum to the Memorial Lecture Room. Books, pictures, and relics were transferred from hand to hand and finally

TEMPORARY THEATRE AT STRATFORD, 1864

Photos: Daniels

GOOD-BYE TO ALL THAT, 1926

deposited in safety well away from the flames. So great was the enthusiasm that two men were able to carry out, with the greatest of ease, an enormous marble bust which required seven men to put it back. It speaks well for the honesty of Stratfordians that not one single relic was lost during this excitement. There were no snappers-up of unconsidered treasures.

The things which were removed to safety, whilst the flames were roaring round about them, included the first four Folios, the Droeshout Portrait, numerous large oil-paintings, hundreds of valuable books, relics of famous Shakespearean actors, a piece of the inevitable mulberry-tree, and a hundred and one other exhibits. Whilst all this was going on the fire was spreading. It looked as though the tower would crash at any minute. The wind was strong and blowing the smoke into the eyes of the tenacious rescue-parties. Would it bring that tower tumbling into the Library while they were still at work? Then a seemly portent happened. Providence performed for Shakespeare on the Avon the trick which it did for Mr. Shaw's St. Joan beside the Loire. Slowly the wind veered round. The smoke was now being blown river-wards. The flames no longer threatened the treasure-house. But still there could be no relaxing. If the wind changed for one minute it might easily destroy all. At last, after three hours, everything was safely housed across the road. The theatre still burned. Part of the tower had collapsed telescopically. The smoke was thicker than ever. Whilst the valuables had been saved the firemen had been more than usually busy, fighting odds which they could not hope to beat. As far as stage and auditorium were concerned, they had lost and the theatre was a complete and utter ruin.

The story was quickly flashed to the outside world along with those results of football matches without which Saturday afternoon would seem unendurable to the British Public. One local journalist, the first, we believe, on the scene, did not bother to send an immediate wire as he felt that "it was too late for the Sundays and could wait for the Monday." Of course, it proved to be a front-page story for the "Sundays." The burning of a theatre is always good "copy," but this was no ordinary theatre. It was a temple as well. It was the very theatre which Bernard Shaw had so heavily criticised less than a year before, the theatre which C. E. Montague had forborne to judge, awaiting the fiery verdict of heaven.

Within a short space of time hundreds of telegrams arrived. They were full of condolence—or congratulations. It was Mr. Shaw who first congratulated the Governors on the beneficence of Chance. Whether or no it was a good riddance of a bad theatre, this fire had come at a cruel time. The Festival was due to open in six weeks. The Company were rehearsing in London under Mr. W. Bridges Adams, who had succeeded Sir Frank Benson as Festival Director in 1919. Everything was almost ready for the 1926 opening. The Governors, who had been elated at the financial result of 1925, were wondering whether they were going to have an equally successful season in 1926. As soon as they heard of the fire they knew they were not to be so blessed. Stratford was in a state of chaos. What about the Festival? What about the visitors? Would this spell ruin for the hotels and tradesmen? Who would give a lead?

Instead of confusion there was quick decision. With dignity and common sense Mr. A. D. Flower kept complete control of the situation and the people of Stratford took his calm advice. They had lost the magnet which was drawing thousands to their town. Their shops were stocked, their inns and restaurants were being got ready. The Bazaar for Bardolaters was all prepared. And now there would be no Bard. No players, no profits. That seemed to be an obvious danger. Naturally everyone looked to Authority for a lead. It can be taken for granted that if the Chairman and his fellow-Governors had not thought and acted quickly the continuity of Stratford's Dramatic Festivals and the prosperity of the town would have suffered severely. As it was, "Business Nearly as Usual" became the order of the Festivals for the next six years. It was on a Saturday afternoon, March 6th, 1926, at about 2.30 p.m., that the Memorial Theatre went up in flames and within twenty-four hours it had been decided that the local cinema—the only one in the town and still thus unique—should be converted into a theatre. Architects had been quickly summoned; so, too, had all the executives. A round table conference was held and the cinema decision was made and announced.

Money was wanted and wanted quickly. The theatre, in those days, was not a rich affair. Although the decision to go forward had already been reached, rightly an appeal was made to the town. Stratford remembered the £20,000 which it had found to build the now burned-out shell; again it met the occasion. Within twenty-four hours the sum of £1,600 had been collected, and this money, together with other cash, was the foundation which assured a further series of Festivals and, incidentally, assured the continuity of the Industry. Shakespeare and relics were once more in common association. There is, in Stratford, an antique shop where you can buy cigarette-boxes made from the burnt timber of the Old Memorial Theatre. These boxes are limited in number and not nearly so numerous as were the various odds and ends made from the one mulberry- and one crab-tree of the legends; yet the amount of charred wood rescued from the smouldering ashes of the 1879 theatre would have been equal to several trees twice as large as Shakespeare's famous mulberry. One of these little boxes was actually used when the earth from the Birthplace garden was sent to fertilise the drama in Texas.

The Great Fire of Stratford, for so it is now named,

was the fourth of a series which commenced in the reign of Queen Elizabeth. The Shakespeare family must have been fire-hardened. The first and second Stratford flare-ups happened in the thirty-sixth and thirty-seventh years of the reign of the Queen, and they both appear to have destroyed some two hundred houses and much valuable property. The third fire occurred on July 9th, 1614, and in less than two hours had accounted for about fifty-four houses. It can be safely assumed that large portions of Shakespeare's Stratford went up in flames and with it, quite possibly, genuine relics, and even papers concerning or belonging to the Poet. The 1926 fire was obviously not so devastating as were the previous outbreaks, but, as Stratford had now become a place of national interest, not only through the performance of the plays but also through the efforts of the Birthplace Trustees, it naturally attracted universal attention.

No tragedy is without its humorous side, and even the burning of Drury Lane Theatre gave the London newspapers something to laugh about. Richard Sheridan, as soon as he heard that his famous playhouse was aflame, rushed to the scene and watched it burn whilst he sat in a comfortable arm-chair in the middle of the road. Authority tried to move him on. "Officer," said Mr. Sheridan, "you cannot stop a man warming his feet at his own fireside." At the time of the Memorial Theatre fire there was, in the crowd, a Scotsman who had a healthy loathing of Shakespeare and who had obstinately resisted the spell of the Poet. He had confessed freely that he had slept through most of the plays and that the players had bored him. An onlooker at the fire turned to him and said: "Isn't it dreadful?" The sacrilegious Scot merely retorted that it was the only good performance he had seen at that theatre yet.

The Governors, being assured of enough money to alter the cinema by enlarging the stage and building dressing-rooms, announced that the Festival would open on the prearranged day. This it did. Stratford was not disappointed. Its £1,000 had proved to be a magnificent investment with a return that could not be reckoned in actual figures. Hotels were as busy as usual. Photographs of the smoking ruin were a new line on the Shakespeare counter. There were the mementoes in charred wood. Most elated of all were the actors and actresses who were taking part in this unique and indeed heroic Festival. They had feared to lose their season's engagement. Now all was to go forward, very nearly as before.

While plans were being made for the alterations to the Picture Palace the Governors of the Theatre were occupied in scheming a campaign whereby they might excite the whole world. Stratford must, this time, make a really big International Appeal. It had the assistance of the London Press, particularly the *Daily Telegraph* and *Punch*. These papers showed a very different attitude to the one adopted when the old building went up. They opened a fund in collaboration with the *Birmingham Post*. They stressed the importance to the world of a theatre at Stratford. They praised the work of the pioneers, of Charles Flower, of Barry Sullivan, of Benson, of Bridges Adams, and last, but by no means least, of A. D. Flower. Here, they said, was a small place in the centre of England which was so easily accessible that it could never starve for the want of a theatre audience. It was a divergent tale from the one they spread less than fifty years earlier. But the motor-car had intervened. The rustic playgoer now moved at forty miles an hour, a very different matter from jogging along in a wagonette at eight.

Support was soon found. Political, literary, educational and artistic leaders, headed by the then Prime Minister, Mr. Baldwin, contributed to the National Appeal by the lending of their names and the giving of money. Whilst the principal daily newspapers were busy organising their New Memorial Theatre Campaign, the Festival Company were accustoming themselves to their new surroundings in the one-time Picture Palace. Audiences, curious to see a Shakespeare play performed in what they imagined must be a makeshift manner, were crowding to view them. There was nothing makeshift about those cinema performances; they were well up to Stratford standard, and thanks for this, in large degree, must be given to the Director of the Festival, W. Bridges Adams, who overcame many of the supposedly insurmountable difficulties with excellent results. For six seasons (1926–1931) the plays were given in this temporary home; it was brave, but it was not "box-office." It cost, in actual loss, some £25,000.

It must have been some consolation to the Company to know that at the conclusion of the Summer Festivals they would be touring the United States of America. These tours were organised in connection with the Rebuilding Fund. Mr. A. D. Flower also went to America and acted as an exalted advance agent for the Festival actors. Despite his years (he was then over sixty), he endured the fatigues of constant travel over long distances. He would spend some time in an American town, immediately prior to the arrival of the Shakespearean Players, and talk about the work done in Stratford and the work that could be done if only a proper theatre could replace the burnèd-out building. As a result of his many public addresses he was largely instrumental in collecting large sums of money for the present finely equipped theatre as well as for guaranteeing excellent houses for the actors who, in their way, were also making sure that Stratford should have its own playhouse once again.

Mr. Flower had laid down his work in England and taken up this fresh quest abroad. In municipal and social affairs, as in the conduct of the family business, which is the brewing of good beer and the conduct of country inns, he was a very busy man, and it must have meant much rearranging of his own work to enable him to carry out his mission. Mr. Flower visited America accompanied by his wife. Their journeys to the United States in 1926 and 1927 were not in connection with the tours of the Company, but in response to an invitation from the American Committee to tell their country what had been accomplished and what could be done with a fine theatre. During these two years they toured most of the great cities, went across Canada and down the coast from Seattle to San Diego before returning through the Middle West. They never asked for money. The Americans claimed that Shakespeare belonged to them as much as to us and, when they realised that here was something worth while, *they* raised more than fifty per cent of the large sum required.

In recognition of this generous support and knowing that many of these donors could not come to Stratford, the Governors decided to send their Company out on a long tour, starting in Canada and going right round the West Coast and back through the Middle West. It was to help to make this visit known that the Flowers went out again in 1928 and travelled as unpaid advance agents a week ahead of the actors, speaking at schools, clubs and Universities. The Company went out again in 1929, and on their way back across America they encountered the big slump, so the Flowers set forth once more and got ahead of them in Washington, Philadelphia and Boston, and a loss was converted into a profit.

Perhaps some of the people who called on Mr. Flower, at his American hotels, were aware of the fact that he was a man with big business interests in England. He received many odd suggestions. One enterprising go-getter suggested that he be employed to dress-up as a preacher and denounce Shakespeare as Satan's right-hand man. That, he claimed, would put Stratford right on America's map and get the Stratford Players capacity business every night. Mr. Flower was not impressed. But he continued to impress America.

Meanwhile, as the funds grew, the plans matured. The new theatre would rise, another Phœnix emerging from the ashes. An architectural competition was thrown open to British, Canadian, and American subjects, with July, 1927, as closing date. The job had peculiar complexity, because the building had somehow to combine scope for the modern picture-stage, the Elizabethan apron-stage, and the Greek orchestra-stage. The judges, architects of the utmost eminence, Messrs. Dauber, Hood and Atkinson, unanimously accepted the design offered by Miss Elizabeth Scott, A.R.I.B.A.* Though Miss Scott was still only twenty-

* *Architectural competitions of this kind can only be held with the supervision of the R.I.B.A.: otherwise its members could not enter. The first judges, Messrs. Dauber, Atkinson and Cass Gilbert (of America), chose a short list of six, three British and three American. These six had half a year in which to complete their work. Raymond Hood, another American, took Mr. Cass Gilbert's place on the panel of judges who finally selected Miss Scott's design.*

nine, she may be said to have had building in the
blood, for she was a grand-niece of Sir Gilbert Scott,
most famous of Victorian architects. She had been
trained in the schools of the Architectural Association for five years, was living in Bloomsbury, and was
practising in association with Messrs. Maurice
Chesterton and Shepherd.

The Great Fire had one great element of good
fortune. It occurred three years before the Great
Slump. Especially in the United States prosperity was
fairly general. The Depression of the thirties had not
yet struck its colossal blow. Britain paid up well:
America, considering the remoteness of Stratford from
its interests, even better. There was an American
Shakespeare Foundation formed to raise money for
the new theatre, and that brought in about £128,000,
while the Building Fund altogether reached about
£250,000. Of this half was called the British Fund,
while the other half was collected in America, Germany, and other countries. The American subscribers
have their names on record in the great "American
Book" now on view in the Theatre Library.

The Foundation Stone was laid on July 2nd, 1929.
There is no formality here about the words "foundation" and "stone," for the theatre, being on the brink
of a somewhat volatile river, much given to flooding,
had to be based firmly.* The start needed much care-

---

* £35,000 *had to be spent on foundations before anything appeared
above ground, as water was discovered seven feet from the surface.*

ful labour. Nearly a year was given to this, and then
the superstructure began to rise and the whole was
ready to be opened on April 23rd, 1932. Before that
day the somewhat stark outlines of the massive new
playhouse had been subjected to a great deal of
abusive criticism. The previous theatre had represented the "knobs-on" style of fussy Victorian roman-
ticism: the present one is perhaps too typical of the
"anti-knob" functionalism of the nineteen-twenties.
A tower might relieve the huge, flat roof which has
evoked angry and repeated comparisons with a jam
factory. (Why, by the way, are jam factories supposed
to look worse than any others?) The red-brick
exterior certainly suits the mellow tints of Stratford's
rufous Waterside, and, when flood-lit at night, it can
appease even those who most dislike its utilitarian
severity by day. Mr. Eric Kennington's sculptures,
on the façade wall, have won general praise. The
interior decoration was far more popular and the
seating was blessedly comfortable. Perfection was no
more to be expected in every detail of the theatre
than in any other elaborate structure. Some features,
such as the acoustics in the stalls, have been criticised,
but, on the whole, the playgoer gets an excellent deal.
There is no better gallery in the country for sight,
hearing and general amenity. The poor playgoer,
whatever his choice of seat, has a really good bargain
and can take his glass of beer in a superb eyrie with a
lovely view over the Avon. Incidentally, this is the

only theatre in the world where it is possible to see eight Shakespeare plays in one week.

The official defence of the building is worth quoting: "It usually happens that the working parts of a theatre, the stage, with its great height, the dressing-rooms, carpenter's shops and stores are hidden away, leaving to the outside view only one façade between other buildings. In this case, owing to its isolated position, the whole theatre is visible from either side, and this is a reason, not perhaps fully realised, why this theatre has met with criticisms that might have been withheld had people understood the requirements which had to be met. In all matters concerning the external design and internal decorations the Architects have had a perfectly free hand. The Governors have consistently refrained from any interference in this respect. Any other course must have led to confusion, for opinions in regard to taste are bound to differ. This is exemplified by the fact that Miss Scott's design has evoked extremes of praise and the reverse. The Governors felt that they could not do better than rely on the judgment of the Royal Institute of British Architects."

Stratford can never have been more crowded than on that April day of the great re-opening in 1932. All hotel rooms had been booked well in advance. The proceedings were to be broadcast nationally. The Press of the world was there. The traffic was on a London scale. The weather, which has often maltreated Stratford on its high days and holidays, was bitterly cold and sleety showers drifted across a town beflagged. Foreign delegates, in unprecedented numbers, might well have preferred snow-caps to their ceremonial top-hats as they shivered in their respectable black overcoats. However, the flags were successfully hoisted in Bridge Street, the Procession to the Church was celebrated with full musical and floral honours, and then a Great Public Luncheon was held in a marquee, since there was no room big enough to hold all who wished to attend. It was no day for the tented field, but appetites had been nipped to keenness by the wind and food and wine were welcome. The oratory, however, as so often happens, outran the public need and demand for it. Sir Archibald Flower, who had been justly knighted in 1932, was very properly once more the Mayor of Stratford in this august year and had an embarrassing time as Chairman. Mr. Baldwin started off well and discharged some of his usual and well-approved line of "Old England" sentiments, but was handicapped because a previous speaker had somewhat lost his sense of situation and so rambled at length and at large as to knock the time-table sideways. Poor Sir Archibald, who had to meet the Prince of Wales now arriving by air and naturally could not keep Royalty on the mat, had to rise and leave the table early.

Meanwhile the wind was blowing keenly down the river on which the Swans of Avon had mustered in

full force to see what all this crowd was about and
what it had to distribute in the way of broken bread.
The more notable members of the public were
admitted to stand in the biting wind upon the steps
of the theatre. They were close to the microphone
into which H.R.H. the Prince of Wales delivered,
somewhat nervously, a speech on the Immortal Bard
and Bardic matters in general, a subject which may
not have been as familiar or congenial to the speaker
as others which overtook him in his way of duty.
However, he went gamely through with it and paid a
just compliment to the American support, and then
all who had seats hurried after the Prince into the
pleasantly warm and comfortable theatre where Miss
Lillah McCarthy recited the Poet Laureate's lines of
greeting and the company were ready with "Henry
IV," Part I. (Part II was given at night.) This excellent, but extremely English, drama can never have
been played before a more august, varied, or cosmo-
politan audience. What all the Foreign Eminences
made of the quarrelsome barons and the conversa-
tional methods of Falstaff and his fellows will never
be known. They sat there apparently undismayed.
Gradually, however, Public Business began to call
them and a stream of imposing motor-cars was slip-
ping out upon the London Road somewhat before
the performance was over.

It was not, it could not be, a good performance.
The actors were naturally nervous, the great ones

in the stalls remained politely inanimate, thawing
torpidly after their stance upon the windy steps outside. The play is not an easy one, and it was suddenly discovered that, however pleasant to the eye the
interior of the theatre might be, it is no easy place for
the comedian to practise his craft. The sliding stages,
by which changes of scene are introduced, make it
impossible to bring a "set" well forward and it is no
easy business to project Elizabethan drama, written
for an apron-stage, from the compromise-stage of
Stratford. The absence of boxes, so common in
modern theatres, creates a difficult gap between stage
and audience and actors at Stratford often complain
of the difficulty of getting contact with and so captur-
ing their "house." It was a difficulty immediately
patent on that first afternoon. There is no more
tricky form of architecture than theatrical construction, so many needs (of the fire-brigade and the caterer
as well as of the actor and the æsthete) have to be
accommodated. Miss Scott had had to meet all sorts
of demands and face all sorts of difficulties of which
many of her critics were totally ignorant. It is easy
to be wise after such events.

When all criticisms have been passed, the fact
remains. The New Theatre at Stratford has been
triumphantly popular. It immediately took its place
as one of the major assets of the Shakespeare Industry.
It became one of the Sights and the public have been
admitted to its splendours at a shilling a head. These

bob-a-nob visitors have evidently agreed that they received their money's worth. Let the figures speak.

The numbers attending plays in the theatre have been since the opening:

1932   115,148
1933   133,705
1934   147,834
1935   150,822
1936   193,362
1937   188,651
1938   181,134

The numbers of those visiting the theatre were naturally greatest at first, but they have remained impressive:

1932   73,800
1933   52,000
1934   43,250
1935   42,750
1936   41,300
1937   35,500
1938   31,000

The superior folk in London first laughed at Stratford's temerity in building on so large a scale, i.e., to hold 1,100. (The old Memorial Theatre had held 850.) Yet soon so many were being turned away disappointed that a large sum had to be spent on extending the excellent gallery to hold 450 instead of 300. The price of admission to the gallery is 1s. 3d., and the Governors regard it as a really important part of the house. Other additions have been made since 1932, especially in the matter of refreshment terraces overlooking the river. Moreover, it is no longer a Summer-and-Shakespeare house only. Stratford, owing to the accessibility given it by the motor-car and the allure for Midlanders of play-going in a really comfortable theatre (perhaps after a good dinner in the theatre restaurant), has become an important winter "date," and touring companies are only too glad to put in a week or a fortnight by the Avon, where only sixty years ago it was deemed hopeless optimism to look even for one or two Shakespearean audiences at the April Festival. Should the D'Oyly Carte company arrive on a dank November day with Gilbert & Sullivan it may be as difficult to book a seat for "The Yeomen of the Guard" as to get entrance at the last minute for a favourite Shakespeare comedy on Birthday Night.

So there it stands, the Industry's chief modern exhibit. The best views of it are from upstream, across the lovely sweep of the old Clopton Bridge which Shakespeare must have crossed so often; the best time is at evening when the slanting rays incarnadine the brick-work and put a Tudor scarlet, solid, beef-eaterish and comforting, upon the building and the scene. Or later, with a moon above and man's artifice of light up-sprinkled from below, it can ride the river with a castle's majesty: the lamps of Water-side lead witchingly to the church and the plash of water on a summer's night may well incline a visitor to prefer an evening stroll and a glass at a riverside tavern to another evening at the play. Yet he need not feel that theatre-attendance in Stratford is just a clocking-in at culture's drill-hall, the answering of duty's roll, or a work of poetry alone. He can sit soft and be enfolded with good sights and lovely sounds, Verona's lyric passion, Illyrian Feste singing of the wind and the rain, and English Bottom in the moon-struck Grecian wood. After all, no other jam factory provides such sweets as these.

CHAPTER XIV

GRAND NATIONAL

"And while the vain world careless sped
Unheeding the heroic name,
The souls most fed with Shakespeare's flame
Still sat unconquered in a ring,
Remembering him like anything."
—G. K. CHESTERTON, *The Shakespeare Memorial.*

THE desirability of a National Theatre seems self-evident to most nations. The British and Americans are supposed to be so rooted in individualism that they cannot endure the thought of public money being devoted to the drama, or public responsibility being taken in any way for the goings-on of actors and their kind. The Puritan tradition in both countries has certainly strengthened the dislike of a National Theatre. If the Theatre is the abode of Satan, surely the honest taxpayer should not help to pay the rent.

That argument, supposedly taken from national tradition, omits the fact that the drama once throve on the patronage and protection of the Crown and that Shakespeare himself, like Molière in France later on, was one of the King's Men. These actors had some social status simply because of that royal connection. Through the Lord Chamberlain the Monarchy has continually concerned itself with our national drama: the trouble has been, in recent times, the hostile and hampering nature of that solicitude. James I spent lavishly on plays and masques at Court, so that his Lord Chamberlain was once valuable in promoting drama; but this official became, under the Georges, a Censor careful to pare the drama's claws and clip its wings by forbidding all political allusion. From politics the Victorians extended the ban to morals.

It is ridiculous to talk about the age-long individualism of our British Drama, which actually grew up under royal favour (the Globe of the King's Men could at least be said to foreshadow a National Theatre), and has since been carefully watched and schooled by the Crown. Now that the affairs of the Crown are so much more merged with those of the Community, and Crown Lands are National Property, it is plain that the Lord Chamberlain, who disciplines our drama, is a Public Official. He is, indeed, a member of the Government. Therefore the idea that we must have no "national action" in our theatre because it is against national tradition is pure nonsense. The British State, at present, does quite a deal about the drama. It censors it, submits it to special and oppressive taxation, and does as much as it can to impede it while actually giving special protective legislation to the film-trade!

Accordingly, to ask for a National Theatre, as a token of State recognition for a great art, in which the

British have conspicuously shone both as writers and actors, is not revolutionary. It is merely to demand a reversal of the Puritan habit and to ask for renewed State patronage of Shakespeare's own profession instead of that persecution to which the Hanoverian hatred of free speech and the Victorian distrust of free conduct subjected the writers and the players from Fielding's time to our own.

The agitation for a National Theatre was heard in mid-Victorian England, when Matthew Arnold, in his campaign against Philistinism, included the theatre as a vessel of light. Impressed by the example of the Comédie-Française, he wrote: "We have in England everything to make us dissatisfied with the chaotic and ineffective condition into which our stage has fallen. We have the remembrance of better things in the past, and the elements for better things in the future. We have a splendid national drama of the Elizabethan age, and a later drama which has no lack of pieces conspicuous by their stage qualities, their vivacity and their talent, and interesting by their pictures of manners. We have had great actors. We have good actors not a few at the present moment. But we have been unlucky, as we so often are, in the work of organisation. . . . It seems to me that everyone of us is concerned to find a remedy for this melancholy state of things, and that the pleasure we have had in the visit of the French company is barren unless it leaves us with the impulse to do so, and with the lesson how alone it can be rationally done. 'Forget'—can we not hear those fine artists saying in an undertone to us amidst their graceful compliments of adieu?—'forget your clap-trap, and believe that the State, the nation in its collective and corporate character, does well to concern itself about an influence so important to national life and manners as the theatre. . . . The people *will* have the theatre; then make it a good one. . . . The theatre is irresistible; organise the theatre." Public opinion found Arnold's enthusiasm all too easy to resist. Nothing was done for some time.

Early in the twentieth century a National Theatre Committee (*not* a Shakespeare Memorial Committee) was set up, and for it the great critic and Ibsenite, William Archer, and the brilliant new arrival on our stage, H. Granville-Barker, actor, author and producer and leader of the advanced Edwardian theatre, drew up a booklet called *A Scheme and Estimates for a National Theatre*. Many leaders of dramatic work in all its branches—Henry Irving, Squire Bancroft, J. M. Barrie, Henry Arthur Jones and Arthur Pinero—allowed their names to be associated with this pamphlet and expressed the opinion "that such an institution is urgently needed." It was hoped that, thus encouraged, some benevolent millionaire might find the necessary £350,000. Andrew Carnegie was approached by William Archer, acting as the Drama's Border Raider. But the Scottish pleader made no impression on the walls of Skibo Castle. Carnegie might be generous to Stratford, but he was not impressed by London's need.

A publisher of public spirit, Messrs. Duckworth, was persuaded to issue a little book on the subject. Perhaps it would catch the eye of the much-needed millionaire who would be moved to assist or, as Mr. Barker puts it, "do the needful." Millionaires, evidently, were not susceptible. None came forward and the Barker-Archer work appeared to be in vain. The first Committee was, however, grateful for the suggestions which these two had outlined, for they formed the basis of the discussions. In a very short time, however, the estimates were quite out of date. Prices had begun to rise—even before the war—and the optimistic scheme had to be temporarily dropped. The Committee remained in existence and, from time to time, deliberated.

Shakespeare, originally, had no place in the scheme of things, except for the acting of his plays. He came into the plans because another august Committee had been formed in 1904 with the express purpose of erecting a National Shakespeare Memorial. Here indeed were the glories of our blood and State. Among its members were the Prime Minister (Mr. Balfour), the Lord Chief Justice, the Archbishops of Canterbury and Westminster, the Chief Rabbi, Lord Roberts, the Ambassadors of all the countries of Europe, of the United States, and of China and Japan, and the Agents-General of all the English-speaking nations overseas. Sir Henry Irving and George Meredith were also supporters. Drama and poetry had their distinguished representation. At the name of Shakespeare everyone applauded. The inaugural meeting at the Mansion House was a great occasion.

It was at first proposed that the Memorial should consist of "an architectural monument (including a statue)," and that, "should a surplus of funds permit, a small theatre for the furtherance of dramatic art and literature, and for the performance of Elizabethan and other plays, might be erected on land adjoining." Later it was agreed that the most appropriate memorial to Shakespeare was a great theatre, in whose repertory his works should hold a steady and sovereign position. This view so appealed to the supporters of a National Theatre that the amalgamation of the two movements became inevitable. The two Committees met and decided to unite and achieve their aims jointly. The erection of the Memorial and the erection of the Theatre were both to be carried out in the name of Shakespeare. (Its title, "The Shakespeare Memorial National Theatre," can be confusing to the general public who, as far as a Shakespeare Memorial is concerned, may think in terms of Stratford or even of the "Old Vic." The National Theatre Committee are, evidently, aware of this misunderstanding and are altering by degrees their title to "The National Theatre founded in the name of Shakespeare.")

Next, Fleet Street, as represented by the *Daily Chronicle,* organised an Honorary Committee in 1908. The *Chronicle's* dramatic critic of that time, S. R. Littlewood, had been a lifelong enthusiast for the National Theatre. This Committee called a public meeting at the Lyceum Theatre. Over two thousand people assembled, including hundreds of men and women distinguished in literature, art and many fields. of public work.

A united General Committee, representative of the two movements, was appointed as Executive Committee. To this Committee was entrusted the drawing up of the scheme and constitution. This was sanctioned at a meeting of the General Committee, held at the Mansion House on March 28th, 1909, at which it was announced that an anonymous donor had contributed Seventy Thousand Pounds towards the sum required by the estimates. When anonymity was withdrawn the Maecenas turned out to be Carl Meyer, afterwards Sir Carl. This seemed likely to set things moving, but Meyer's example was not infectious and the English millionaires held back. The Committee proposed the building of a National Theatre in London within seven years, so as to have it ready for the Shakespeare Tercentenary in 1916. £50,000 of the £70,000 bought a site in Bloomsbury in 1909, just behind the British Museum. Then came the war and again the Committee was frustrated. During this period the site was rented to the American Red Cross, for an annual figure of about £3,000, and used for "The Shakespeare Hut," whither came soldiers on leave for entertainment and refreshment.

After the war the Committee found that building costs had risen disastrously: it had its site and a little money, but not nearly enough to build. It therefore adopted the seemingly sensible policy of running a mobile theatrical company with Shakespeare as the basis. Accordingly the New Shakespeare Company came into being with W. Bridges Adams as Director and W. H. Savery as General Manager. This Company was to run the Stratford Summer Festival of 1919 and also to go on tour, financed by the income derived from the rent and other sources. To conduct its Stratford work a sub-committee of the National Theatre Committee was formed, representing the National Theatre Committee and the Stratford Memorial Theatre Governors.

The work of the New Shakespeare Company was much approved, especially by those critics of a National Theatre in London who said that a truly National Theatre to Shakespeare would be a Company touring nationally. London already had plenty of Shakespeare, whereas, with the rapidly spreading invasion of the "pictures," the country was being starved of the drama, especially of a classic kind.

In the early part of 1922 the Committee decided

to share their annual income between the New Shakespeare Company and the "Old Vic." Just at this time
the Bloomsbury site was disposed of, and whilst legal
matters were being settled the parent body were
advised, by the Charity Commissioners, that they
could not dispose of their income in touring ventures.
The New Shakespeare Company had taken to the
road as well as supplying Stratford with its essential
summer Festival. So the proposed payments for the
two companies concerned fell through and the
National Theatre Committee was left with its capital,
but no site, and no immediate prospects of finding
another Meyer or setting the builders to work.

The interference of the legal experts meant that
the National Theatre Committee was now unable to
command a company. It had seen this company as the
nucleus of that greater band which, in due course,
would occupy the stage of their ideal theatre. It also
meant that Stratford found itself, without any warn-
ing, bereft of its actors. The direct outcome was that
the Stratford-upon-Avon Festival Company came into
existence under the management of the Governors.
Previously this body had been theatre-managers only,
engaging a theatrical company to perform the plays.
Now they became managers of the Company as
well.

The National Theatre Committee made various
efforts to stimulate the sluggish sympathies of the
public. Support for a National Theatre, in London,

is by no means unanimous, even among those who might be expected to favour it. Some theatrical managers dislike the idea of a subsidised rival. Some actors fear the dead hand of bureaucracy. Some authors are individualists to the end. Still, there was a tremendous turn-out of stage players for a Shakespeare Matinée at Drury Lane, organised with characteristic energy by Mr. Sydney Carroll on behalf of the National Theatre Appeal Committee. The bill consisted of Shakespearean Snippets and Shakespearean Snippets tend to be a bore at their best. Not all were at their best on this occasion and the programme did seem to go on for a very long time. While funds were raised, enthusiasm was not.

Meanwhile the capital sum accumulated gradually and the Committee was much strengthened by the increased time now given to it by Mr. Geoffrey Whitworth, who had proved his capacity as an organiser by his skilful as well as unremitting service to the British Drama League. Throughout its life the National Theatre Movement has been fortunate in the zeal of its members, but public apathy has made its work extremely hard. Londoners are notoriously short of civic spirit and it is difficult to persuade a citizen of Tyneside or Clydeside or even Deeside to subscribe for yet another playhouse on the distant Thames.

A fresh and spectacular move, however, was soon made. A site in the Royal Borough of Kensington

(South) was purchased and the choice was at once attacked by those who spoke of it as Museumland and discussed as absurd the idea of a National Theatre without a central location. The Committee could plead the excellence of the site's communications, the suitability of the price, the difficulty of finding an alternative, and the reasonableness of dodging the enormous rents, rates, and overheads of the Shaftesbury Avenue area.

The Committee then had to enter upon long negotiations with the London County Council before anything could be done in the way of designing the theatre. There also was much debate as to whether there should be a competition for the architect, or whether they should appoint one architect directly. The advantages of an architectural competition are obvious, but the disadvantages are considerable. One cannot always be sure that the winning design will meet the needs of the theatre. Theatre-building is an extremely technical matter, and any competition has to be conducted by an outside Board of Assessors appointed by the Royal Institute of British Architects. It is true that a competition may discover an unknown genius. On the other hand, the most eminent architects do not, as a rule, enter for competitions. After viewing the position from all sides, and being fully conscious of the merits of a competition, the Executive Committee finally decided to appoint Sir Edwin Lutyens, with Mr. Cecil Masey as his technical colleague. Mr. Masey has a very wide experience of theatre construction and Sir Edwin is not only President of the Royal Academy but the present acknowledged master of domestic, commercial, and governmental buildings in all forms. He also designed the Cenotaph.

So, on a rather dull and draughty afternoon in the spring of 1938, an assemblage of theatrical notables, pressmen, photographers, and others gathered in Cromwell Gardens before moving on to tea and buns in a neighbouring hotel. They descended into a hole in the road behind a wooden palisade, where there was the customary battery of cameras ready. Here the National Theatre is to rise, when the funds permit. And it is open to those who criticise the site of this hole to stop making jokes about museums and find a "better 'ole" at the price. On that afternoon Mr. Bernard Shaw, after doing some ceremonial things with site-deeds and twigs and sods of earth in his best mulberry-planting manner, advised the company to accept the public apathy as normal and go straight ahead. "People ask me," he said, " 'Do the English people want a National Theatre?' Of course they do not. They never want anything. They have a British Museum, but they never wanted it. They have Westminster Abbey. They never wanted it, but now that it stands there, a mysterious phenomenon that came to them in some sort of fashion, they quite approve of it and feel the place would be incomplete without it. What we have to do is to produce this phenomenon."

The argument was that, once you have forced on the community some good thing which it does not want, it will be compelled by shame into maintaining that good thing later on, just as the British people now keep the National Gallery and the British Museum. This policy, in brief, is to present the tax-payers with a handsome baby and then leave it to them to hold, should the infant have no legacy or silver spoon in its mouth. But, of course, that is not a necessary view. Some would not build a National Theatre until enough has been collected to endow it privately. In either case it is noticeable that the British National Theatre, thus envisaged, is in origin not a State Theatre at all but a private gift to the public. Opinions differ as to what should follow. Can the public then be cajoled into supplying its gift-horse with the necessary oats? Mr. Shaw thinks that it can.

Meanwhile, the campaign goes briskly on. The Committee is a strong one and there are no jealousies between it and the administrators of Stratford and the "Old Vic." Indeed, the Chairman of the Shakespeare Memorial National Theatre Committee is the Earl of Lytton, who is also Chairman of the "Old Vic's" Board of Governors, while the Stratford Governors are represented by Sir Archibald Flower and others of their body, including Mr. Whitworth.

A special campaign was started for the endowment of seats in the National Theatre in honour of famous persons, especially of famous persons connected with the stage. Some of the endowments are very interesting. Two famous critics, Clement Scott and J. T. Grein, were thus fittingly remembered by Lord Camrose and Lord Kemsley, the present proprietors of their newspapers, the *Daily Telegraph* and the *Sunday Times,* while the family of C. E. Montague of the *Manchester Guardian* were responsible for a seat in his name. The Earl of Lytton honoured his grandfather, the great Bulwer Lytton. Lord Esher chose Nell Gwynne. Mr. Bernard Shaw named Barry Sullivan "the travelling tragedian," who was connected with the first Stratford Festivals. Lady Astor endowed a seat for her native Virginia, an interesting point because, as we saw, Shakespeare was so closely in touch with the founders of the Virginia Company and thus made a species of American contact. The great Danish dancer, Genée, now Madame Genée-Isitt, gave a seat to honour the Kronborg of Elsinore, Hamlet's home, of which we shall have more to say. Many others have thus paid tribute to dead relatives of distinction or poet-dramatists of Shakespeare's time. Among living recipients of the honour is Sir Seymour Hicks. And there, as they say and while we write, the matter rests. There are a site, some funds, and high hopes of an early start. The National Theatre founded in Shakespeare's name can hardly be said, as yet, to stand. But it is considerably nearer to arising than ever before. Its enemies, we fancy, may have soon to look it in the face. Its face, since Sir Edwin Lutyens and Mr. Masey will be the fashioners, should be a fair one and able to confront with pride the dreaming spires of South Kensington.

CHAPTER XV

OUTWARD, ONWARD, UPWARD

"There's hope a great man's memory
May outlive his life half a year."
—*Hamlet*, III, 2.

REALLY there is no escaping William Shakespeare now. Ether joins land and water as his kingdom. Broadcasting, nimble as Puck himself, as swift and invisible as Ariel, puts its girdle round the earth and runs upon the sharp winds. Broadcasting of Shakespearean plays has been a regular feature of B.B.C. programmes and, by choosing Sunday afternoons, the directors have been able to recruit casts of exceptional power. Now Shakespeare has been televised as well, "Othello" being an early choice for this approved experiment. Then again while we listened on a recent Boxing Night to the "ace" of American Broadcasters, Mr. Alexander Woolcott, expounding the sad life and sweet songs of Stephen Foster, we suddenly heard the speaker introduce his theme by a quotation from Heminge and Condell and their preface to Shakespeare's First Folio. That Columbia has long hailed Warwickshire and sent its pilgrims in the steps of Washington Irving, whose name now marks the largest hotel in Stratford-upon-Avon, we have already seen: we have noted too that loyalty in far-flung Texas which finds so puissant a magic in the Stratford earth and Avon water that it will import the same, consigned and sealed by authority, for the fructification of drama in the West.

An interesting side-line of the Shakespearean fervour and the Shakespearean Industry has been the tendency to extend the cult and commerce, which have a natural home on the banks of Avon and of Thames, to places and lands about which the poet merely happened to write. It is not enough to celebrate the composition of "Romeo and Juliet" and of "Hamlet" in Stratford and London: the veneration must extend to Verona and to Elsinore. Nearly thirty years ago Verona made its gesture of gratitude for the fame conferred upon it by erecting a statue of Shakespeare, standing by the reputed tomb of Juliet. This work, by Renato Cattani, has not sufficed. Even the recent divergences between Shakespeare's land and Juliet's in matters of foreign policy, even the anti-British feeling avowed by the imposition of "sanctions," did not deter the Veronese from further acts of homage. Verona is now instituting a Shakespeare Museum; its first exhibit might well be a brace of Stuffed Gentlemen to match the stuffed alligator favoured by Romeo's chemist.

In this Verona is the companion or rival

of Elsinore,* where the recent performances, with international star-actors, of "Hamlet" in the castle-yard, have been so well attended that further Danish gestures of veneration are in hand. The royal castle of Elsinore had nothing to do with the original Amleth, a Prince of Jutland whose life is buried in the mists of the tenth century and its Nordic Sagas. Elsinore is in Seeland and the Castle was, in fact, just being built when Shakespeare was writing "Hamlet." He turned the Jutlander into a nobleman of the Restoration, who returns to Denmark as a University Man (M.A. Hons. Wittenberg?) with a somewhat surprising knowledge of London theatre politics in the year 1600. None the less, Hamlet and Elsinore are so closely associated in the common mind all over the world that, since the former is generally accepted as the greatest of Shakespeare's characters, the latter naturally tends to become one of the holiest plots of all Shakespearean ground. It has been suggested that Shakespeare may have visited Elsinore with a troupe of actors and thence picked up some of his local information, i.e., about the heavy drinking of the Danes, a point which was tactfully dropped from the Folio of 1623, because a Danish lady was then Queen of England. On the other hand, if Shakespeare had been to Elsinore he would scarcely have made Horatio mention "Yon high eastward hill," for the neighbour-

---

* Helsingor in Danish. For convenience we retain the Shakespearean form.

ing coast of Southern Sweden is extremely flat and
he could not possibly have seen

> "the dreadful summit of the cliff
> That beetles o'er his base into the sea."

The sea-walls of the castle are comparatively low and
there is no sign of a summit. Whether Shakespeare
went to Elsinore or not, there, to the general delight,
does his fame go marching on. So do the pilgrims.
The Danes are determined to satisfy their visitors'
thirst for knowledge about Amleth of Jutland, son
of Horwendil and Gerutha and slayer of Horwendil's
usurping murderer Feng, and also about that wise
and witty and world-conquering gentleman and
master of the English tongue, our own Shakespearean
Hamlet, slayer of Claudius and Prince in Denmark.
Elsinore's Kronborg is at present mainly used as a
maritime museum, but, suffering a land-change, it is
to have a Hamlet Section.

The participation of Denmark in the Shakespeare
Industry was, in the long run, as inevitable as it was
just. The Danes are people of great taste, as all are
aware who have enjoyed their food and their
furniture. When it became apparent that the Port
and Castle of Elsinore must at long last be "featured"
as, in their tongue, a considerable "Shakespeare-
Minder" (Shakespeare-memento), the Danes went
very decently about the work of "minding."

They—

"Nothing common did or mean
Upon that memorable scene."

A charming people, they went gracefully into action.
Elsinore, now an hour or so's journey north of
Copenhagen through woodlands, park, and pleasant
sea-shore villadom, is a harbour and ship-building
town with some clang of industry, some agreeable old
squares and streets, and the Renaissance Kronborg
dominating the little peninsula which juts out toward
the Swedish shore. About a mile from the Kronborg
is a piece of rising woodland looking out over the
narrow water which parts Denmark from Sweden.
This was once the monastery garden of the Blessed
St. Anna, but it became, as did so much monastic
property in Protestant countries, Crown Land. It was
used as the site of a Country Palace, and the pleasant
eighteenth-century building was called Marienlyst by
the Dowager Queen in 1767. (Marienlyst is the
Danish for "sea-pleasure.") The Danish monarchy has
been extremely generous in its gifts of land, and the
huge royal deer forest at Klampenborg, six miles
north of Copenhagen, has been turned, for example,
into one of the loveliest and best-timbered commons
in the world: its noble beech-woods and open grass-
lands are much used by the Danes for riding, golf,
and family junketing of all kinds.

True to tradition, the monarchy handed over
Elsinore's Country Palace of Marienlyst to serve as a

public hospital in 1848. But it was found unsuitable. The municipality of Elsinore acquired the estate and made a public park of it. Then, being made forcibly aware of the Shakespeare Industry by the influx of Hamlet-hungry tourists, the townsfolk realised that something had to be done. So, while the building of the Country Palace was used as a museum for the display of domestic crafts, the grounds suddenly became "Hamlet's Garden." A notice at the gate now announces, in four languages, that "The surroundings which inspired the poet have been preserved through the succeeding centuries." That Shakespeare ever visited or was inspired by Elsinore is, as we saw, pure guess-work. However, the garden itelf, with its trimmed hedge of beech and yew and elaborate patterns of box-bordering, is simple and serene; the lawns are beautifully kept and one can easily imagine a performance of "Twelfth Night" or "Much Ado" being delightfully staged there on one of those evenings of high summer when the light never wholly fades from the steel-blue bowl of the Scandinavian sky and all natural features stand out in that dry, clear air, with a clarity which has a kind of magic most theatrical.

On the sea-shore in front of Hamlet's Garden stands the famous hotel of Marienlyst, once the summer resort of the Russian aristocracy as well as of the local nobility and gentry. Traces of its grandeur still remain. Here alone, for example, in Denmark is

Public Gaming still permitted. But the Dane likes no flaunting of a lordly extravagance. The Little Horses circulate nightly in summer between the respectable hours of eight and ten and the odds are so discouraging (six to one for a winner, with nine horses starting) that only "mad dogs and Englishmen" are likely to play for more than a casual throw. Marienlyst, however, is not all gaming and gaiety. Here, too, Hamlet is remembered and if, in utter despair at your gaming losses, you go forth to seek a diet of worms in the garden, you may do so at Hamlet's feet. For in the grounds stands a modern statue of the Prince under which is intimated, in English, that he is once more asking his all-too-familiar question about the relative values of being and not-being.

The Prince is habited Elizabethanly. The feature which especially distinguishes this statue by Herr Frank is the presence of a moustache without beard. That Hamlet was conceived and performed as a bearded fellow the text implies and a beard was the common wear of a young nobleman in 1600. But the moustache is certainly odd. There is now to be a new statue in bronze of Hamlet and Ophelia by Herr Tegner, in the public gardens. Herr Tegner has offered the statue free and incidental costs of erection are likely to be borne by the Carlsberg Foundation, to which the profits of the Carlsberg Brewery now flow. In Denmark the beer is excellent in itself and a source of excellence in civic life. The more Carlsberg you drink (and a most agreeable lager it is) the more do you endow science, learning, and works of art. In the solution of the "liquor problem" Denmark certainly has given the world a civilised and prudent lead. Since the proper honouring of Shakespeare in his own town has been so largely dependent on the public spirit of a brewing family, it is interesting to find the same genial industry assisting the cult, along with all other forms of art and knowledge, upon the Danish shore of the Sound.

There remains the matter of Hamlet's Grave. Tomb-lust is a strong form of human appetite. A shrine without a grave is deemed utterly deficient by sightseeing man and so many visitors have demanded Hamlet's Grave almost with menaces that the Elsinore wing of the Shakespeare Industry has naturally had to produce some sort of visible and tangible response. The answer is an astonishing-looking object in the Marienlyst Park. It seems to be a genuine antique. It is a stone coffer with strange carvings. On one side a lion appears to be devouring a pregnant snake. On the other a sea-horse with the wings of a bird and a fish's tail is in full gallop. This panel chiefly suggests a collision between a Derby winner and the Loch Ness Monster. What is really buried or contained therein is a mystery: some rudely say a cat. When Sarah Bernhardt, on her pilgrimage to Elsinore, saw this object, she received "a sorrowful impression." "It

HAMLET'S (OR THE CAT'S) GRAVE AT ELSINORE

did not seem to be genuine at all," she wrote. "On the journey home I stood dejectedly on the deck. Do not let us talk any more about Hamlet's empty grave, but about Hamlet's living castle and let us make it Hamlet's real castle."

To that end, the celebration of a Shakespearean shrine with a Shakespeare play, Denmark has recently striven with great success. In June, 1937, the English "Old Vic" Company headed by Miss Baylis, Mr. Tyrone Guthrie, who had directed "Hamlet" brilliantly in the spring, and Mr. Laurence Olivier, who had given a no less brilliant rendering of Hamlet's part, accepted an invitation to give open-air performances in the Court-yard of Kronborg. The usual curse of bad weather, which seems well-nigh inevitable at Shakespearean revels, descended upon the company, who had to rehearse all night and later to act in driving rain upon a soaked and slippery platform in the vast cobbled yard which can, in gusty weather, house those nipping airs mentioned in the text. One especially remembers Miss Baylis very busy with hot coffee and good cheer. It may indeed be a chilly spot, fit for such ghostly walkings as Claudius was wont to undertake. On the first night, when an august company, including the Crown Prince of Denmark, was expected, the performance was washed out altogether and the players, with great spirit, retired to their hotel, the Marienlyst, and there gallantly improvised a presentation in the ballroom, using its little cabaret-stage and the floor-space immediately below it.

This was, in fact, to repeat the Elizabethan model of the mummers on the road. The players had come to Elsinore: they dressed up and clapped to it like charade-players in a drawing-room. They had had no rehearsal in the room which they were using. Shakespeare's plays were written for any sort of circumstance and they stand up to this kind of spontaneous, let's-pretend method of staging better than they do to heavily scenic and elaborated presentations. All present on that night agreed that it was a most moving and exciting performance. The Danes are first-rate linguists, so much so that they might almost be called a section of the English-speaking Union. True, Shakespeare's English is by no means ours, but with a little preparatory reading-up the play was well followed and much appreciated. Later, with a lift in the weather, it could be acted in the great court of the Kronborg, as had been the purpose all along. It was hoped that in the following year Mr. Leslie Howard would be able to give his "Hamlet" there, but he could not make the necessary arrangements, so Germany intervened with its own Prince of Denmark. Herr Gustav Grundgens, a distinguished German actor, was the chief figure of the second Elsinore Festival which took place in July, 1938.

Needless to say, the British Empire has not been far behind in acknowledging the Bard. Not only has Shakespeare followed the Flag: he has, with the aid of the British Empire Shakespearean Society, assisted in carrying the best of English poetry to the farthest verges of the far-flung culture-line. This Society was founded in 1901, partly because Sir Henry Irving, its first President, said that the world needed it. Mr. Acton-Bond, its first Director and now a Vice-President, has put an enormous amount of work into its affairs. It is its special object to stimulate local Shakespeareans to read and perform the plays and to respect Shakespeare's language by cultivating a good, vigorous diction. South Africa and New Zealand have their branches and a membership of nearly 10,000 has been reached. One of the strongest centres has been Sheffield, where a membership of 1,000 was reached a year or two after the foundation of the branch. Stratfordians may be interested to learn that, under the Society's auspices, Mr. and Mrs. A. D. Flower (now Sir Archibald and Lady Flower) performed on the stage of Stratford's old Memorial Theatre, the former as Antonio in "Twelfth Night" and the latter as Portia.

The Tercentenary of Shakespeare fell during the war. It was celebrated by the B.E.S.S. with a tremendous effort in aid of the Red Cross and War Relief organisations. The Society organised the Shakespeare Festival of Mercy and distributed for sale on behalf of the charities concerned millions of Shakespeare Medallions, that is, miniature reproductions of the Droeshout Portrait with a pin for attachment to

the coat. A fund was raised so that every London
County Council schoolchild should wear the
Medallion on April 23rd, 1916. Very large sums were
raised all over the country and overseas—in Pretoria,
Cape Town, Toronto, and Christchurch. Much abuse
has been hurled at the Droeshout effigy, but, during
the war, it served.

Shakespeare's American contacts have already had a
chapter to themselves. Hollywood's approach to Stratford's "Monarch of the Mind" still remains to be
described. A play combining sex and sadism was
naturally the first to attract the film-mind. An early
silent picture of "The Taming of the Shrew" was
made and followed by a talkie version, featuring Miss
Pickford and Mr. Fairbanks. An English music-hall
comedian, when asked to guy this, replied that bur-
lesquing a burlesque was not his idea of fun. Warner
Brothers next encouraged Reinhardt to make a picture of "A Midsummer Night's Dream" and, needless to say, no expense was spared. This excursion
of the camera into fairyland won some praise as well
as sneers, but the public did not encourage Warner
Brothers to encourage Reinhardt to go any farther
in this direction. Then Metro-Goldwyn came along
with its Hollywood Verona, featuring Mr. Leslie
Howard and Miss Norma Shearer as Romeo and
Juliet. This picture was notable for many things. On
the credit side was the decorative work of Mr. Oliver
Messel. Mr. Howard, a very quiet and rather passion-

less and unpoetical Romeo, had his handicaps to face.
He was, for example, first discovered amid a flock of
sheep. Presumably Mr. Thalberg, the director, had
some sheep handy and meant to use them, although
the unforeseeing Shakespeare had made no allowance
for Love among the Fat Stock. The Publicity
displayed the caption:

> "Boy Meets Girl, 1436.
> Romeo and Juliet, 1936."

and also contained, under Mr. Thalberg's signature,
the unforgettable remark:

> "But Shakespeare did more than write a perfect
> scenario. He wrote magnificent poetry."

Hollywood was learning things. Yet evidently Shakespeare's talent as a film-scribe was, if perfect, still inadequate for Metro-Goldwyn, who further employed
for screen-adaptation Mr. Talbot Jennings and as
Literary Consultant, Professor William Strunk, Jr.
The latter's initials at least were on the right lines.

The preparation was tremendous. Miss Shearer was
cast as Juliet. "Then," we were told, "began one of
the most rigorous novitiates since the time of Ignatius
Loyola. Miss Shearer retired into the Italy of the
15th century. . . . Practically nothing that a girl
of fourteen of that day would have thought, known

or done remained foreign to Miss Shearer." While Miss Shearer was completing her omniscience and her Experiment with Time, Metro-Goldwyn were preparing 60,000 square feet of plaster, 75,000 feet of heavy lumber, 35,000 square feet of composition board, 24,000 pounds of tiling, 20,000 yards of cloth, 90,000 flagstones, 60 trees, 100 pigeons, 500 lipsticks, 40 Veronese ducats, and hundreds of jewelled daggers. Miss Shearer, despite all this, made an effective Juliet and the civil strife of Verona was vigorously portrayed. Above all, of course, the crimson glory of those 500 lipsticks burns in the mind for ever.

Another effort to film Shakespeare, this time in England, was Miss Bergner's appearance as Rosalind in "As You Like It." Our own description of this was "Elizabeth in Her German Arden." Others, owing to the quantities of livestock employed, preferred to think of it as a Day at Whipsnade. Whether the screen Arden was German or Zoological, many held that the result was a long way from Warwickshire.

The reception given by the film-public to filmed Shakespeare has not, apparently, justified further experiments, at least on the large, the 500-lipstick, scale. It is typical of the Film Mind (or lack of it) that so far no English producer has been invited to "talkify" Shakespeare. Shakespeare, as we visualise him, had an omnivorous appetite for all forms of experience and of art. He altered the technique of his own plays to meet the changing needs of his theatre and he would probably have welcomed the resources of the modern screen. There is no blasphemy in filming Shakespeare: but there is banality in packing the "set" with irrelevant livestock on the assumption that Shakespeare could not make his human beings interesting and must be helped out with sheep and goats. A great Shakespearean film can and will be made when the director is told to spend less than was ever spent before and not to assess his spectacle by the livestock-and-lipstick standards so dear to Hollywood.

One thing we take to be fairly certain. Shakespeare was not a tremulous and wincing highbrow who would shrink from meeting the Big Noises of the Talking Screen. He might have enjoyed their company, for he was "a good mixer," and he would certainly have enjoyed their cheque for his script. Further, he might have taught them to make better film-versions of his work. Meanwhile, the Knowles statue of Shakespeare, planted by Baron Grant in Leicester Square, presumably because it was the heart of theatre-land, now surveys and points its text: "There is no darkness but ignorance," towards a hideous medley of picture palaces with not one single niche left for the actor appearing in person. Empire, Alhambra, Daly's, all are gone. The Square is now, as architecture, confusion's masterpiece. Why leave poor William in this derisive desolation? Our policy is to shift the Bard elsewhere and substitute a colossal

group in marble and gold of All the Warners, surrounded by the Metro-Goldwyn Lions, Five Hundred
Symbolic and Sky-scraping Lipsticks, and as much
sculptured livestock as Hollywood deems proper to
the site and to the glory.

A foreigner visiting England has for his earliest
view a Shakespeare Cliff. Had he entered London
at the close of 1938 he would have discovered no
"National Theatre Founded in Shakespeare's Name,"
but he could have seen first-rate performances of the
two most popular Shakespearean comedies. Had he
gone in search of Christmas cards he would have discovered that one sixpenny store had commissioned a
special series of Stratford Views, including the new
Memorial Theatre as well as the church and the old
cottages. He would have seen dozens of Shakespeare
Calendars and he would, more astonishingly, have
been confronted, in the window of a chemist's shop,
with a replica of Shakespeare's Will, price 3s. 6d. Why
this document, reproduced in its original form, which
is almost totally illegible by the modern, should be
deemed a Yuletide attraction, or a proper companion
for pills and cosmetics, we cannot say. To the mysteries of the Shakespeare Industry there is no end.

Had our stranger, feeling indisposed, consulted his
newspaper as to a gastric stimulant he would have
read as an advertisement for a saline draught: "Old
Salt Quotes Shakespeare." The Salt, blissfully purged,
is halloing to the reverberate news-columns, "Richard

THE FAMOUS INITIALS AT WINDSOR

is himself again," and we can leave our foreigner, doubtless a well-read Bardolater, to place the quotation. Feeling better, the visitor goes sight-seeing at Windsor, where on the stone-work of St. George's Chapel the initials W.S. and the date 1606 have been graven. Immediately the Industry pounces. The letter "S" has the peculiar curl at the top which is noted in the accepted Shakespearean signatures. Therefore the poet went there with the children of the Chapel Royal . . . therefore he spent his time, somewhat vulgarly, scratching his name on the sacred stones. Believe it or not.

Making for Stratford the foreigner will pass close to a Shakespeare Farm in Buckinghamshire. Why? Because Aubrey said that Shakespeare on his London journeys used to stop at Grendon, and there found the character of Dogberry. In Stratford every visitor may be surprised to receive first impressions that are not antique. He might have hoped to arrive in Ye Olde Tudor Traine. Certainly the branch-line from Leamington is not conspicuously modern in its methods and equipment. But Stratford Station— might not that have been a Timbered Piece as "Olde" as any of the structures recently contributed to the town by our well-known and well-intentioned banking firms?

It might. But there seems to have been an accident. When Stratford first received a railway-station, the railway directors intended it to be "reminiscent of

the Birthplace." But for some reason they changed
their minds or the plans were muddled. They gave
Stratford a standardised product of British railway
architecture and rather oddly bestowed the black-
and-white-timbered Shakespeare Station on Kidder-
minster, more famous for its carpets than for cantos
and for comedies. Once in Stratford the stranger can
buy any kind of Bardic "memo" as well as genuine
antiques. He cannot sleep in any inn that Shakespeare
actually knew in its present form, but he can stay in a
house of the poet's period. What is now the Shakespeare Hotel was then, and had been for some time,
the Great House of the Clopton family. It probably
became the Shakespeare Inn before Garrick's time.
Since Garrick mentions the Stratford habit of naming
rooms after plays and characters, the Shakespeare
Hotel's labelling of bedrooms in this manner may
be as old as the Garrick Jubilee. The Falcon, which,
being opposite New Place, the eighteenth-century
legend-builders turned into the poet's much-used
house of call, did not, in fact, become an inn till 1645.
Here the dinner-bells have Shakespearean names. The
White Swan has mural paintings, which must have
been there when Shakespeare was a boy in Henley
Street.

Should our visitor happen to strike Stratford out
of season, say in the old hiring holidays of October,
Mop Fair and Runaway Mop, he might discover
Shakespeare used as a slogan (and misquoted at that)

in the very heart and centre of all Shakespearean shrines. One showman, proclaiming some sort of Ghost Train for the excitement of the farmers' boys and girls who came crowding in for "The Mop," hung out a huge sign: "Hamlet, I am thy father's bogy." This textual emendation might have been kept for some other town.

Overwhelmed by the bucolic din and pressure of the autumnal Mop, or even by the tourist-thousands of high summer, our foreigner may proceed to Birmingham. Birmingham has had, since 1868, its own Shakespeare Memorial Library, containing 28,000 volumes, forty-four bound volumes of Play-bills from 1764 onwards, and books on the Bard in fifty-six different languages. The Four Folios are there, many precious Quartos, early copies of Holinshed's Chronicles (1577 and 1586–7) and of North's Plutarch (1579), and also the Forrest Collection of Shakespeare with its enormous aggregation of pictures and illustrations of all kinds bearing on the plays. Birmingham's loyalty to Shakespeare has made and kept this the greatest library of its kind in our country, despite a disastrous fire which destroyed all but 500 volumes in 1879.

Books and broadcasting, scholarship and salesman-ship, the zeal of the faithful and the ingenuity of the forger, honest passion for a mighty poet and dis-creditable eagerness to cash in on culture's chances and fool the pilgrim into emptying his purse—what a mixture it all is! Ubiquitous now and unquenchable, outward, onward, upward go the story, the glory, and the commerce. The existence of a Shakespeare Industry is not only inevitable: it is desirable. Were there no Shakespeare shrines, no dramatic festivals, no proper care of his boyhood places, his garden and his grave, no Birthday offerings of flag and flower as well as performance of his written word, the world would deem us to be thankless barbarians, unworthy of our fortune. It would be said that we always honoured our merchants, never our men of letters and the arts. The last person to deplore the Shakespeare Industry would have been, in our opinion, William Shakespeare himself. He was, as well as a poet of infinite perception, a man of property, a shrewd investor, and fond of a bargain. Surely he would have been the first to see that reasonable chances were not missed. Some aspects of the Industry have been discreditable and some ludicrous: but many others have been essential, decorous, and creditable tributes to our sovereign genius. Stratford has got rid of its old scandals. The foundations of the Amazing Monument are now above suspicion. We trust that where we have smiled at the Industry the laughing mood was justified and that, where honour was due for honourable homage to the greatest of all our poets, playwrights, and masters of the English tongue, we have duly paid that debt to the good servitors of Shakespeare's name.

INDEX